This is Service Design Thinking.

This book is printed on acid-free paper. ♾

Published by John Wiley & Sons, Inc., Hoboken, New Jersey.

Published simultaneously in Canada.

For general information on our other products and services or for technical support, please contact our Customer Care Department within the United States at (800) 762–2974, outside the United States at (317) 572–3993 or fax (317) 572–4002.

Wiley also publishes its books in a variety of electronic formats. Some content that appears in print may not be available in electronic books. For more information about Wiley products, visit our web site at www.wiley.com.

ISBN 978–1–118–15630–8 (paper)

Printed in the United States of America
10 9 8 7 6 5 4 3 2 1

Basics — Tools — Cases

THIS IS SERVICE DESIGN THINKING.

Marc Stickdorn

Jakob Schneider

John Wiley & Sons, Inc.

THIS IS SERVICE
DESIGN THINKING
BEHIND THE
STICKY NOTES.

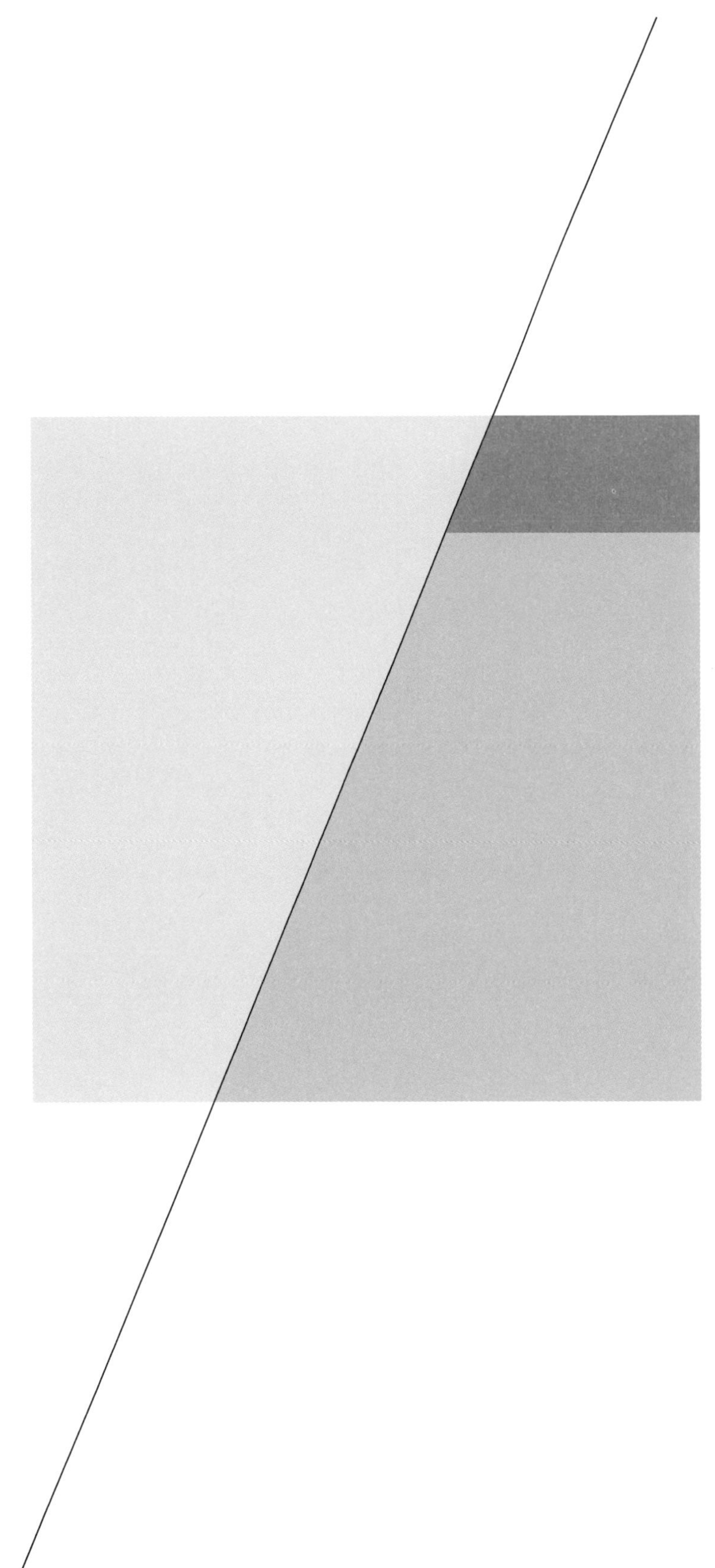

Introduction

What is Service Design?

Who are these Service Designers?

How does Service Design work?

What are the tools of Service Design?

Cases

Applied Service Design

Deep Service Design thinking

Appendix

PREFACE

This book aims to be a textbook on service design thinking – an interdisciplinary approach that offers great value for entrepreneurs and innovators in the field of services. No matter whether service design thinking already made it into your everyday vocabulary or you just hear about this the very first time, no matter whether you're a student, teacher, researcher, manager or company owner, and no matter whether your background is in design, management, engineering or any other profession, this book will serve you as an introduction, reference and case study book. Moreover, it is supposed to be a source of inspiration and motivation for your future work.

The book is structured into three main parts. **Basics** illustrates the fundamental concepts of service design thinking and its relation to service marketing. In particular, this chapter explains various gateways into service design thinking from backgrounds like product design, graphic design, interaction design and design ethnography, but also from strategic management and operations management and in addition rather new fields like social design. **Tools** explains the iterative process of designing services and shows methods and tools of service design as a kind of toolkit that we hope you will be able to implement in your own work. **Cases** exemplifies how the basics, processes and tools come together through five different case studies. **At the end of the book,** service design thinking is wrapped up in three articles on how motivation as a fundamental component of human behaviour is a precondition for designing services, an overview of recent service design research publications, and through consideration of how service design thinking integrates with other philosophical approaches. However, **before we start** with the actual content, the design beyond the design provides a summary of how

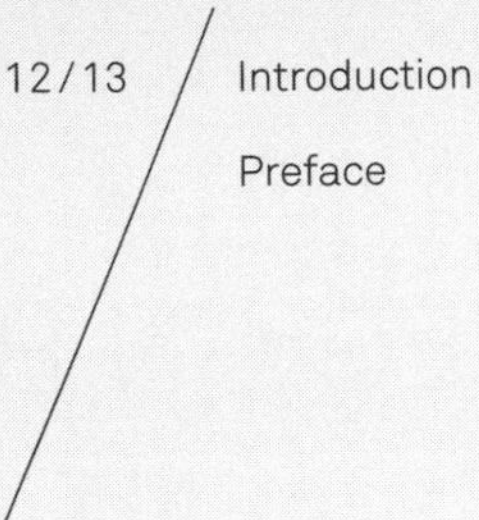

we adopted a service design thinking approach to the design of this book itself and besides that you'll find a short description on how to use this book.

This book project attempted to follow the principle of practice-what-you-preach. It is not only created for the growing service design community but to a large extent by and with the service design community. Thus, we want to thank all our co-authors, contributors and everyone who provided feedback on the publication. We have tried to mention everyone who helped us during the progress of this project and we apologise if we have forgotten someone along the way. There are a few people, we want to thank personally. First and foremost we want to thank Fergus Bisset who supported the project from the start, by setting up the first crowdsourcing website, right through to co-editing most contributions. Furthermore, Bas Raijmakers, Geke van Dijk and Luke Kelly helped us reviewing, editing and illustrating the tools and methods. Finally, we want to thank our publishers, for their belief in the project and their great support!

Mostly, however, we want to thank you – the reader. Only your interest in this book and your interpretation of the information contained in it generates real value from this project! We thus look forward to hearing more about the people reading it, how you are using it and what you think about it. So, please keep in touch!

The editors, Marc & Jakob, August 2010

THE DESIGN BEYOND THE DESIGN: A DIFFERENT APPROACH TO DESIGNING A TEXTBOOK

MARC STICKDORN
JAKOB SCHNEIDER

While colloquially the word design is used to refer to the appearance or styling of a particular product or outcome, the proper meaning goes far beyond that. In particular, the approach of service design refers to the process of designing rather than to its outcome. The outcome of a service design process can have various forms: rather abstract organisational structures, operation processes, service experiences and even concrete physical objects.

Since service design is a still young and emerging approach, service design education is even younger and just developing. There are various courses and recently even study programs on service design, but so far there are no textbooks explaining this approach. One could argue that an approach like this does not need a textbook, since it is something you potentially have to learn by doing. Without a doubt, you cannot learn what service design is and how to do it just from a textbook. You need to try, fail, learn from your mistakes, improve, try again and thus educate yourself.

Service design education is therefore rather a kind of briefing and tutoring process. Besides explaining the big picture, it is all about giving hints, proposing methods and tools, and showing how to use them while working on a project. The main question we asked ourselves in spring 2009 was how could we make teaching and learning service design easier and more pleasurable?

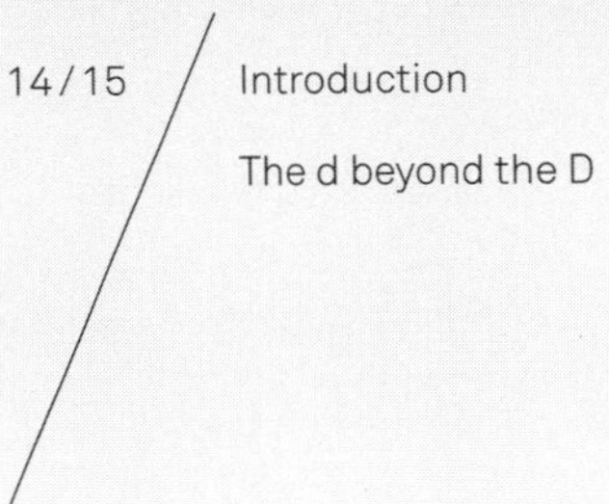

Motivation and inspiration

Based on the insights of a service design course Marc gave in spring 2009, we started a series of interviews with both service design course participants and educators to understand what the main difficulties are of learning how to design services. In this context we tried to understand who teaches service design? What is the content and how is it delivered?

In our interviews we discovered the need for a serious and static reference opposed to the ever changing blogosphere.

Who attends respective courses and workshops? Answering these questions gave us the motivation and initial inspiration to start this project. Following the principle of practice-what-you-preach, we applied methods and tools of service design on the process of designing this first textbook on service design. Thus we consider this book rather as a service to you – the reader – than as a mere physical object we offer for sale. The durability and experienced sustainability of print media made us do a book rather than a website or App. Moreover, in our interviews we discovered the need for a serious and static reference opposed to the ever-changing blogosphere. Besides, a book is still one of the most reliable forms of media; a book is portable, tangible, durable and never faces problems of low battery or bad reception.

Since service design is an interdisciplinary approach, different people teach and learn service design in different ways; all of them with their individual backgrounds and motivations. However, during our interviews we realised that they all share the same problem: they miss a textbook. This variety of people with differing needs led us to the question of which author has the knowledge and authority to write such a book? The author would need to share all these different backgrounds to exemplify the interdisciplinary nature of service design and in order to know all the methods and tools service designers use. We knew many authors capable of doing this: the service design community as a whole.

Experiences and expectations

Using a crowdsourcing approach to develop the book's content involved a lot of planning and communication. Certainly an aspect that both of us underestimated at the beginning. To illustrate the interdisciplinary character of this approach, we asked service design professionals with specialist backgrounds to describe the connection between their original discipline and service design. However, in order to find out which methods and tools the service design community uses, we simply needed to ask them. With the help of Fergus Bisset, we set up a Wordpress website, where people could contribute methods and tools and comment on other contributions. This website was promoted online through Twitter, Facebook and various blogs, and through the online service design communities like the Service Design Network or Wenovski. We collected more than 50 descriptions of service design methods and tools. In a following step, these were evaluated through a Uservoice forum, where a sum of 1188 votes decided which ones should be printed in the book. Subsequently Geke van Dijk, Luke Kelly and Bas Raijmakers helped us to write, edit and illustrate the selected methods and tools.

Based on the insights we gathered during spring 2009, Jakob started a series of workshops on the design of textbooks throughout the summer and fall. He conducted contextual interviews with 24 teachers and students from distinct disciplines, such as physicians, medical students, physicists, physics students, lawyers, law students, teachers and

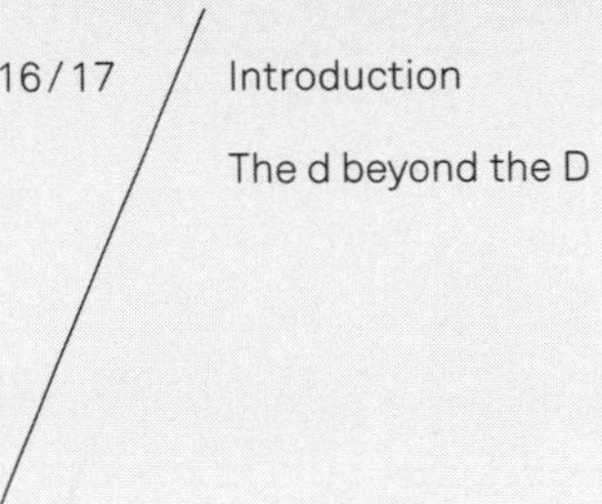

prospective teachers. Each discipline showed and discussed a few examples of textbooks – both good and bad ones – to present a range of perceptions about what constitutes a good textbook. During the second phase insights and ideas were further generated about what makes a good textbook through a moderated group discussion with six students from all of the mentioned disciplines and additionally two designers, intentionally without experience in book design. In particular the layout of the

This project needed to be authentic to itself: a book about service design must itself be understood as a designed service.

book as well as its academic and linguistic level was discussed. Yet again it became clear that this project needed to be authentic to itself: a book about service design must itself be understood as a designed service. How is the book used, which is the most relevant information and how do you find it? Even how do you hold a book when you're using it during workshops, e.g. sitting, standing, walking?

Ideas and concepts

Developing a structure, layout, tone of voice and visual language took us quite some time. We started in fall 2009 and agreed on our final concept in spring 2010. Considering the insights we gathered earlier, we defined a few associations the book should evoke. To test these, we used various methods from different backgrounds. We published an early draft of the "five principles of service design thinking" to gain feedback on both content and layout. Using Panoremo, a tool developed to generate emotional feedback for 360° environments, we gathered 168 emotional hotspots for these five pages. Furthermore we produced realistic dummy prints. Although content-wise only the headings and highlighted sentences referred to the topic – the other text was Goethe's "Werther" – we were able to observe the emotional reactions to the layout and haptics. From this we were able to evaluate whether the solutions found in the abstract contextual interviews work for the main target group of service designers and those who are interested in it. We've been to various meetings of service designers, such as the First Nordic Service Design Conference 2009 and a Wenovski MiniUnConference. We rejected impractical approaches and those causing undesired associations. By doing so, we improved the concept iteratively and developed metaphors for complex relationships (infographics and pictograms) and visual systems for the linking of contents.

An awkward title

One of the repeatedly raised questions referred to the awfully long title. Each of the topics of service design and design thinking is complicated enough. Why must we confuse the audience even more with a title like "This is Service Design Thinking"? The service design community still struggles with exact formulations. Some want to find a completely new name for the things we do, some want to show that this is not new at all; some consider themselves as service designers, some as design thinkers and others as design strategists or new service marketers. However, we all share a certain approach. Services can be designed from various perspectives, using different methods and tools of various disciplines and thus also using different terminology. Service design is interdisciplinary and therefore it cannot be a discipline in itself. However, this book illustrates that designing services in the interdisciplinary way entails a certain way of thinking. This is service design thinking.

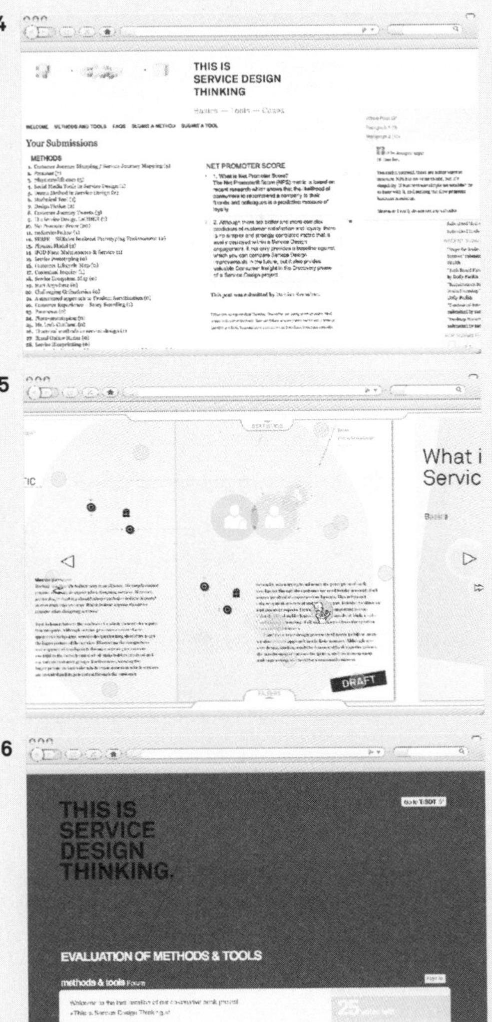

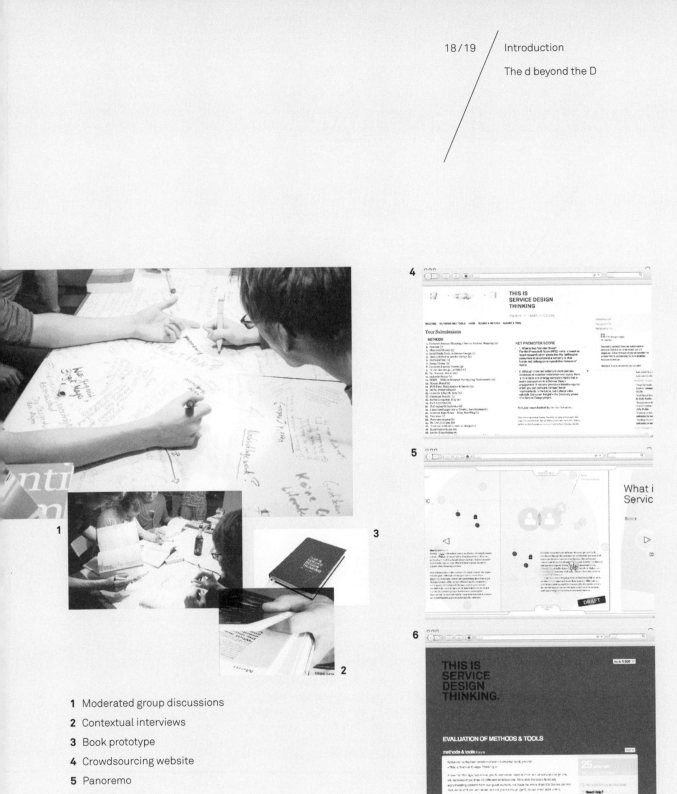

1 Moderated group discussions
2 Contextual interviews
3 Book prototype
4 Crowdsourcing website
5 Panoremo
6 Uservoice forum

CROWDSOURCING MAP

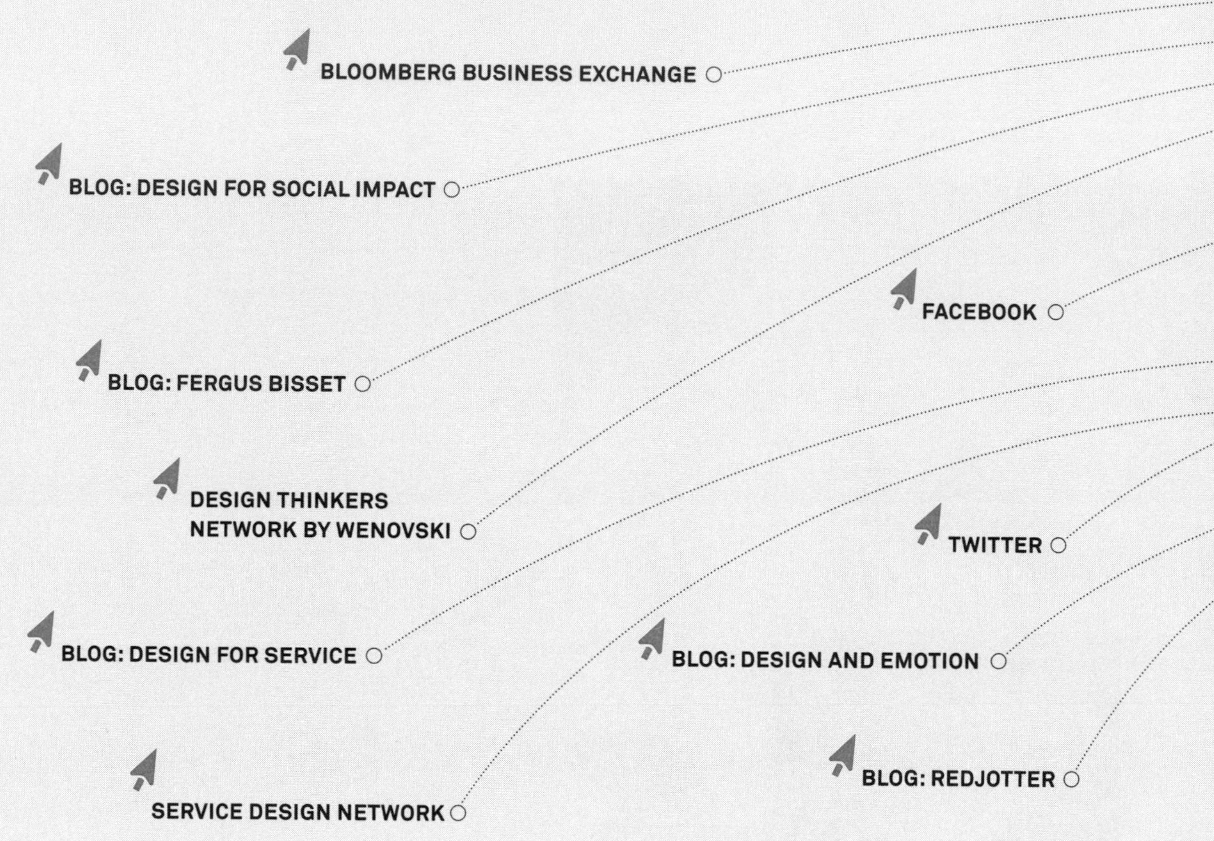

BLOOMBERG BUSINESS EXCHANGE The site linking to our project page —bx.businessweek.com /
DESIGN AND EMOTION Marco van Hout mentioning the project —design-emotion.com /
DESIGN FOR SERVICE Jeff Howard talking about the project on his blog —designforservice.wordpress.com /
DESIGN FOR SOCIAL IMPACT Kate Andrews talking about the project on her blog —kateandrews.wordpress.com /
DE-THINKING SERVICE, RE-THINKING DESIGN Visiting the First Nordic Service Design Conference with a prototype of this book; talking to professionals about content and structure; testing layout principles /
FACEBOOK Several profiles of the service design community reporting on this project —facebook.com /
FERGUS BISSET Fergus Bisset talking about the project on his blog —fergusbisset.com/blog /
FLICKR Photos of the dummy of the book have been published here for people to comment on —flickr.com /

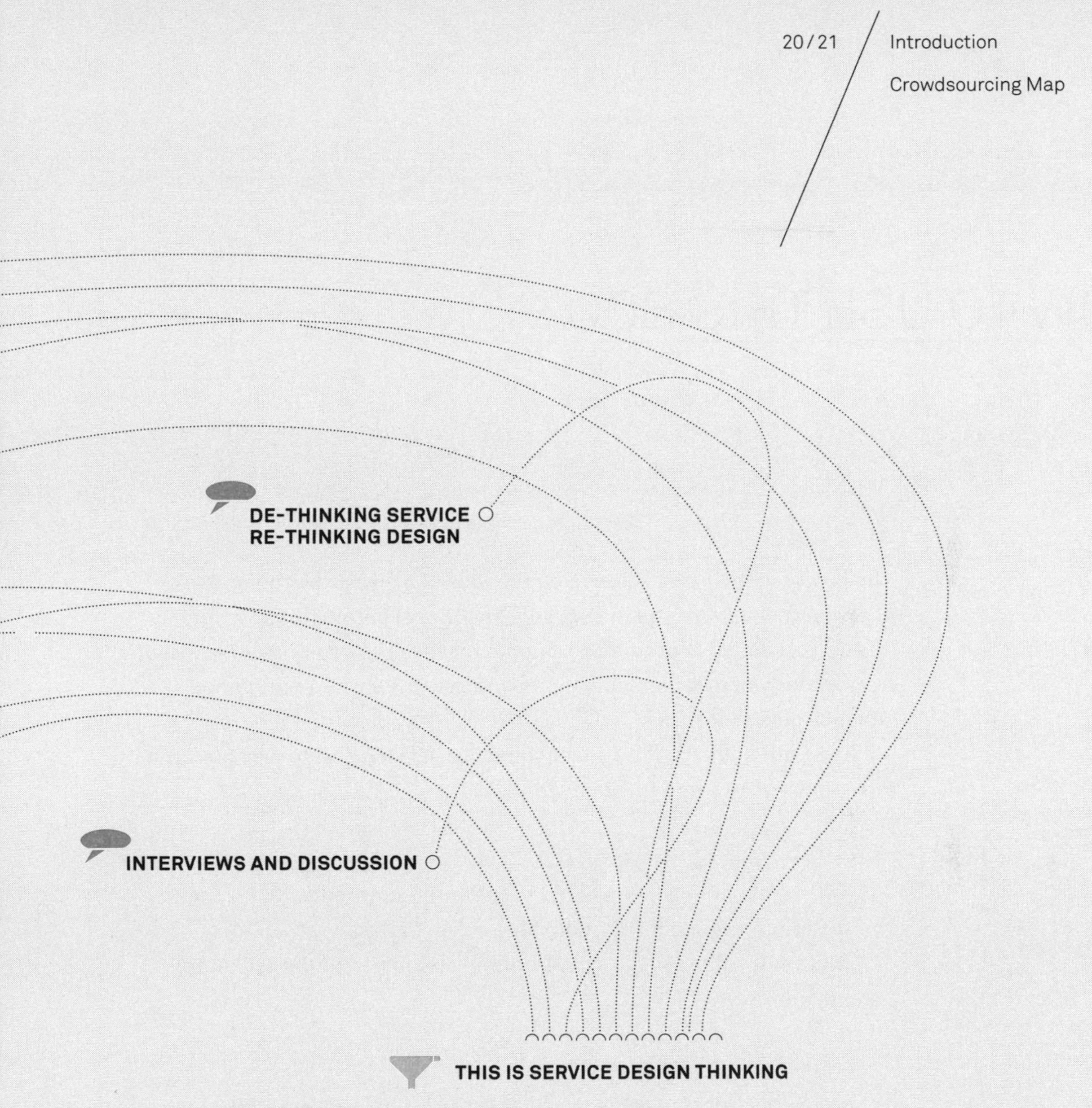

INTERVIEWS AND DISCUSSION Interviewing students and professionals from Germany and Austria about expectations towards a fundamental book on service design thinking /
DESIGN THINKERS NETWORK BY WENOVSKI Social network on design thinking initiated by Arne van Oosterom reporting about the book project —designthinkersnetwork.com /
REDJOTTER Lauren Currie talking about the project on her blog —redjotter.wordpress.com /
SERVICE DESIGN NETWORK SDN informing about the possibility to contribute —service-design-network.com /
TWITTER People twittering about this book project and inviting contributions —twitter.com /
THIS IS SERVICE DESIGN THINKING Gathering input from all over the net —thisisservicedesignthinking.com
(In alphabetical order)

HOW TO USE THIS BOOK

The layout of this book is based on the idea of a classic textbook. We do not want to interrupt you during your reading experience. However, this book is aimed at offering additional means of information visualisation in order for you to understand context more quickly and remember content more easily.

Since this book itself is the outcome of a service design process, let us introduce you to some special features:

— As you noticed, this book is structured in three parts through different colours. Sticky-note blue refers to Basics, green to Methods, yellow to Cases. Additional chapters and the appendix appear in grey.

— Service design is the world of sticky notes, and so is this book. The turned sticky notes (sticky side up) indicate page references while the colour represents the respective part.

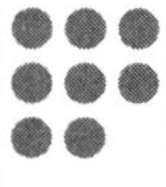

— At the end of the book you will find an overview page. This page shows all icons that are used throughout the publication. After a short period of time you will remember the icons by heart and can spot relevant points without reading details.

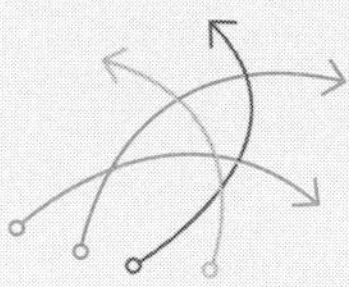

— This book is full of visual connections that will help you understand and follow topics, which are contextually related. You will quickly discover how this is done by lines and arrows, and special typographic emphases.

What?

— Nearly every page spread is entitled with a question on the top left, which repeats the topic you are going to get answers to. These answers are offered by breakout sentences. Note that these sentences are underlined in the main text so that you can easily see where the answer is taken from.

— Pictograms representing the methods of service design are introduced in the second part. Every time a method appears in other texts, its icon appears as well. The overview page at the back of the book provides you with an overview of all icons and symbols.

— In order to keep the texts in this book tight and legible, all textual references are provided at the end of the book. Furthermore, there you will find an index structured by the three colours. Thus you can decide in which part you want to look up a word.

After all, these explanations should be considered optional. Design that has to be explained rarely is good design. All visual hints are developed to be understood intuitively. So, don't let us keep you from getting started with this book any longer.

www.thisisservicedesignthinking.com

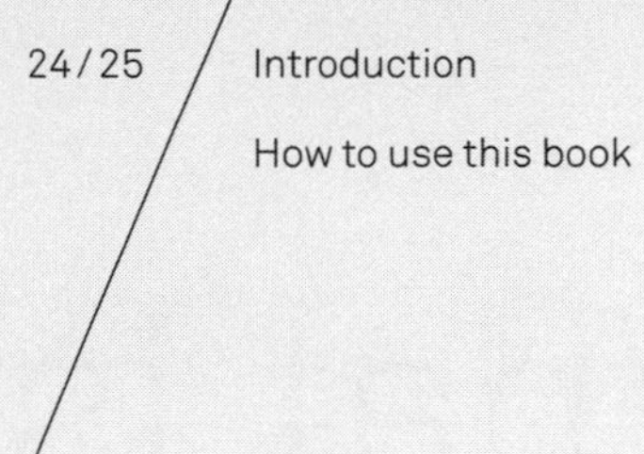

THE CUSTOMER JOURNEY CANVAS

At the online touchpoint of the book we provide you with a canvas developed to support you when designing services. You can use it not only for yourself to get a quick overview of certain service processes, but also with providers for a self-portrayal and with customers and other stakeholders to explore and evaluate services. Besides visually simplifying existing services, you can also use it to sketch service improvements and innovations. It supports many of the tools presented later in this book. The Customer Journey Canvas is available under cc license on our website.

Try it, adapt or modify it, take a snapshot and share how you use the canvas through our website. Watch out for service design thinking!

NOTE: All visual material in this book is provided on the website for download. The high-quality files are available under cc license.

What is Service Design?

Basics

DEFINITIONS: SERVICE DESIGN AS AN INTER-DISCIPLINARY APPROACH

MARC STICKDORN

Frankly, one of the great strengths of design is that we have not settled on a single definition. Fields in which definition is now a settled matter tend to be lethargic, dying, or dead fields, where inquiry no longer provides challenges to what is accepted as truth.

— RICHARD BUCHANAN, 2001

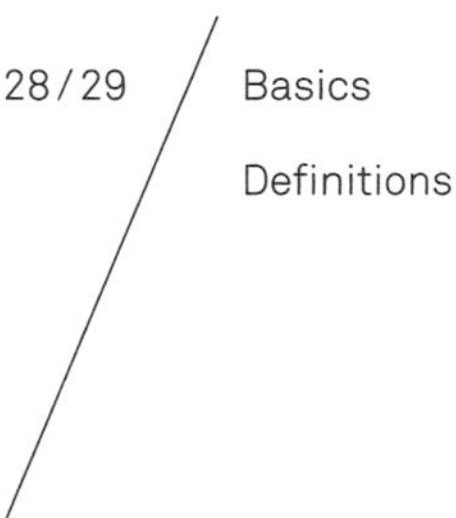

If you would ask ten people what service design is, you would end up with eleven different answers – at least.

Service design is an interdisciplinary approach that combines different methods and tools from various disciplines. It is a new way of thinking as opposed to a new stand-alone academic discipline. Service design is an evolving approach, this is particularly apparent in the fact that, as yet, there is no common definition or clearly articulated language of service design.

A single definition of service design might constrain this evolving approach, whereas a shared language is undoubtedly important for the further growth and development of service design thinking. Therefore, this book strives to propose the basis for a common language of service design.

With this intent and building upon the basis that a working definition of service design is as much to be found in the combination of various examples and attempts to define service design as in any single one of them, the following pages exemplify different points of view within and across this emerging field.

What is Service Design?

Academic approaches for service design definitions

Service Design is an emerging field focused on the creation of well thought through experiences using a combination of intangible and tangible mediums. It provides numerous benefits to the end user experience when applied to sectors such as retail, banking, transportation, and healthcare.

Service design as a practice generally results in the design of systems and processes aimed at providing a holistic service to the user.

This cross-disciplinary practice combines numerous skills in design, management and process engineering. Services have existed and have been organised in various forms since time immemorial. However, consciously designed services that incorporate new business models are empathetic to user needs and attempt to create new socio-economic value in society. Service design is essential in a knowledge driven economy.

— THE COPENHAGEN INSTITUTE OF INTERACTION DESIGN, 2008

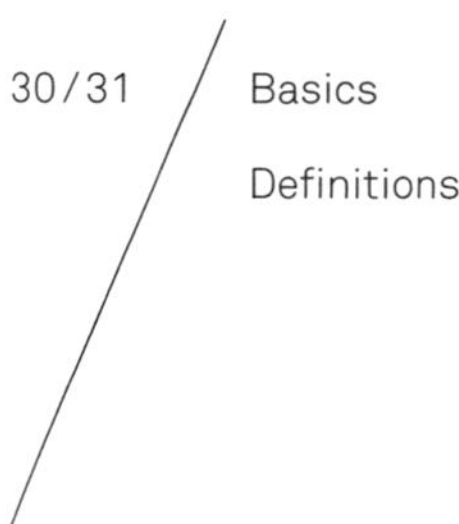

Service Design helps to innovate (create new) or improve (existing) services to make them more useful, usable, desirable for clients and efficient as well as effective for organisations. It is a new holistic, multi-disciplinary, integrative field.

— STEFAN MORITZ, 2005

Service design is all about making the service you deliver useful, usable, efficient, effective and desirable.

— UK DESIGN COUNCIL, 2010

Service Design aims to ensure service interfaces are useful, usable and desirable from the client's point of view and effective, efficient and distinctive from the supplier's point of view.

— BIRGIT MAGER, 2009

What is Service Design?

Agency approaches for service design definitions

Service design is a design specialism that helps develop and deliver great services. Service design projects improve factors like ease of use, satisfaction, loyalty and efficiency right across areas such as environments, communications and products – and not forgetting the people who deliver the service.

— ENGINE SERVICE DESIGN, 2010

Service design is a holistic way for a business to gain a comprehensive, empathic understanding of customer needs.

— FRONTIER SERVICE DESIGN, 2010

Developing the environments, tools, and processes that help employees deliver superior service in a way that is proprietary to the brand.

— CONTINUUM, 2010

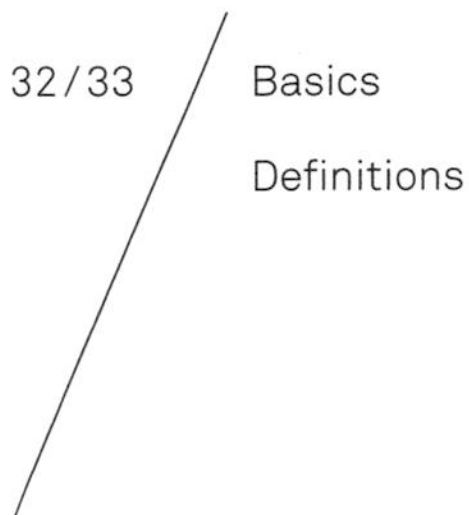

Service Design is the application of established design process and skills to the development of services. It is a creative and practical way to improve existing services and innovate new ones.

— LIVE|WORK, 2010

When you have two coffee shops right next to each other, and each sells the exact same coffee at the exact same price, service design is what makes you walk into one and not the other.

— 31 VOLTS SERVICE DESIGN, 2008

5 PRINCIPLES OF SERVICE DESIGN THINKING

MARC STICKDORN

1. USER-CENTRED

Services should be experienced through the customer's eyes.

2. CO-CREATIVE

All stakeholders should be included in the service design process.

3. SEQUENCING

The service should be visualised as a sequence of interrelated actions.

4. EVIDENCING

Intangible services should be visualised in terms of physical artefacts.

5. HOLISTIC

The entire environment of a service should be considered.

A dynamic language for a dynamic approach

Since there is no common definition of service design, this book instead outlines the way of thinking required to design services. The following pages attempt to illustrate service design thinking through five core principles.

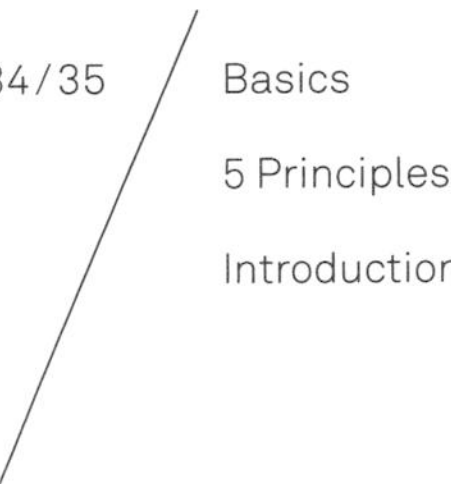

CUSTOMER

SERVICE PROVIDER

STAKEHOLDER

SERVICE DESIGNER

TOUCHPOINT

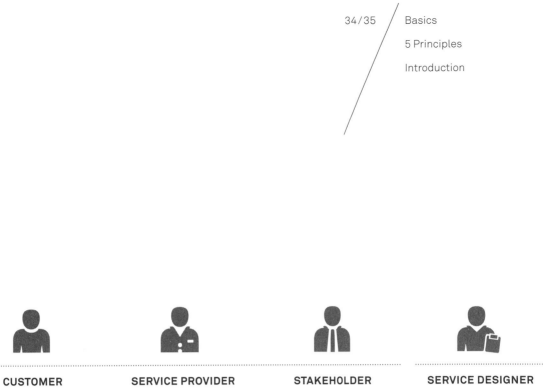

every contact point between a customer and the service provider

SERVICE EVIDENCE

a tangible artefact related to a service process

SERVICE PERIOD

pre-service / service / post-service — current period of a service

1
IT IS USER-CENTRED

Agree on a common language!
To deliver services, a certain degree of customer participation is necessary. Think of any service offered by a design consultancy or public transport operator. None of them would be able to operate without the involvement of the customer. Services are not tangible or standardised goods that can be stored away in an inventory. Instead, services are created through interaction between a service provider and a customer. The inherent intention of a service is to meet the customer's needs and, as a result, be used frequently and recommended heartily. This is often not the case.

How can we design services in a user-centred way?
Think of two customers. Both were born in 1948, male, raised in Great Britain, married, successful and wealthy. Furthermore, both of them have at least two children, like dogs and love the Alps. One of them could be Prince Charles and the other one Ozzy Osbourne. Though statistical customer descriptions are important, a true understanding of habits, culture, social context and motivation of users is crucial. We need to put the customer at the centre of the service design process. This requires a genuine understanding of the customer beyond mere statistical descrip-

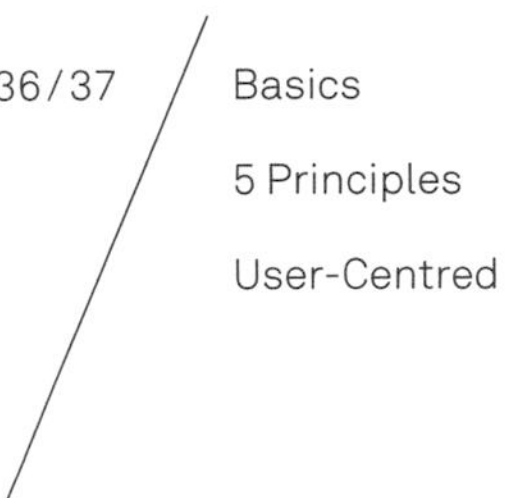

tions and empirical analyses of their needs. Gaining authentic customer insights includes the application of methods and tools that enable the service designer to slip into the customer's shoes and understand their individual service experience and its wider context. We are all customers – though with different needs and mindsets. The understanding and disclosure of these disparate mindsets is where service design thinking begins.

If you remember an occasion when you tried to get technical assistance, like using a telephone helpline for example, it is common to have problems in how both parties involved understand each other. You and the hotline agent literally speak the same language, and yet it is often difficult to communicate because you exist in different realities. The same of course can be true when you work in interdisciplinary teams; managers, engineers, designers, marketers as well as front-line staff and customers, can often misunderstand one another – simply because we all have individual backgrounds and experiences. The ability to make use of this knowledge during the development of services is crucial for its later success. A user-centred approach offers a common language we can all speak; the service user's language.

2
IT IS CO-CREATIVE

Everyone can be creative!

Putting the customer at the centre of a service design process involves facing the reality that potentially there is more than just one customer group, and each group possesses different needs and expectations. Furthermore, providing services also demands consideration of the various stakeholders, such as front-line staff, back-office employees and managers, as well as non-human interfaces such as vending machines or websites. Thus, a single service proposition can involve a number of actors and different customer groups as well as different employees and interfaces. During a service design process we need to involve customers as well as all other stakeholders involved in exploring and defining the service proposition.

How can we integrate the stakeholders of a service into the process of designing it?

Think of the various stakeholders involved in creating, providing and consuming a service, for example managers, marketers, engineers, designers, front-line staff and customers. Now that we have agreed on the common language of our customers, we need to come up with some ideas about how to design a new service or improve an existing service.

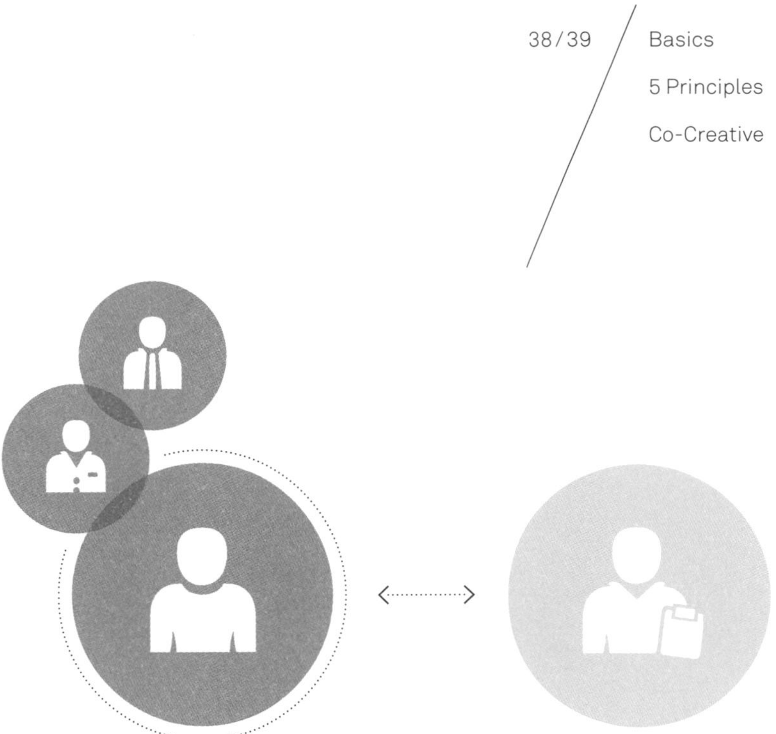

Therefore, we should involve all these different people in the process and we need to be creative. However, creativity is not so much a gift as a process of listening to the ideas "flowing" through one's head and being prepared to articulate them. Service designers consciously generate an environment that facilitates the generation and evaluation of ideas within heterogeneous stakeholder groups. There are a variety of methods and tools for gaining genuine insights from different user perspectives in the creation of services and for the development, prototyping and testing of these service concepts. This is co-creation, and facilitating this in groups representative of your stakeholders is a vital aspect of design thinking and a fundamental part of service design.

Furthermore, co-creation during the design process facilitates a smooth interaction between the stakeholders during the actual service provision – essential for both sustainable customer and employee satisfaction. Through co-creation customers get the chance to add value to a service in partnership with the service provider early in the development of the service. The more a customer gets involved in the service provision, the more likely this service is of evoking co-ownership which in turn will result in increased customer loyalty and long-term engagement.

3
IT IS SEQUENCING

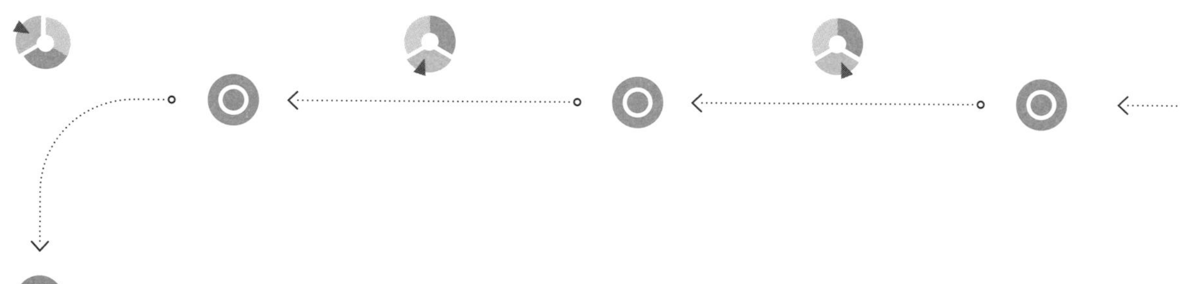

Imagine a service as a movie!
Services are dynamic processes that take place over a certain period of time. This service timeline is crucial to consider when designing services, since the rhythm of a service influences the mood of customers. We might get bored if something progresses too slow (e.g. waiting at the airport check-in) or we might get stressed out if it goes too fast (e.g. rushing through the airport security check).

How can we influence the rhythm of a service?
Imagine a very simple example of a service such as going to a hairdresser. Now try to visualize this service process as a stage play or movie.
This movie would consist of a series of static pictures, which would be combined to create a moving sequence. Service design thinking uses this analogy to deconstruct service processes into single touchpoints and interactions. These, when combined, create service moments. Touch-point interactions take place human-human, human-machine and even machine-machine, but also occur indirectly via third parties, such as reviews from other customers or via print or online media. Every service process follows a three-step transition of pre-service period (getting in touch with a service), the actual service period (when the customers

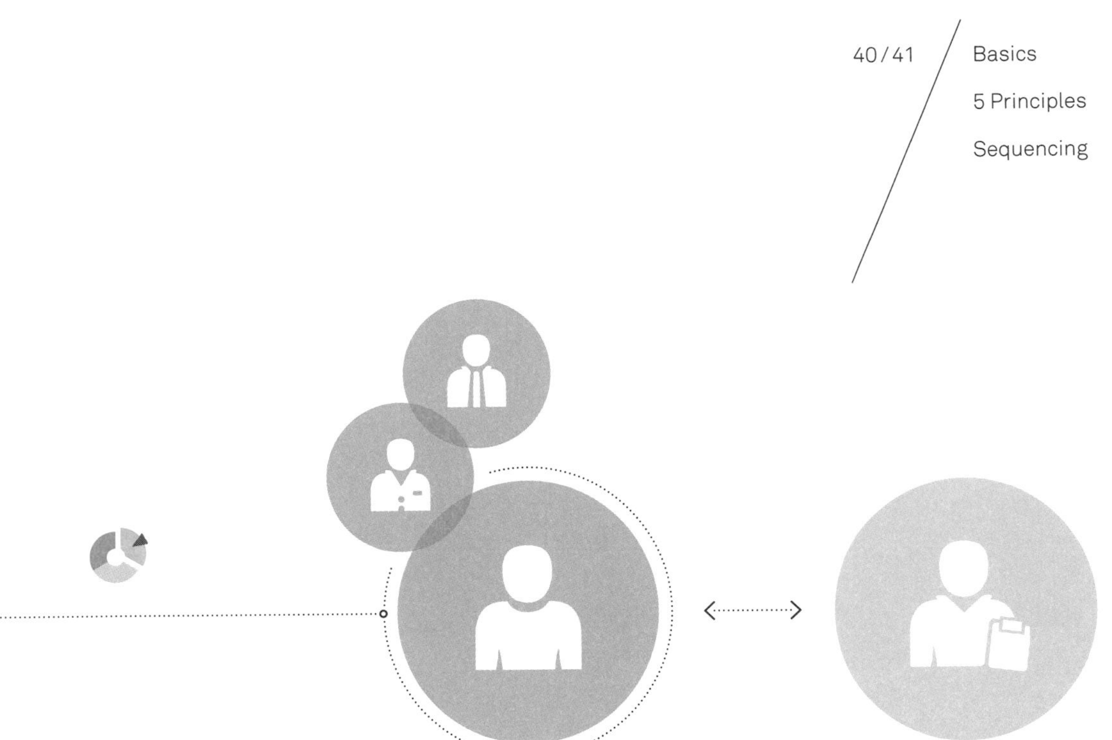

actually experience a service) and the subsequent post-service period. To stay with thc cxample of a hairdresser, the first touchpoint of the pre-service period would be the moment when a customer perceives the need for a haircut and thus learns about the service offer, through an advertisement, by walking past the shop or by hearing about the hairdressers through word of mouth.

Just like any good stage play or movie, a superior service should keep a sense of expectation without exacting strain upon the customer. This typically entails holding the customer's interest with a good narrative. The sequence of service moments should thus be well orchestrated to achieve a pleasant rhythm, ensuring a climactic progress of the customer's mood and communicating the story inherently to the service through each touchpoint. Like a stage play, a service moment not only consists of what is happening front of stage, it also includes multiple backstage processes such as cleaning of the shop floor to prepare the front of stage for action. To achieve an excellent theatrical performance, actors have of course to run through many rehearsals; services are no different. We need to prototype services and iteratively test their impact on customers.

4
IT IS EVIDENCING

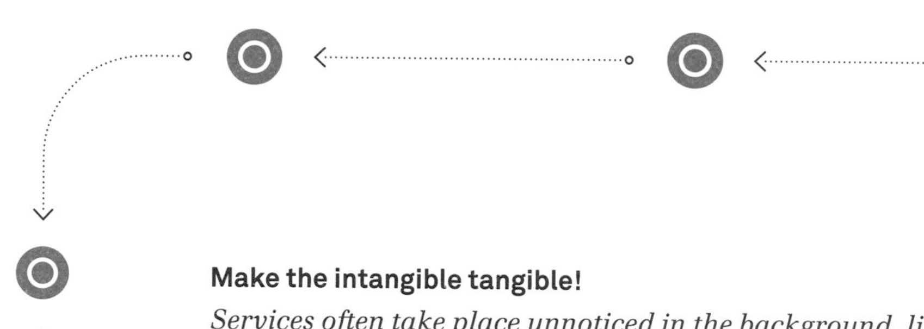

Make the intangible tangible!
Services often take place unnoticed in the background, like the housekeeping service in a hotel. In fact, services like these are intentionally designed to be inconspicuous. However, if paying a bill is the first moment customers become aware of such backstage service processes, their inconspicuousness might create a disparity in customer expectation and potentially result in their disaffection with the service.

How can we make customers aware of intangible services?
Think of your last holiday. Did you bring home any souvenirs? Did you place them somewhere, where you can see them from time to time? And do you remember the good time you had when you take a look at them? Physical evidence or artefacts such as souvenirs or small bottles of shampoo from your hairdresser can trigger the memory of positive service moments and thus, through emotional association, continue to enhance customers' perceptions of the service they have received. Service evidence can thus prolong service experiences beyond the mere service period far into the post-service period. Utilising this effectively has the potential to increase customer loyalty and for customers to recommend the service to others.

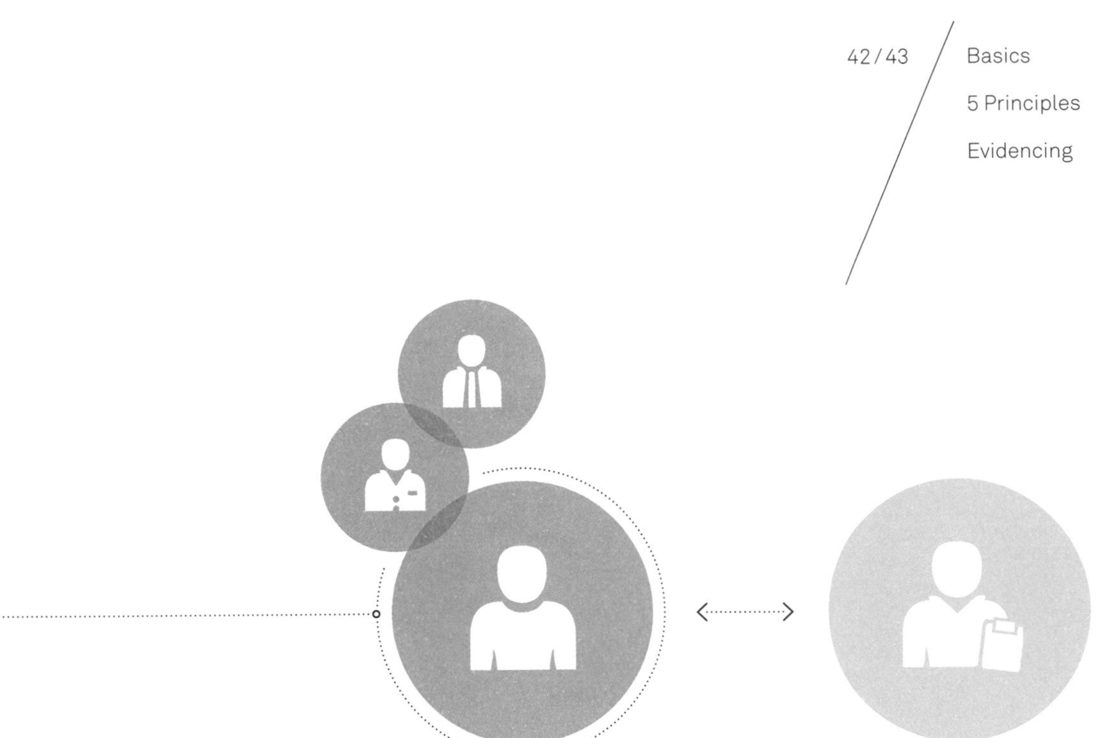

In addition, evidence can explain certain aspects of a service touchpoint or process, a sign next to an electric hand dryer pointing out that the proprietor knows that customers would prefer to use real towels but that costs or the environmental impact do not allow this can generate appreciation and empathic engagement. Evidencing can occur in a variety of forms: bills, mail, emails, brochures, signs, souvenirs or other products. These add a tangible component to what would otherwise have been an intangible experience. Making the service more tangible is, however, not always desirable to service users – think of junk mail as an example of evidencing gone wrong.

Service evidencing can thus help reveal inconspicuous backstage services. Sometimes even promoting the once inconspicuous to become standard service signals such as the folded toilet paper representative of housekeeping in hotels. Service evidence needs to be designed according to the service's inherent story and its touchpoint sequence. If a service process is like a movie, a better understanding of the work behind the scenes (i.e. the backstage processes of services) can result in an increased customer appreciation of the service experience.

5
IT IS HOLISTIC

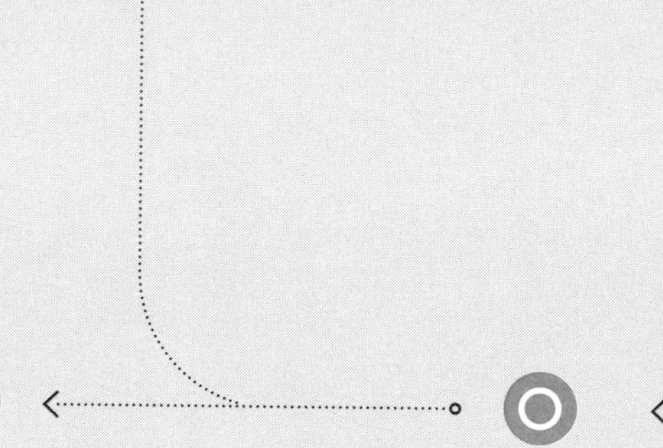

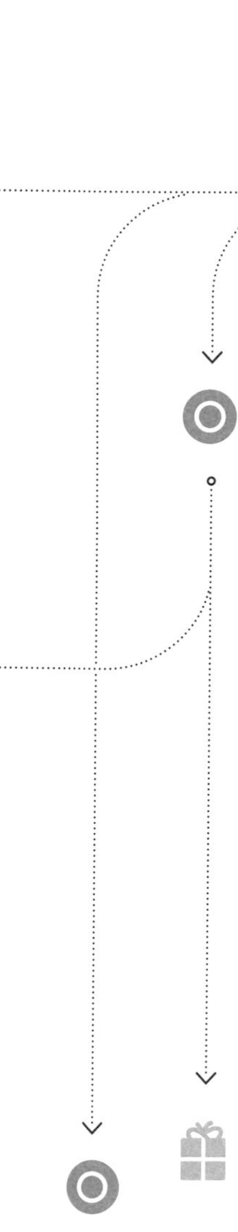

Keep the big picture!
Although services are intangible, they take place in a physical environment, using physical artefacts and do in most instances generate some form of physical outcome. Subconsciously, customers perceive this environment with all their senses. We see, hear, smell, touch and taste the physical manifestation of services.

Which aspects need to be considered when designing services?
Genuinely working in a holistic way is an illusion, it is simply impossible to consider every single aspect of a service. However, the intention should always be to see the wider context in which a service process takes place.

At the level of individual touchpoints and service moments, the focus should be on the environment where the service takes place. The conscious awareness of what customers might otherwise perceive subconsciously with their senses can have a profound impact on the experience of the service itself.

At the level of the service sequence, there should be a focus on alternative customer journeys. There are always a number of alternative touch-

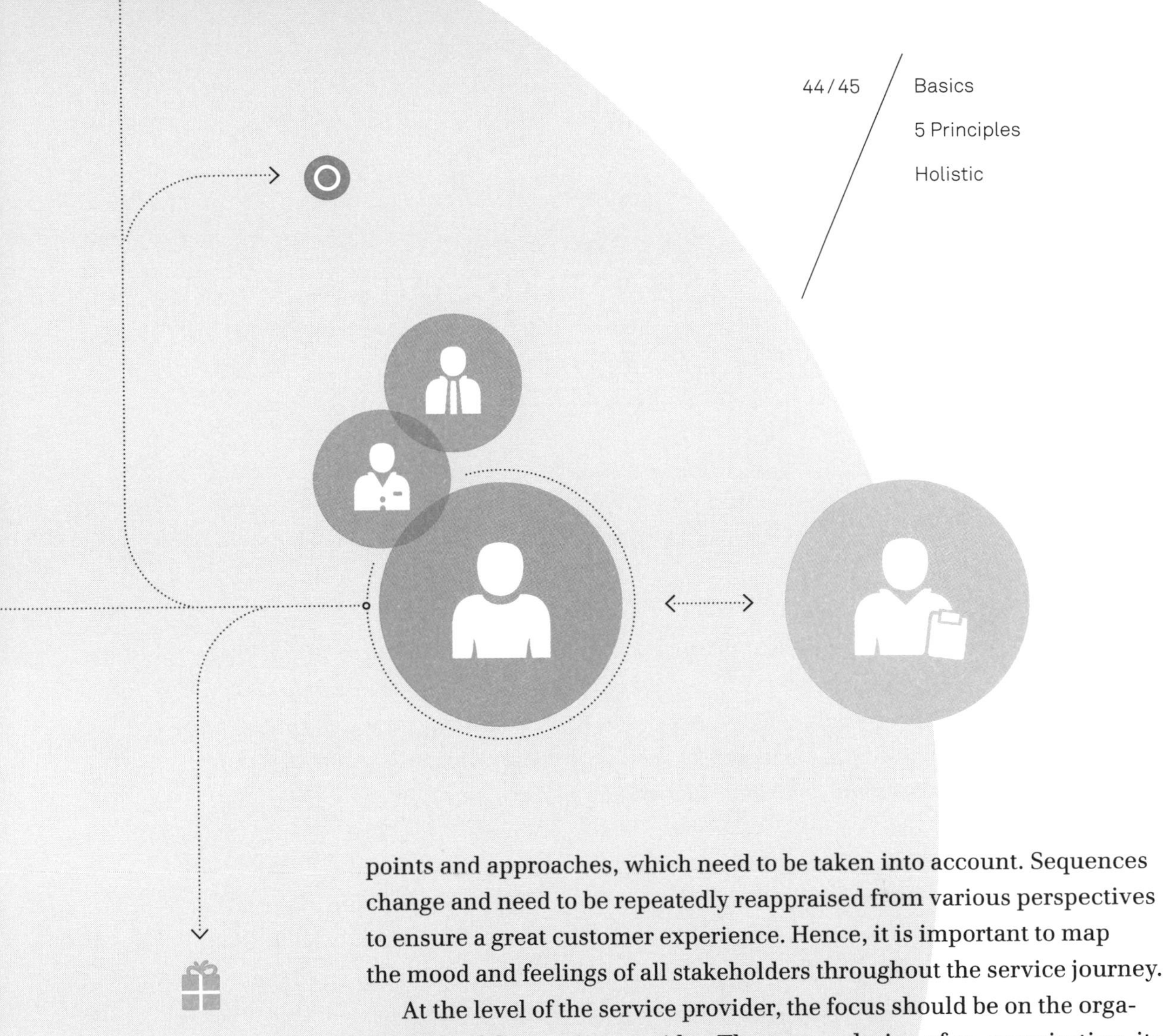

points and approaches, which need to be taken into account. Sequences change and need to be repeatedly reappraised from various perspectives to ensure a great customer experience. Hence, it is important to map the mood and feelings of all stakeholders throughout the service journey.

At the level of the service provider, the focus should be on the organisation of the service provider. The system design of an organisation, its inherent culture, values and norms as well as its organisational structure and processes are important issues for the design of services. Disparities between the corporate identity embodied by the organisation's management and staff and the corporate image perceived by the customers need to be ironed out. This can help promote a service mindset within the organisation and to articulate the importance of employee and customer motivation.

To summarise, service design thinking supports the co-operation of different disciplines towards the goal of corporate success through enhanced customer experiences, employee satisfaction, and integration of sophisticated technological processes in pursuing corporate objectives.

MARKETING: CONNECTING WITH PEOPLE, CREATING VALUE

LUCY KIMBELL

Service design thinking takes as its focus humans rather than organisations, and finding ways to help organisations and stakeholders co-create value. This essay shows how some of the core concepts in marketing underpin designing for service and it also suggests where design practices can contribute to marketing.

The emergence of marketing

Of all the disciplines that have something to contribute to service design, marketing is probably the one that can claim to already have done so in significant ways. Like other management fields, marketing theory and practice have changed over time influenced by wider social, economic and political developments. One of the main shifts in marketing was a move from a production orientation to a marketing orientation. When goods were scarce, for many firms, marketing consisted of efforts to sell what they produced and of analysing relationships between buyers and sellers. But as new manufacturers increased competition, marketing began to turn away from selling goods to customers. Instead, they tried to understand what customers might want and then produce that – not the other way round. This marketing orientation has had an enormous influence on the world in which we live.

Organisations make huge efforts to find out what customers want or need, especially in consumer goods, and try to differentiate their products and services to attract distinct market segments. Studying the ways marketing organisations try to reach consumers using diverse media

shows how embedded these ideas are in contemporary culture in developed economies.

Contemporary definitions of marketing explain it as being centrally concerned with identifying customers and then initiating and maintaining relationships with them in ways that create value both for customers and organisations. Recent research includes developing theories of consumption, to understand what influences people to buy, how customers make decisions, the role of different factors in shaping consumption including access to information, other peoples' activities, and the wider

Of all the disciplines that have something to contribute to service design, marketing is probably the one that can claim to already have done so in significant ways.

context including global marketing and social marketing. To develop strategies, marketing professionals turn to quantitative methods, such as surveys, and qualitative methods such as ethnography.

Services marketing

Much of the early focus in marketing was on goods. Services became an important topic in marketing from the 1970s onwards as researchers realised that the economic value of services was beginning to exceed that of other kinds of activity. Some of the early effort was working out how to define services, often as what goods are not or as additional offerings complementing products (Vargo and Lusch, 2004b). Four characteristics summarised by Zeithaml, Parasuraman and Berry (1985) from a survey of existing research – intangibility, heterogeneity, inseparability, and perishability (IHIP) – have since been shown to be not generalisable

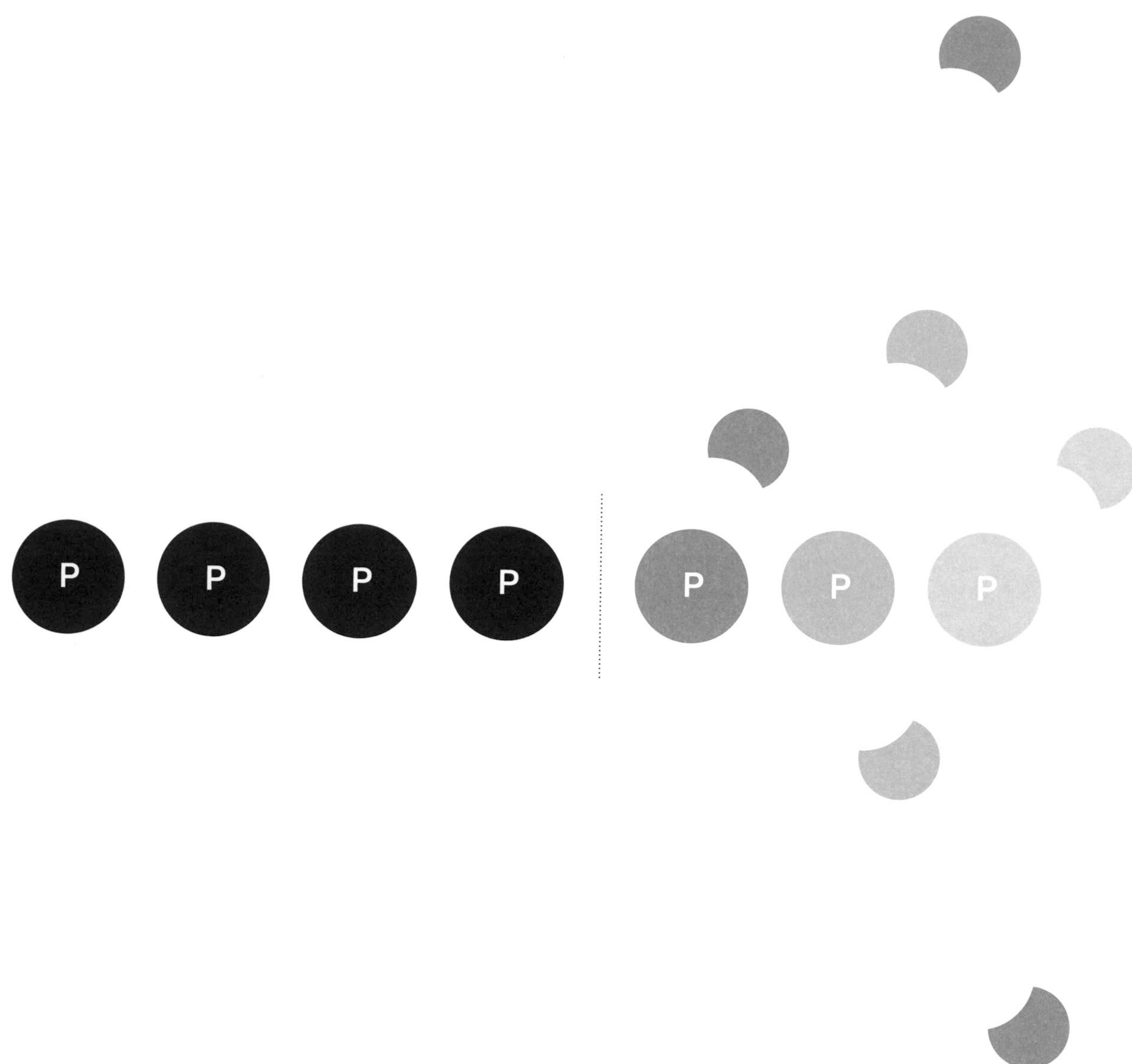
P
P
P
P
P
P
P

across all services and to be applicable to some goods (Lovelock and Gummesson, 2004; Vargo and Lusch, 2004b). Further developments in conceptualising services have lead to what is currently an unresolved question. Either (a) everything is service, as suggested in by Vargo and Lusch's (2004a) articulation of a service-dominant (S-D) logic, proposing that the conventional distinction between goods and services does not matter; or (b) new ways need to be found to understand the specific qualities of organising for and consuming services, such as highlighting ownership and access to resources (Lovelock and Gummesson, 2004).

While the debate continues about what constitutes service, researchers have also focussed on specific aspects of service. They began to move away from traditional marketing's emphasis on pricing and transactions towards understanding in more detail the processes through which individual customers interacted with firms. An example of these changes was the addition of three extra factors to the classic "4 Ps" of the marketing mix of product, price, promotion and place: participants (the human actors involved in the service encounter), processes (procedures, mechanisms and flows of activities) and physical evidence (the physical surroundings and tangible clues) (Booms and Bitner, 1981). Researchers also began to emphasise service quality perceived from the point of view of the customer for whom the service encounter constituted the service (Zeithaml and Bitner, 2003). Research on customer relationship management brought to attention the relations between customers and organisations and lead to an understanding of creating value with customers (Normann and Ramírez, 1993). Relationship marketing emphasised the roles of other actors such as partners in constituting value through alliances with a wider group of organisational actors (Grönroos, 2000).

Marketing or design?

Even a brief review of the main ideas within marketing has shown to what extent they have diffused through contemporary design, in particular service design. Indeed it is perhaps hard to identify two distinct fields, such is the close correspondence between them but there are some important differences, shaped in part by the influences of the social sciences within marketing and by the educational backgrounds of many service de-

Understanding value and the nature of relations between people and other people, between people and things, between people and organisations, and between organisations of different kinds, are now understood to be central to designing services.

signers in art and design schools. Marketing is about organisations creating and building relationships with customers to co-create value; design aims to put stakeholders at the centre of designing services and preferably co-design with them. Marketing scholars and practitioners have developed tools and concepts including blueprints, service evidence, and a focus on the service encounter; designers use these tools and develop others that often focus on individual users' experiences as a way into designing services. Marketers define who the customers of a service are or could be and the broad detail of the kinds of relationship an organisation might have with them; designers give shape and form to these ideas, and can enrich and challenge assumptions by making visualisations. Marketing researchers study customers to develop insights into their practices and values; designers can use insights as the starting point for design and add a focus to the aesthetics of service experiences. Marketing has a view of new service development that is shaped by

problem-solving; design professionals have an understanding of an iterative design process that involves exploring possibilities and being open to serendipity and surprise.

It probably does not matter whether service design is part of marketing, or vice versa. The ways ideas spread and how organisations in different market sectors are organised are likely to shape how service design plays out in different firms. What does matter is that understanding value and the nature of relations between people and other people, between people and things, between people and organisations, and between organisations of different kinds, are now understood to be central to designing services. The field of services marketing has been concerned with such questions for several decades and has contributed some important concepts. But marketing on its own is just one element of any organisation's effort to innovate in services. It is a multidisciplinary approach combining marketing with other specialisms that serves to create value as services are designed and enacted in the interactions between individuals and organisations.

Who are these Service Designers?

Basics

FIELDS OF SERVICE DESIGN

Service design thinking as an interdisciplinary approach includes and connects various fields of activity. The following articles provide a comprehensive overview of how different design and management disciplines incorporate service design thinking and how these disciplines facilitate service design.

The selection of disciplines makes no claim to be complete. In fact, many more disciplines could be included here, such as engineering, IT, architecture, psychology to name but a few. However, this exemplary assortment illustrates the implementation range of service design thinking.

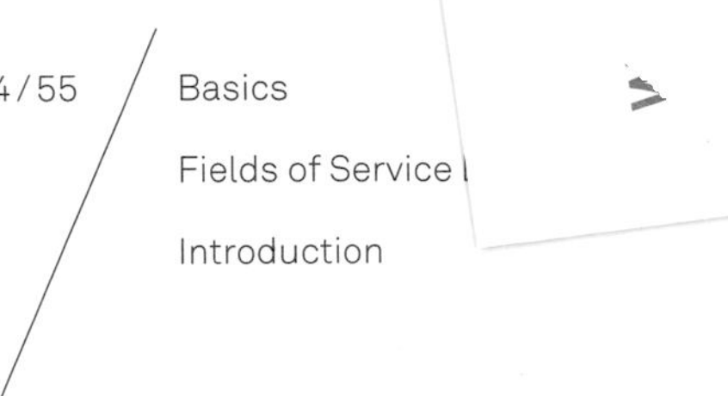

SATU MIETINNEN, FINLAND
Product Design

JAKOB SCHNEIDER, GERMANY
Graphic Design

SIMON CLATWORTHY, NORWAY
Interaction Design

KATE ANDREWS, UNITED KINGDOM
Social Design

RALF BEUKER, GERMANY
Strategic Management

KATE BLACKMON, UNITED KINGDOM
Operations Management

GEKE VAN DIJK, THE NETHERLANDS
Design Ethnography

PRODUCT DESIGN: DEVELOPING PRODUCTS WITH SERVICE APPLICATIONS

SATU MIETTINEN

This chapter looks at the influences of service production upon product design and considers the implications of the evolution of product designers from designing just products to designing services too.

Conceptual design and iteration

The roles of designers have changed as well as the methods they use in their design work. Valtonen (2007) demonstrates this in her study of how the role of an industrial designer has diversified. Designers are now working in managing design processes in companies, working as researchers and contributing to consumer research.

Product design, also known as industrial design, has undergone changes during past decades. The design of objects is no longer restricted to form, function, material and production. Design is arguably now focused on the interaction between people and technology, and products serve as platforms for experiences, functionality and service offerings (Buchanan, 2001). The Industrial Designers Society of America defines industrial design as a professional service of creating and developing concepts and specifications that optimise the function, value and appearance of products and systems for the mutual benefit of both user and manufacturer (IDSA, 2010). Thus it can be perceived that industrial design is itself a service that benefits users and manufacturers of products and services.

Design seeks in practice to identify problems and latent needs in various aspects of people's lives that can be used to inspire creative generation of artefacts. People's needs and problems change as their social,

technological, and economic living environments change. Design responds to the emergence of new environments and user needs. Designers study users and their usage of artefacts to develop better products and generate knowledge that can be embedded into artefacts. Users generate knowledge through interpretation of this embedded knowledge in artefacts. They need to be able to understand the value, meaning, and the ways to use the artefact in different situations of their daily lives.

The role of an industrial designer has diversified. Designers are now working in managing design processes in companies, working as researchers and contributing to consumer research.

The International Organisation for Standardisation (ISO) introduced a process guideline (ISO 13407) on "human-centred design process for interactive systems" with an emphasis on user participation in the system development process (Sato, 2009). The Human Centred Design (HCD) process model can be applied to organise HCD approaches into problem framing, information gathering and interpretation, solution ideation, development and evaluation phases. Each of these phases represent the different parts of the product and service development process that design can help inform.

Stakeholders' activity levels can be used as an organising principle in HCD approaches to product and service development. Stakeholders in the design process can also be considered both designers and users whilst representatives of the design community can be considered to be design engineers, industrial or interaction designers or user researchers. They take part in the design process by contributing their expertise in defining and specifying technological solutions, helping define the key user characteristics or by articulating the visual appearance of the product.

Users within the HCD process can be considered as either anyone exposed to interaction with a product or service or so-called secondary users such as service personnel and employees of the service provider who are involved in the provision of the service. User expertise like these individuals may provide is useful in building a clearer picture of the contexts and practices in which users might interact with the product. Other such stakeholders are customers, suppliers and third-party de

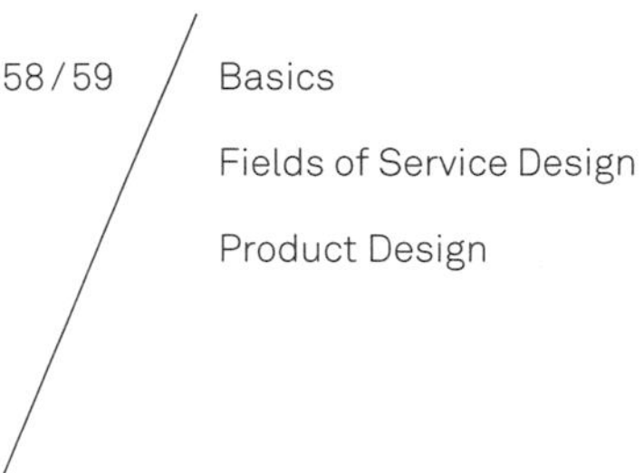

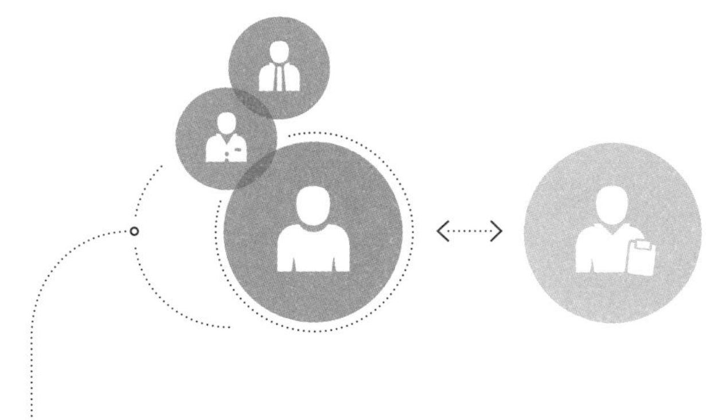

evelopers all of whom may participate in the HCD development process by contributing contextu

THIS IS CO-CREATIVE.

The concept of activity refers to participants' interactivity, initiative and style of collaboration and contribution in design events. User roles may vary from proactive participation where users contribute to solving and framing design challenges to passive roles where designers instead interpret user data without any direct engagement with the user community (Keinonen, 2009).

al information of domain specific expertise.

Product design is always linked to a manufacturing process. Typically, there are a large number of engineering processes that have to be integrated to support the production of a complete product. By considering product design holistically as a service, it is possible to consider how all the processes are connected to the business of exchanging goods and marketing. Product design can, and must, therefore assist in the fulfilment of the demands of the delivery and maintenance processes as well as the user experience of a service.

The use of these human-centred design tools characterises the product design process. In turn these help facilitate creation of suitable product specifications to meet all relevant engineering and user specifications. Product design can also be used for corporate communications, brand building, technology development and marketing (Keinonen, 2006).

Conceptual product design focuses on combining several product design perspectives: a user-centred design approach, a variety of qualitative and quantitative research and data gathering approaches, and visualisation techniques such as sketching, imaging and prototyping. Where the product design process aims toward a product launch, conceptual design can play several roles in supporting a company's business

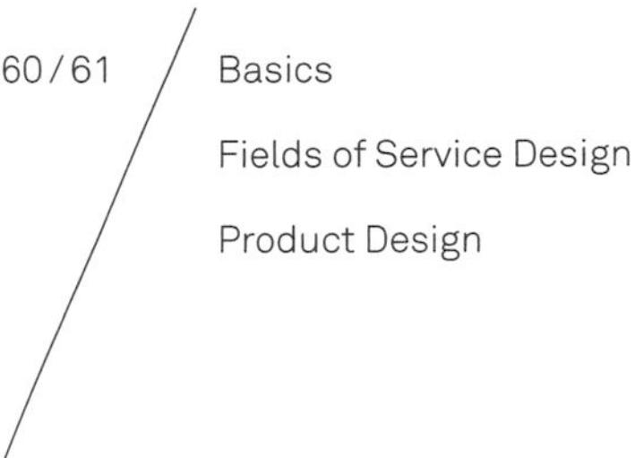

objectives and organisational processes. The objective of concept development is not articulation of a product specification that comprehensively defines a product as described previously. Instead, product concept development outlines the product's characteristics and begins a process where the organisation can consider how it would need to evolve or adjust to accommodate actual development of this concept in the future. Product development concepts can make a major contribution to later phases of product development. Emerging concepts are created either as a result of technical research and development or through modification of existing products in an attempt by the organisation to enter radically different markets. They make user needs understandable and help the company's learning and decision-making processes for future product generation. Visualisation of such concepts is typically accomplished through development of scenarios in anticipation of forthcoming technological development and future research. Very often these concepts are not aimed at implementation. Visions are also used to outline and communicate a company's brand and future marketing strategies. (Ibid.)

Conceptual product design focuses on combining several product design perspectives: a user-centred design approach, a variety of qualitative and quantitative research and data gathering approaches, and visualisation techniques such as sketching, imaging and prototyping.

Iterative design development helps to solve problems found in user testing. There must be a cycle of design, testing and measurement, then redesign, repeated as often as necessary. This is a way to incorporate results of behavioural testing into the next version of the system. Making a system user friendly and easy to operate is the goal of this approach (Gould and Lewis, 1985). Iterative design is a design methodology based on a cyclical process of prototyping, testing, analysing, and refining a work in progress. Typical product design development embodies this iterative design approach where, as detailed previously, stakeholders can assist in refining the outcome. Creation of product development concepts can be part of iterative design work. Both conceptual and iterative design approaches are important phases in the service design process. The challenge is to design user-orientated hybrids that incorporate both the customer facing products and that help articulate the service they assist in offering.

Product-service hybrids

In the era of industrial production it has not been customary to sell services. Or at least it has not been customary to consider industrially produced products as part of a service proposition. If wishing to embrace this reality, industrial producers face the challenges of developing a business culture of service development as well as requiring the practical knowledge of pricing and maintaining services. The aim is largely to increase profitability, growth and customer retention through the development of service propositions. Companies producing consumer products are now being challenged to develop hybrid products. Koivisto (2007) defines hybrid products as products where the service has been designed as an inseparable part of the product. A good example of this is Apple's iPod and iTunes product package (Apple, 2010). Developing such a hybrid product means that both the product concept and a service system are developed in tandem.

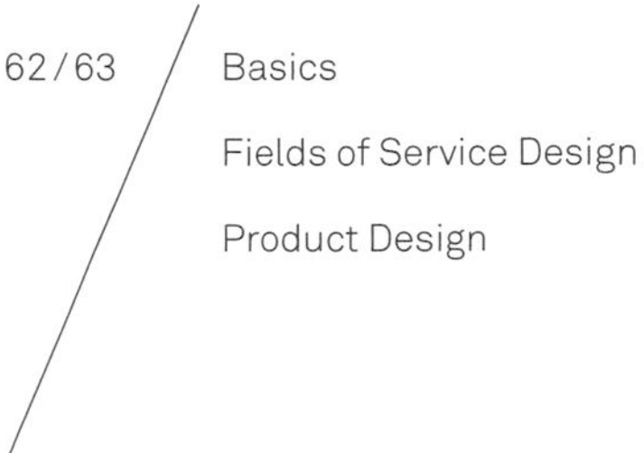

KONE is a business-to-business provider for complete solutions for the installation, modernisation and maintenance of elevators, escalators and automatic building doors (Kone, 2010a). The challenge is to communicate the service business that KONE offers to the customers. Kone's customer portfolio consists of a variety of differing customer requirements, development of new machinery as well as provision of maintenance and service products to customers. As a result, Kone's service business is significant. The company's objective is to offer the best people flow experience to their customers by developing and delivering solutions that enable people to move smoothly, safely, comfortably through their customers' premises without waiting in buildings. They seek to offer this in an increasingly urbanising environment – giving them clear potential to innovate and expand their market.

Lea Lehtinen from Kone Corporation Service Innovation unit discussed the development process of the KONE Deco™. The KONE Deco™ is a new interior decoration solution that can be installed in both a new and existing lift (Kone, 2010b). It covers the full service from the planning of the decoration to material installation and replacement. The decoration can be changed to suit the place and event, even several times a year. Customers can choose replaceable design panels for the back wall to create a unique character for the elevator or, for example, to bring a marketing campaign into the lift. An airline might show scenes from its newest destinations. If the route changes, the design elements can easily be changed. The KONE Deco™ is an example of the hybrid product where the service and physical product are integrated across, and to ensure the efficient lifecycle of the product.

Myyrmanni shopping mall, as another customer, had a development need: Customers did not rise to the second floor of the shopping mall by using rustproof steel-car lifts (Myyrmanni, 2010). They were queuing for the landscape lifts. To ensure efficient customer flow this had to be changed. The mall had tried out a new lighting design and attempted to guide the people flow with arrows in the floor. A new concept to change the flow of people had to be developed. This is how "The Incredibles" concept emerged and solved the problem.

KONE has a wide range of customers of different sizes. Close co-operation with business partners thus makes effective service development possible. Faced with this challenge, service design should be included as part of the organisational process of the company. Service design should be included in every aspect of the process from order to delivery as well as installation and material sourcing. It is important to use the company's own core know-how of its service context and harness the organisational

A successful service design project requires integrating stakeholders as earlier as possible in the project development process.

understanding of institutional practices in the product development process. This occurs in the case of KONE by using the knowledge of the maintenance and installation staff in elicitation and development of the maintenance requirements for the service.

A successful service design project requires integrating stakeholders as early as possible in the project development process. Opportunities to iterate the product development process together with the stakeholders involved in the project should be created as soon as possible. This will in all likelihood result in an increase in proactive solutions. Management buy-in needs to be secured to support the process. There has to be constant communication, continuous sales work and partnership with the

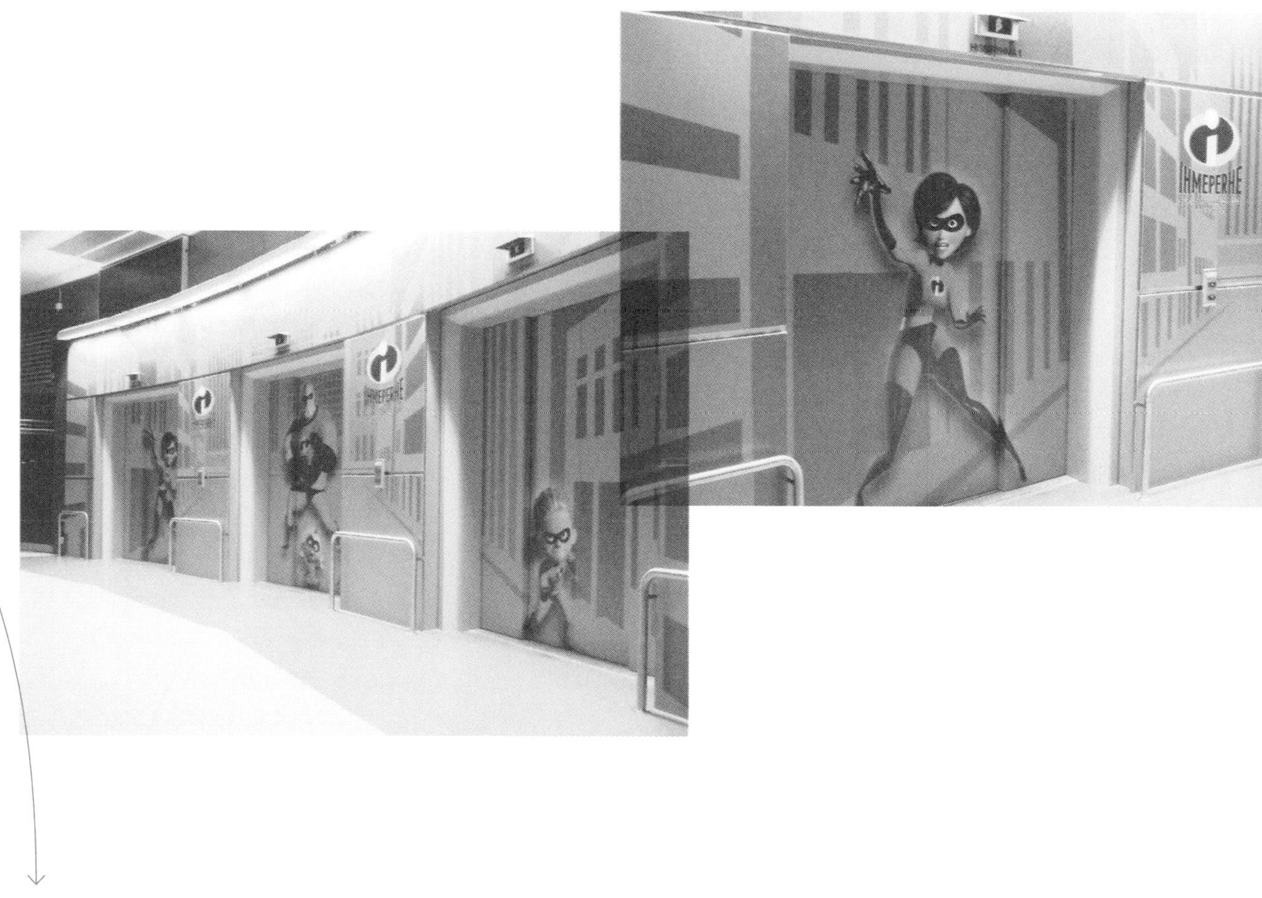

Steel car elevators were decorated with the pictures from “The Incredibles”. This created an improved atmosphere and made the steel car elevators attractive to the shopping mall customers. The people flow was changed and the problem was solved.

designers. It is also necessary for everyone in the organisation to understand this interdisciplinary way of working and the business logic this demands.

Service design has been brought to KONE Corporation with an unprejudiced attitude, utilising organisational information broadly and exploiting the benefits of designers and psychologists co-operating with one another. Brainstorming with the customer using storyboards is one of the service design methods used at KONE. The advantage of service design in this context is that it makes the service visible and understandable for the customers. Other methods utilised are, for example, customer focus groups and different electronic mock-ups and product prototypes. Increasing technologisation has led to a fragmentation of user needs, but if understood correctly it also presents significant opportunities for organisations like KONE to innovate extensively with their product and service offerings. Good service design projects can also help find answers to the customer's present and future needs. As this example has helped articulate, service design methods can be used both for developing a hybrid product as well as developing an out-and-out service product.

Creating value propositions with users

Sanders (2005) points out that companies are seeking and experimenting with new tools and methods for human-centred design research. Design research has thus moved away from experiential design, such as just observing people using the product, into more generative approaches to product development where enquiries are conducted by design researchers to generate ideas or to uncover new product development opportunities at the starting phase of the design process.

Mark Jones, Lead of Service Innovation at IDEO, says that from his perspective the design process begins with understanding the product's context of use, and observation of users' experiences by moving into the field to observe users and how they interact with the product. In a typical development project pre-research, work is done before one or two workshops with the stakeholders. Subsequently, the development case needs up to six or seven iterations and mock-ups as part of the iterative product development process.

Typically, a design team would consist of an engineer and designer. When you start designing actions, systems or product service systems, this range of expertise needs to be expanded through the involvement of a human factors expert. Design's role is to illustrate and represent the complexity of the system to make it more understandable as well as represent the added value that the product brings to the company. Participatory design methods are used in the development work and this involves relating extensively with clients. How the methods are chosen depends on the business case.

When the product service systems or service-product hybrids are developed it's not only about what kind of services are co-created with users but also about what the service's role is within the organisation's business model. When designed and considered well, the product service systems and service-product hybrids detailed here can make key contributions to the overall value proposition and desirability of the products offered by an organisation.

GRAPHIC DESIGN: PROVIDING VISUAL EXPLANATION

JAKOB SCHNEIDER

It is nearly impossible for any product or service to be available on the market without a graphically designed element. Wayfinding systems, user interfaces, pictograms, packaging, forms or manuals are all graphically designed. To be successful, these offerings have to be well designed and thought through in terms of their graphical impact and how the information they contain is structured.

An individual's perception of the world is much more dependent on visual impulses than ever before. At the same time, people have to deal with a plethora of sources of information, increasingly distributed by digital media. It is therefore necessary to develop mental filter systems, or mechanisms of perception through which individuals can continue to make sound decisions about the information and perceptual stimuli presented to them.

Mental models help an individual's orientation in the world; they are the abstract and reductive mental representation of the complexity all of us face in everyday life – the schemas by which all of us understand the world around ourselves. If, however, a user is confronted with a situation they have never previously experienced, they cannot fall back on an existing model. Knowledge about the payment process at a supermarket, and the mental model of how this system works in their head might or might not necessarily be helpful for understanding how to interact with a new online shopping process. The metaphor of the online shopping cart for example, promotes the development of a new mental model,

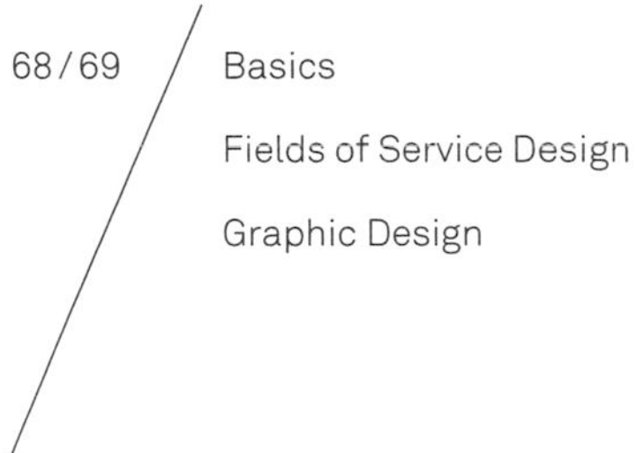

through reference to an analogous experience. The individual can draw upon known mechanisms and functionalities associated with, in this case, shopping carts to understand a novel and largely intangible online system of payment. Even though online shopping is phenomenologically different from previous experiences the user might have of "offline" shopping.

It is the graphic designer's task to trigger an individual's apriori mental models, or at least to positively influence the accrual of such cognitive representations of meaning.

It is thus the graphic designer's task to trigger an individual's a priori mental models, or at least to positively influence the accrual of such cognitive representations of meaning. This chapter explains what graphic design is capable of and what role it can play within service design – from the perspective of a graphic designer.

Two tasks: information and branding

Historically speaking, graphic design has its origins in the applied arts. It has its roots in the professions of poster artists and sign writers. However, today there are two big fields of activity for a graphic designer, while boundaries of these two fields are fluid.

Branding refers to helping an offering establish a visual identity and familiarity in the eyes of customers. Thus graphic design taps into and adopts a number of patterns of which the customer already has a mental model: use of the colour green in packaging can, for example, suggest an association with the user's ideas of freshness, organic products or, more recently, environmental friendliness.

Information design, on the other hand, pertains to the task of making complex and abstract content accessible in a simpler way. Through logical composition, visual hierarchy and the use of visual metaphors, viewers are supported in their absorption and comprehension of information.

Branding supports the customer to emotionally approximate himself with the theme or emotional context of the experience. Within this setting, information design leads to a satisfactory and positively associated user experience.

Branding and information design are not opposed to each other. They rather operate with a high degree of interdependency. The branded visual environment reduces inhibition thresholds of participants through its use of familiar motifs. This supports the customer to emotionally approximate himself with the theme or emotional context of the experience. Within this setting, information design leads to a satisfactory and positively associated user experience. Nevertheless, these two fields have different focuses. There is no disputing that branding is an essential part of market positioning, as it creates the atmosphere that motivates the user to become aware of and consider the offering in the first place. Information design has far greater underlying and explicit influence in the service design process, since it changes how society handles information, and moreover has the power to affect users' perceptions of the value of a service proposition or indeed of any of the information transfers between service provider and the service recipient that is integral to the service experience.

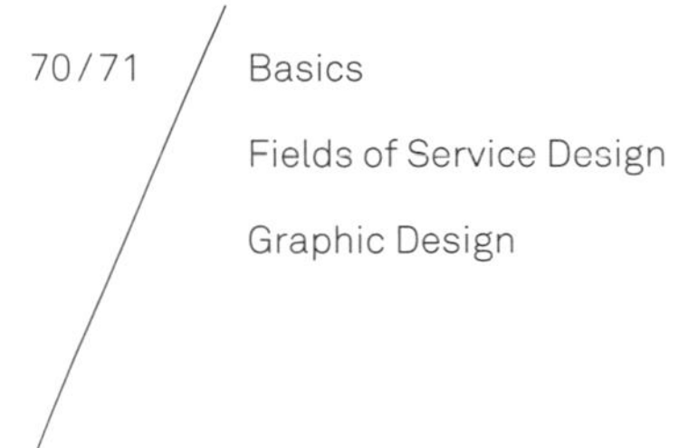

The works of a pioneer of graphic design, Henry C. Beck (1902–1974) are a good example of this. He created the prototype of all public transportation maps. Beck's plan of the London Underground adapted the geometrical clarity of an electrical circuit board for the geographical position of the Underground stations. In doing this, he made the complex system more understandable and accessible through visual abstraction. His approach of combining two fundamentally different topics – electrical wiring and public transportation – helps the user develop their own mental model. In fact, he changed our way of imagining the Underground's conglomerate of tubes and stations.

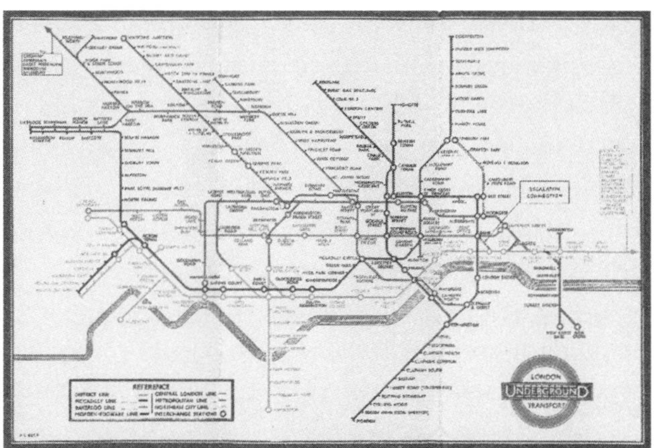

Henry C. Beck's plan of the London Underground from 1936 adapted the geometrical clearness of an electrical circuit board for the geographical position of the Underground stations. His approach of combining two fundamentally different topics – electrical wiring and public transportation – helps the user to develop their own mental model.

The need for orientation and reliability

After decades of progressively more empty public advertising and the obvious manipulation of advertising promises, the customer is fed up with not being taken seriously and seeks authenticity. (Gilmore, J. H. and Pine, B. J., 2007)

It is necessary to accommodate this mind set. How authentic is a cleaning service whose visual presentation is itself messy? How believable is a grocery market, specialised in organic products, which shares a similar corporate design to a multinational convenience food company? How much trust is warranted for an online tool that appears inconsistent with the Internet's visual language, or uses web aesthetics that are ten years old?

Customers today have a strong sense of how a product with service components can be integrated into their everyday life. Such products are often sold on the basis of helping to simplify their life, not to create further confusion. Users become increasingly annoyed when they feel a product is irrational – for instance: having to press the start button, to shut off a computer; being debited after pressing "proceed", despite wanting to check again the entered address before you confirm a purchase online or noticing two screws are on the wrong position when the cupboard has already been built.

A negative feeling occurs, at least unconsciously, if one encounters bad graphic design or disparities in visual communication such as those mentioned above. An improper presentation of an organisation makes the customer uncomfortable and produces inhibitions and sometimes even anger. Moreover, if the use of an offering is perceived as difficult and exhausting, this may cause unwillingness or denegation. It may be forgivable for a customer that their bank's corporate identity does not really

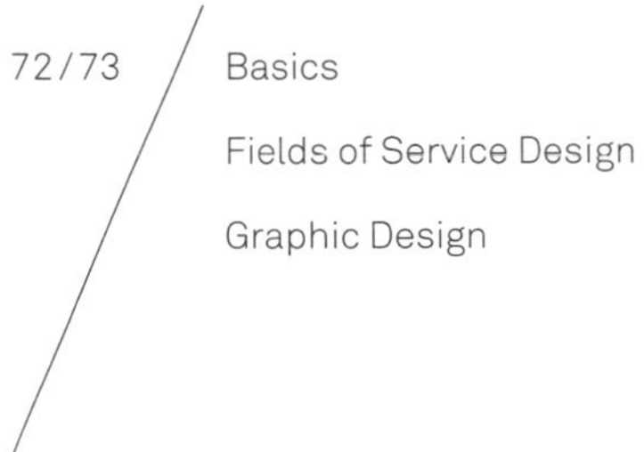

inspire confidence, but they become upset when they cannot see their balance because the pixelated letters on a screen are too small to read.

Visual presentation plays an important role in three ways. It pre-empts the actual service process, it controls customer expectation, and it can promote trust during interaction. The so-called look and feel can evoke a positive prevailing mood, or even make the service usable in the first place through visual aides. Lastly, the visual appearance acts as an anchor that links the user to the positive experience. Visual control is henceforth a key competence in the conception of design propositions.

Visual control

"These days, information is a commodity being sold. And designers – including the newly defined subset of information designers and information architects – have a responsible role to play. We are interpreters, not merely translators, between sender and receiver. What we say and how we say it makes a difference. If we want to speak to people, we need to know their language. In order to design for understanding, we need to understand design." —Erik Spiekermann, graphic designer

When standing in front of a cash machine, previous design propositions determine if you, or maybe your own grandmother, will be able to interact successfully with the machine. Putatively banal parameters like letter size, fonts, colours, positioning and notably a logical formation and formal organisation of the given information is critical.

For graphic designers it does not matter if they are working on a product or a service offering. Whether they have to create a print product, an interface or a three-dimensional presentation, it is imperative for the graphic designer to know what they want to offer the customer on a visual level, in order to adequately convey the thoughts and concepts standing behi

Who are these Service Designers?

THIS IS HOLISTIC.

Graphical elements of any kind never stand alone. Their impact on the user is dependent on the physical and emotional environment.

nd the design proposition. If they want to see how and if their design is working appropriately they

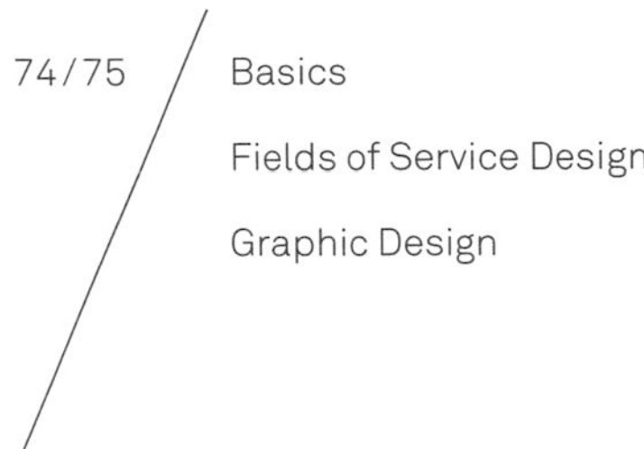

BEAUTY AS A SIDE EFFECT OF A FUNCTIONAL TASK

The design agency schneiter meier külling (smek) from Zurich developed a new packaging concept for Helvepharm, a Swiss producer of generic medicine. Analysis of the product environment brought certain uniformity in medicinal packaging to light. This was by no means identified as an aesthetic problem only. Patients face the threat of confusing completely different preparations.

Smek eventually developed an especially easy information design for Helvepharm's packaging. An explicit colour code paired with clear typography presents immediately to the customer what sort of medicine he is taking, and how he has to deal with it.

The visually independent positioning in the market competition is more of a side effect and actually roots in the functional task.

have to see the entire context and the surrounding system as a whole. Assume a local community ce entre wants to redesign its waiting room and hires a qualified graphic designer, granting him absolute freedom. The designer might identify the touchpoints: doors, seats, signs, service counter and a cashier window. Facing these constraints, they ask two questions: Which emotions should be aroused in each area, and how can it be explained to the citizens what they have to or can do in this location?

The role of a graphic designer does not lie in sticking a previously developed logo on each and every surface.

The answer to both questions could lie in a structured process outlined through bold lines on the floor. These could lead the user from the door, to take a queuing number, to the seat, the counter and then finally the cashier window. Additionally, a big sign could explain the whole process. A distinctive colour code, consistent with the colours on the sign and the stations, can on the one hand communicate the station's meaning in an emotional way, and on the other hand assist in structuring the room spatially. On the already installed display panel it could be explained why the citizen has to wait and for how long, by using an information graphic.

After a consistent and functionally designed system has been established, these exemplary measures could be recursively applied to all further touchpoints. Ultimately the visual orientation system could be embedded in a corporate design, which stands for openness, clarity and reliability, achievable for example through a clear, simple visual language.

It is nonetheless important to understand that the role of a graphic designer does not lie in sticking a previously developed logo on each and every surface. The complete visual appearance consists of far more factors

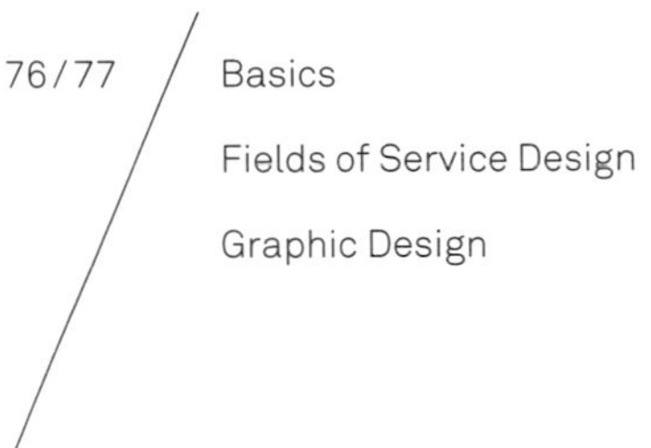

than just such signage. The use of colours, text, photographs, the chosen medium, the type of production – there are countless ways to keep an image consistent and also countless ways to dilute it. As many parameters decide what is told by whom, as how it is told.

The orchestration of these factors requires designers to be open to current trends and familiar with previous trends to best enable them to understand the world of their target audience. There are certain photographs that most viewers would consistently place as from the nineties, which could be very unfortunate if this aesthetic is not what is desired by the organisation. At a detail-focussed level of typography, which could be seen as the equivalent to pronunciation and pitch of voice in the design world, the viewer can be addressed loud and clear, quiet and playful or serious and outdated.

The given example of the community centre illustrates the relationship of branding and information design in a meaningful way. In the case of service design, however, the team works out its focus group very precisely, it analyses and modifies operations on and offstage and verifies the designed outcome in repeated experiments. It is able to plan and accompany the process with the necessary expertise. These examples of how graphic designers think and operate should indicate that they are indispensable members of a service design team.

How graphic designers contribute to a service design process

The creation of a comfortably usable form, the development of a pictogram system, the design of an information graphic, the concept of user guidance in digital media, and in fact every kind of visual positioning in the branding of services and service organisations, needs the experience and expertise of professional designers. Today, such designers work typically at the end of the process: The strategic planners develop a concept, lasting several weeks, and the designer is asked to "create a couple of nice pictures" just before the deadline. Doing it in that way wastes an opportunity. The full integration of visual designers in an interdisciplinary team from the beginning should be as self-evident as the hiring of a project manager.

Graphic designers have a distinctive visual imagination and think early about how a planned idea will work in practice. They depend in their work on thinking mostly about the moment when the user comes into contact with the product or service offering. This special perspective contributes to the development process right from its onset. The creative team benefits from the designer's ability to create mock-ups and prototypes with relative ease. These can already have certain functions and can therefore help in detecting misconceptions, making it easier for team members without creative background to play the user's role and integrate themselves with the creative process.

Regardless of the specific task at hand, the graphic designer is an asset because of their own way of analysing the environment. The special perspective they possess in interpreting how graphic information and culturally coined visual codes work is valuable for creating functioning design propositions.

ORIENTATION AND STYLE AS A NECESSARY COMBINATION

büro uebele from Stuttgart developed a signage system for the Stuttgart Trade Fair. Visitors of different nationalities have to orientate themselves on the extensive convention area. The system guides them to the right place. And to make the walk seem shorter, it's entertaining: outside they are greeted by bright flags, inside by distinctively striped signs and big walls of colour. The chord of colours, like colourful wallpaper, makes the uptake of information both pleasant and easy. The coding of the various destinations works subliminally: pink leads to the congress, blue to the exits, red to the halls.

Branding and information design complement each other in a symbiotic way. Function and emotion combined define the concrete parameters like typography, colours, form and composition.

INTERACTION DESIGN: SERVICES AS A SERIES OF INTERACTIONS

SIMON CLATWORTHY

This chapter explains what interaction design is, and what it can do for you and your service. Interaction design is becoming an important part of services, and becoming more important by the day. Giving it due focus can make you money and save you money at the same time. Read on to find out more.

Services are a series of interactions between customers and the service system through many different touchpoints during the customer journey. As the sole way that customers relate to your services, you would think that interactions would be centre stage for all service providers. So, why are so many services so bad? When Demos, a UK think tank, talk of a fundamental disconnection between services and people, one of the main reasons they give is the poor consideration of the interactions between the service provider and the customer – the interaction design. To value your customer, you need to spend some time understanding the interactions they have with your service, and that means two things. Firstly, viewing your service through the customers' eyes, and secondly, designing in such a way that customers receive consistent experiences over time which they consider valuable. It's strange, but repeatedly we see companies ignoring both of these aspects, with the consequence that customers feel ignored and value is lost.

One of the key characteristics of services is that they often include employees in the customer interface. Although this is rapidly being replaced by technology, it is still true for a great many services. Interaction

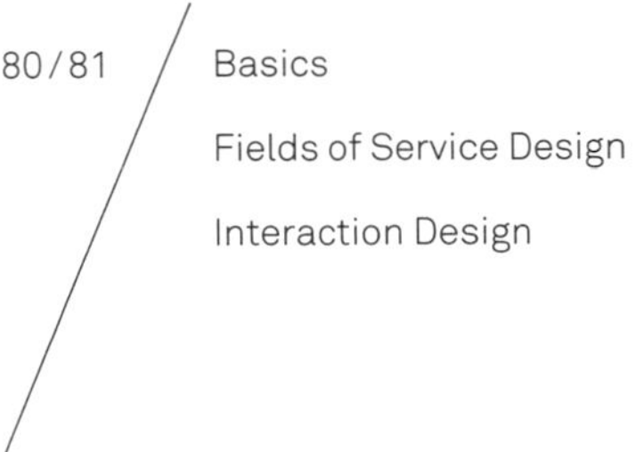

design for services therefore relates to the design of desired employee behaviour, as much as design of interactions with technology. The focus of this chapter is, however, upon the design of interactions for digital interaction. This is not because personnel behaviours are not important, but because digital interaction is an area that is becoming more and more central for service delivery. Self service, co-production and social networks are all aspects that recently have placed a focus upon digital interactions, and their design. There is a separate discipline called interaction design, which focuses upon the design of interactions in products and services. It's a rapidly growing discipline, and recently it has been championed by Apple, but Microsoft does a good job too, and Nokia was the king of mobile interaction until a few years ago. They all employ numerous interaction designers, who make life easier and more pleasurable for us.

> Self service, co-production and social networks are all aspects that recently have placed a focus upon interactions, and their design.

Desirability is king in the land of interface design

Desirability in a service fires desire in the customer. Desirable interactions are something you tell others about and which give trust with, and loyalty to, the service. Finally, and this is becoming more and more important, desirability has a strong emotional dimension, often giving a pleasurable experience from the interaction. Apple, Amazon, Nintendo, Samsung, Nokia and Sony all understand that this makes them money. Sounds good, but it's not an easy thing to do, mostly because desirability requires collaboration across traditional silos in a service organisation.

Utility – It just has to work at the functional level
Desirability depends upon the service offering functional benefits that your customers need. This might sound simple and pretty banal, but scoring highly in terms of utility demands that you really understand your customers and their needs, together with an understanding of the functional benefits of your design offering. Not all organisations know these things and continually view the world from their own point of view rather than that of their customers. To get a high score on the utility level you need to offer people what they need but no more and this is not always an easy thing to pull off. There is a big tendency for feature creep in interactive services – hey let's add that feature, it doesn't cost extra! This leads to a service that has strayed from the core offering and which customers find vague or fuzzy. Utility is about what your service does.

Usability – Keep it simple, stupid (KISS)
While utility is about what, usability is about how. Usability is all about how easy it is to get to the offering (utility value) when using the service. It's all about ease of use, which often relates to how quickly ar

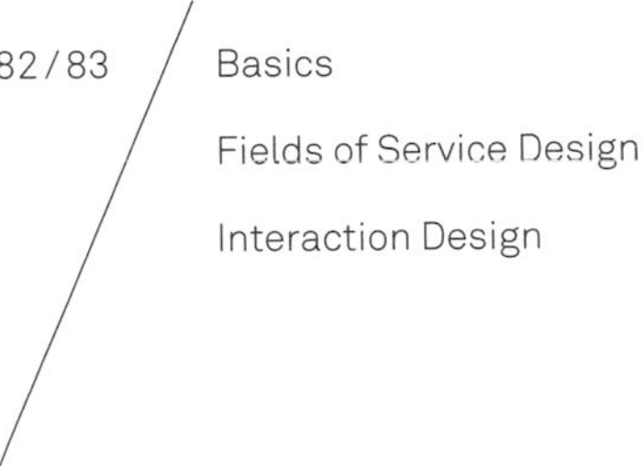

THIS IS SEQUENCING.

The series of interactions outline a so called customer journey through the offerings of the respective service.

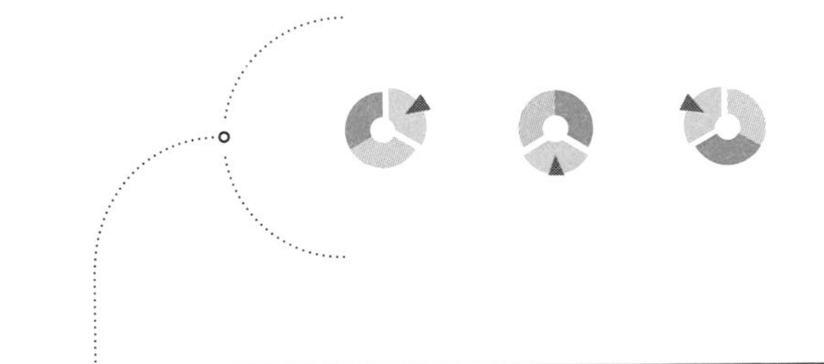

nd smoothly a customer can move through the service journey, and the risk they run of misunderstanding something and making errors (and error recovery of course). Its key metrics are time, errors and flow.

Usability relates strongly to how the interaction is strung together, often in terms of the design of the dialogue between the (online) service and the customer. Within interaction design, this is often termed the interaction architecture, and describes the functional divisions between the different parts of a website, and upon the functional layout of a page. A website needs to be structured according to the customers' expectations of structure. This is described as the customers' mental model, and ideally, your website structure should mirror the customers' mental model. This is not always a simple task to sort out, but luckily there are skilled information architects out there who can help you with this. A good means of finding the customers' mental model when designing a service is to ask customers to structure the site for you, and there are several methods available to help them do this in a structured way.

There are three keys to unlock the door to usability: frequency, sequence and importance. Frequency says that things the customers do most frequently (e.g. next, back, search etc.) should have a prominent position in the sequence. Sequence says that activities that occur in sequence should be presented in sequence (i.e. you pay at the end of a transaction, not in the middle). Importance means that important pieces of information need to be given clearly and at the right time (e.g. if you only ship within the EU, then a customer trying to buy from India needs to know this early on – not at the end of a six-page check-out dialogue). Understanding the customers' mental model and applying the frequency, sequence and importance rule will crack most of your usability needs. But, beware, like all rules, you cannot follow them blindly, and there are always tradeoffs that have to be made between these elements.

Pleasurability – the pleasure principle

We like things that make us feel good. In fact, we use a lot of time, effort and money on pleasurable things. Why is it, then, that when it comes to digital interactions, most of it is designed to be neutral at best? It's as if we have all been brainwashed to expect utilitarianism in everything digital. Luckily, we are entering into the experience economy,

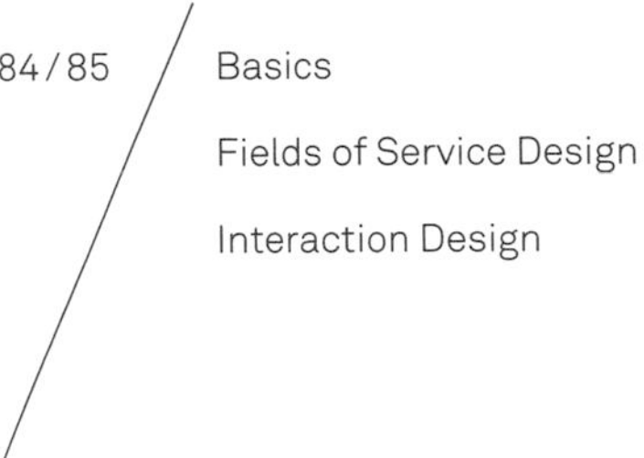

in which, finally, pleasurable experiences are recognised as central in today's markets. Ten years ago, Nokia accelerated past its main competitor, Ericsson, by making more pleasurable mobile phones. At that time, Ericsson was better at (and actively advertising) their battery life and antenna sensitivity, but the phones were frustratingly difficult to use. Nokia introduced the pleasure principle through design, advertised the phones with images of expensive perfumes, luxury clothes and Belgian chocolates. The rest is history.

Pleasurability is about how the whole solution makes you feel. It relates to a sum of details within your service, and often relates this to culture from the world outside. Pleasurability relates to the way the interaction is designed. The way it looks, the way things move, the feedback it gives you. It relates to style, but it also relates to much greater things. It relates to your brand and to what people expect from you. Pleasurability is not something for everyone. Ryanair, for example, is focussed upon the utilitarian value and explicitly distances itself from highbrow style in their interaction design, with great success. It focuses upon utility and usability as part of its utilitarian approach, and this links to its no-frills offering very well.

For a long time, customer input to services has been limited to physical input through a keyboard (and a mouse), while output has been purely visual. This is a totally unnatural form of interaction, but one that technology has dictated and forced upon us through the past thirty years. Radical things are happening within interaction design now, because finally we are being freed from keyboards and mice. Interaction pleasure is now becoming central to our service experience as a result of Apple redefining this in music players and mobile phones whilst Nintendo has done the same for gaming consoles. It's all about the physical and tangible, and this is a breath of fresh air for interaction design and customers alike. Flicking between images with a finger, pinching to change size, or dragging with your finger are all direct forms of interacting with systems that are pleasurable and natural. Not only this, movements such as these are hard wired from our fingers into our pleasure zones, giving a double bonus, both usability and pleasurability together.

A high level of desirability requires strong internal alignment, a strong brand and knowledge of managing design. However, it is a very strong differentiator and gives a mind share amongst customers.

Desirability – moving from good to great

If you put some effort into your interaction design you will be able to make a perfectly good solution, but if you are searching for true desirability you need to work hard. The benefits can make it worth it, but you have to be very confident of your offering, your position, and have a crystal-clear brand to be able to move up the desirability scale. Firstly, you need to think of the three elements of utility, usability and pleasurability as a mixing desk so that you can fine-tune your interactive solution and find your own mix.

A high level of desirability is not for everyone. It requires strong internal alignment, a strong brand and a good knowledge of managing design. However, it is a very strong differentiator and gives a mind share amongst customers that can give a market lead for a considerable amount of time. Examples such as Amazon, Nokia, Apple and Nintendo have shown that focus upon desirability creates strong value in the longer term. However, differentiating in such a way through interaction design is not for everyone.

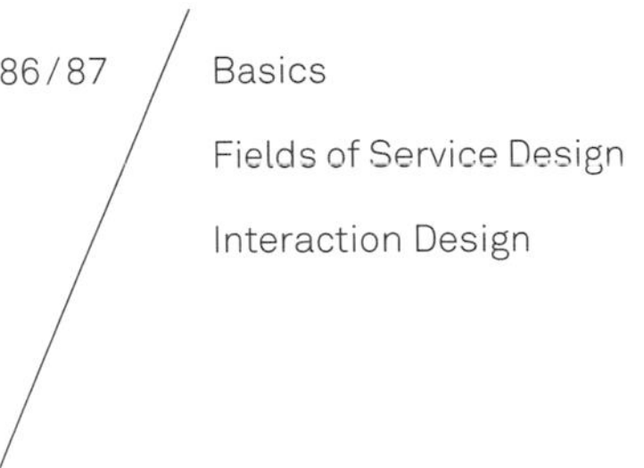

DESIRABILITY IS MADE UP OF THREE BASIC ELEMENTS:

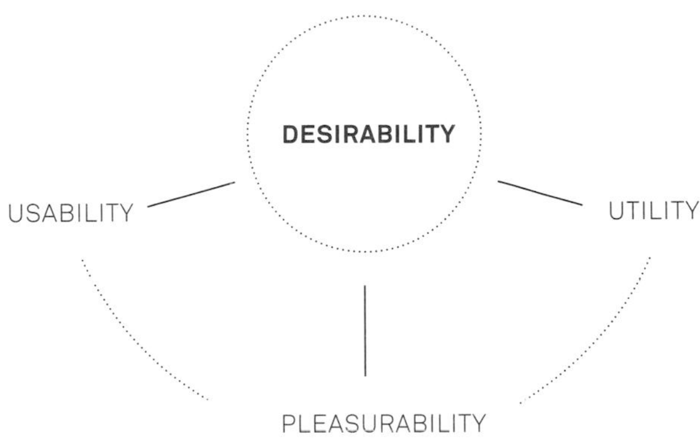

UTILITY — what the service does, or offers the customer, at the functional level
USABILITY — how easy it is to interact with the service
PLEASURABILITY — how pleasurable the interaction is at the emotional level

Conclusion

To conclude then, it's time for you to think about the mix of utility, usability and pleasurability that fits your service. The answer to this lies in understanding your customers, your offering and your brand strategy and in finding an alignment between the interactions you design into your service and what your company is all about.

Interaction design can retain customers that you have, gain new customers and most likely create efficiencies that easily will be visible on the bottom line. Not only this, typical service attributes such as friendliness, pleasurable experiences and exceeding expectations are all outcomes that interaction design can offer you.

SOCIAL DESIGN: DELIVERING POSITIVE SOCIAL IMPACT

KATE ANDREWS

Intentionally or unintentionally, design and its processes have formed and styled the world we live in. Design surrounds everyday life to such an extent that designers and their processes have become largely invisible, vastly misunderstood and subsequently undervalued by society. Service design is playing an important role in shifting these perceptions, by breaking down preconceived notions of creativity, actively illustrating the significant and wider social application of design, and involving more people in the design process.

It is common for design graduates to stand at their degree exhibitions, with little more than a 1m square board on show to illustrate three years of thinking, development and visual and physical output. Such constraints perhaps breed a naive confidence that together with good grades, someone in the industry crowd might recognise the depth and direction of the work that the student displays.

From this perspective, there is much to query and explore in the broader role of design disciplines and how they are positioned alongside other disciplines. Designers possess more than simply an ability to style products; they are practitioners of an applied process of creative skills: identifying problems, researching, analysing, evaluating, synthesising and then conceptualising, testing and communicating solutions. Design, whatever the discipline, is not only about an end product, but rather a systematic process of identifying problems, then researching, creating, testing and implementing solutions.

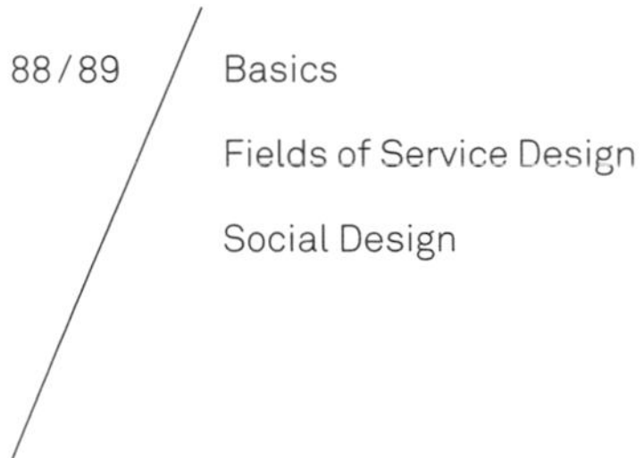

One can look to the design profession for inspirations on style, but further investigation will show that design offers more than solely the creation and promotion of consumer goods. It is also possible to observe that designers have, through their broad and adaptable skill set, a service to offer to all areas of society. Such broader applications of design have variously been termed "innovation" and "design thinking", two terms that have seen David Kelley's IDEO and D-School gain kudos in the pages of Business Week. This broader application of design was consolidated

Service design is playing an important role in shifting former perceptions, by breaking down preconceived notions of creativity, actively illustrating the significant and wider social application of design, and involving more people in the design process.

in 2009 with the publication of *Change by Design* by IDEO CEO Tim Brown and *The Design of Business: Why Design Thinking is the Next Competitive Advantage* by Roger L. Martin. Design Thinking is now very definitely part of the social consciousness. But to what end?

Exploring the philosophical and historical position of "design thinking", Robert O'Toole explains:

"Design thinking is taking shape as an attitude, as a methodology, as a philosophy. And perhaps also as an approach to learning and designing learning. Certainly if its methods are able to deliver on the promises, unlocking potentials, setting creativity free, but in a collective and collaborative context, aiming for durable and sustainable ends, then it more than envisages an exciting and viable future. How can this be tested? Imagine, discover, think, prototype, test, iterate, implement."

Who are these Service Designers?

As demand for, comprehension of, and the value of design thinking have evolved, a mass of socially motivated designers have united further. Thinking very differently about design, they are using strategic processes to tackle critical issues such as sustainability, unemployment, mental health, homelessness and poverty.

Employing the design process to tackle a social issue or with an intent to improve human lives is known as social design. Although the term is used in an array of contexts and subsequently put to very different uses, social design exists as a way of thinking about what, why and how design (product and/or process) can or does address the ever-changing needs of a society.

Whilst designers have worked with a social conscience, and with a view to modifying societal perceptions for many years, the evolution of this practice has previously appeared embryonic and unsustainable. Methodologies of co-design, social innovation and service design have dramatically broadened the application of "design thinking", giving impetus and stability to a social design movement. One could argue that through these new methodologies, designers are better communicating the value of their creativity.

Social design exists as a way of thinking about what, why and how design (product and/or process) can or does address the ever-changing needs of a society.

In a 2010 feature, written for DesignObserver.com, designer Justin Kemerling explained the potential of interdisciplinary collaboration as a method for delivering positive social impact: *"There's a good chance [that] any given area has people who are good at graphic design, illustra-*

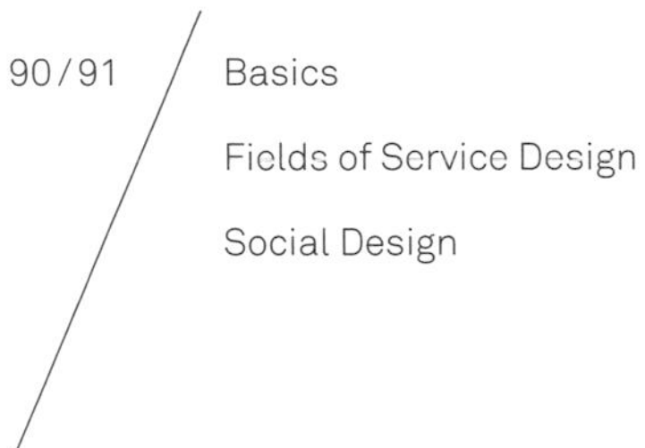

tion, web design, programming, writing, event planning, connection making, community organising, public speaking and joke telling and want to get their hands dirty. Put all those together and you've got something that's ready for positive impact."

Recognising the growth of a potential new design movement, many designers have begun forging multidisciplinary networks with the aims of social improvement through design. Identifying social projects that could benefit from design expertise, and sharing examples of successful practice online, designers have begun to identify how their transferable skills could be utilised, and how intangible ideas can be visualise

Model Aidpod in a Coca-Cola crate

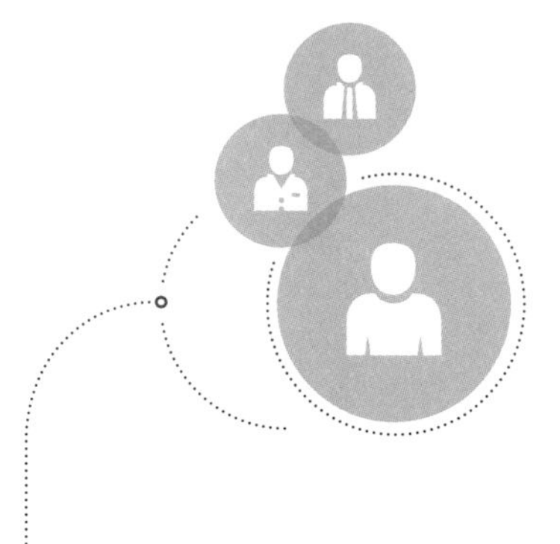

ed, communicated and implemented. One example of where a multidisciplinary design team successfully supported a socially focused project is with the story of ColaLife.

In December 2009, as the decade closed, design journalist Alice Rawsthorn confirmed how the "new wave of social designers" had successfully redefined design as more than a creation of "things", however, in her closing line she asked; "Was it enough? Sadly not. Let's hope design does better in the next decade." So, what's next? How do we "do" better? How do we upscale the success of the previous decade and ensure a sustainable social role for design?

The tools and methodologies being developed by service designers provide a unique opportunity for all designers, whatever their discipline, to consider, approach and tackle social issues. As the processes of design become more transparent and accessible to audiences, clients and end users, a better understanding of design's social value will emerge, helping to facilitate a broad and sustainable social application of design.

THIS IS CO-CREATIVE.
CASE STUDY: COLALIFE

In September 2008, ruralnet|uk Chief Executive Simon Berry presented an idea he had to ask Coca-Cola to utilise their global distribution channels to get medical equipment to dying children in Africa. Such a bold ambition demanded consideration of the project holistically, to identify the various systems Coca-Cola employed in its distribution networks and how it might be possible to utilise these for humanitarian purposes. This project would demand an innovative approach to work on new ways of addressing aims and objectives of all stakeholders involved with a view to ensuring maximum social benefit.

The project was heavily marketed through social media channels, something that helped bring together and facilitate the sharing of the different skills of designers interested in taking up this challenge. In effect, social media united participants in pursuit of this bold idea and helped turn it into something simple and accessible for a broad audience to understand, support and participate in. Simon was able to uncover people globally who had skills to aid the project's development. In under a month the Facebook group grew substantially and Simon gained international press coverage. Within six months the project was branded as ColaLife, had its own website, voluntarily designed, had its own animated advert, and an online and offline community of multidisciplinary designers and other supporters backing the campaign.

In 2010 and 2011, ColaLife made it into the idea index of Buckminster Fuller Challenge. Simon and his partner Jane won an UnLtd* Award in June 2010. In the same month they both gave up employment to focus full-time on ColaLife on a voluntary basis. As of today there are local partnerships in Zambia to implement a pilot of ColaLife in 2011. Partners include UNICEF and the local Coca-Cola bottler SABMiller.

This success sprung from a number of designers beginning to think holistically about a given problem and collaborating together effectively through social media and web technologies in pursuit of an innovative and practical solution to a pressing social problem.

STRATEGIC MANAGEMENT: WHY CORPORATIONS DO WHAT THEY DO

RALF BEUKER

In 2005 W. Chan Kim and Renée Mauborgne came up with their concept of "Blue Ocean Strategy" (BOS), which demonstrates how to overcome the traditional management paradigms of positioning, generic strategies and value chains. Besides recapping these established management concepts, this article explains how service design thinking at different strategic levels makes the perfect ingredient for creating a Blue Ocean in uncontested market spaces.

When following the manifold on-/offline discussions about service design these days, one could easily get the impression that the community thinks that businesses are deliberately delivering bad service in light of the obvious gains that are connected with good service design. With this in mind, please allow for a short exercise and close your eyes for a moment. Try to recall the latest service interaction you've had with, say, your mobile phone provider. Whatever comes to your mind, do you really think they've done this deliberately? While I definitively don't think so, what I do believe is that corporations and their employees have their very individual reasons for doing what they do even though it might result in bad service. But please don't get me wrong, I don't want to justify or accept bad service as such, but instead I want to understand why bad service takes place by firstly identifying causes before remedying the symptoms. Accordingly, the aim of this article is to address the following questions:

- Why do businesses create/accept bad service?
- What is the role of management education in this context?
- Why don't the most common management models offer sufficient arguments for better service design?
- What is the role of Design Thinking in overcoming this situation?
- How can service design create a Blue Ocean by Design Thinking?

Service design has gained a lot of attention over the recent years even though the field as such is not new. Amongst others some comprehensive research goes back to the early 1980s and is closely connected to the writings of Marketing Professor Valarie Lethal (http://bit.ly/zeithaml). As a matter of fact, her approach to service design is largely driven by gaining insights into the nature of services and as such by exploring ways of creating value for business by systematic service management. Accordingly, the recent attention to service design by design professionals (Satu Miettinen and Mikko Koivisito, 2009) focussing on the interactive processes that take place when services happen makes perfect sense and brings the field to another professional level.

Corporations and their employees have their very individual reasons for doing what they do even though it might result in bad service.

Back to the roots of … strategic management

So why is it that, despite all these insights, bad service is still around us? Let's face it, managers and not necessarily service designers usually make decisions about the level of investment in service concepts. Accordingly, from a broad management perspective the service that is usually accompanying a product or transaction is usually one tiny element of a larger set of value-adding activities. As a consequence, one needs to gain a better understanding of the mental models that (still) frame the decisions being made by managers on the three strategic levels – corporate, business and operational – in which they operate.

Corporate strategy

Ever since the late 1970s Harvard B-School Professor Michael Porter and his 5-Forces Model (1979) have shaped the education and thinking of business students across the globe. Within this model a company's strategy is the result of an external setup of industries and markets. The dominating variable here for strategic decisions is the overall attractiveness of an industry. As a consequence, a service on this level is mainly an attribute of a product and/or transaction rather than something that is shaping the nature of an industry as such.

Business strategy

This level deals with decisions about how and by which means a company is competing in a given market. While there are numerous B-School models that could be cited, it is again M. Porter and his Generic Strategies model (1980) that should be highlighted. He identifies three generic strategies that a company should pursue: cost leadership, differentiation and focus. From these three business strategies he stresses the idea that only one strategy should be adopted exclusively by a firm and failure to do so will result in a "stuck in the middle" scenario. According to this logic, "Service" is rather a means of differentiation than of cost leadership and thus results in above-average costs. Potential mid- to long-term benefits resulting from higher customer satisfaction are usually neglected since it is an input-dominated model.

THE 5-FORCES MODEL — M. E. PORTER

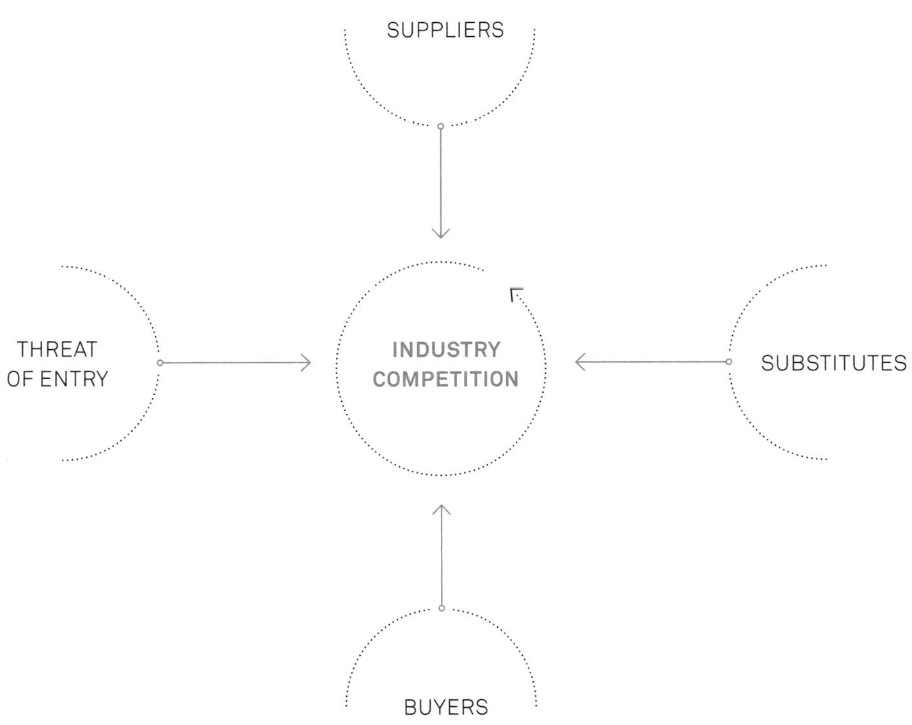

Operational strategy

Last but not least, Porter (1985) also described the Value Chain Analysis for the first time. From a broad perspective a value chain illustrates the major business functions that add value to a company's products and services. These functions consist of research and development, product design, manufacturing, marketing, distribution and customer service. The difference between the aggregated costs of these functions and the final sales price is referred to as the "margin". This means wherever reductions in costs are realised within the value chain, the higher the resulting margin for the company is. It doesn't need to be mentioned that as long as customer service is ranked at the end of this chain, any savings are being realised here and not at the top in, for example, R&D.

Exploring new options: design thinking

What we've learned so far from the paragraphs above is that none of the dominant management models on each strategy level provide sufficient argument for a reasonable service design culture. In my view the most critical obstacle that prevents investment in service design is the assumed exclusiveness between cost leadership and differentiation on the strategic business level. It has taken the relentless communication of Roger Martin (2007), the dean of the Rodman Business School, to allow corporations to start realising that "design thinking", also known as the iterative process of "both ... and" thinking rather than "either ... or" logic, offers a means to overcome such exclusivity. In his view the iterative nature of the design process, and hence the designer as a key stakeholder, facilitates new organisational designs and processes beyond that of traditional management procedures. The break-up of the exclusivity between cost leadership and differentiation may only be one such result.

Implications for service design

In a lecture series for the Association of Registered Graphic Designers of Ontario (RGD Ontario) in 2001, design management pioneer Peter Gorb (http://bit.ly/PeterGorb) gave some basic but very helpful advice: *"And what designers need to learn, and this is the most important thing, is the language of the business world. Only by learning that language can you effectively voice the arguments for design."* In conjunction with my elaborations above, this certainly does not mean that service designers now all have to become managers. However, a closer fram/

THIS IS HOLISTIC.

The relevance to think out of the box not only applies to service innovations, as often quoted, but in particular to one's background and language.

hing and/or adaptation of service design concepts into the logic of management thinking might bring the discipline closer to the boardroom. In 2004 W. Chan Kim and Renée Mauborgne came up with their concept of Blue Ocean Strategies (BOS). Blue Ocean Strategies are about creating a market for something that did not exist before, and marketing it in a space free of competition. Smart service design clearly has the potential to act as a key facilitator in creating such BOS's as the chart illustrates. This might even result in a "less service is more" concept as the example of easyjet.com demonstrates. Concluding my arguments I would recommend treating the growing number of service design tools, methods, models and approaches as means to an end rather than an end in itself.

Whenever possible try to integrate service design logic into management models and management thinking and create cases for integrative service design thinking.

BLUE OCEAN STRATEGY – ACTIONS FRAMEWORK

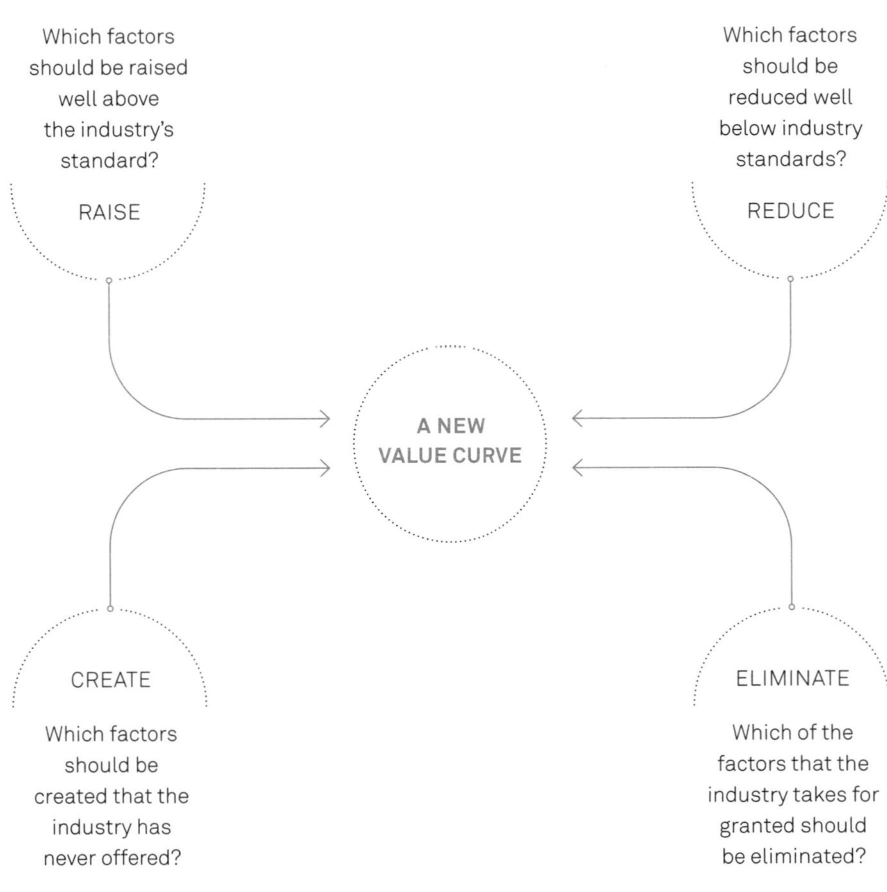
Which factors should be raised well above the industry's standard?
RAISE
Which factors should be reduced well below industry standards?
REDUCE
A NEW VALUE CURVE
CREATE
Which factors should be created that the industry has never offered?
ELIMINATE
Which of the factors that the industry takes for granted should be eliminated?

OPERATIONS MANAGEMENT: THE RELENTLESS QUEST FOR EFFICIENCY

KATE BLACKMON

Operations management (OM) is concerned with the design, management, and improvement of the processes through which an organisation's products and services are delivered. The underlying value is based on the efficient use of "men, methods, materials, and management" (a phrase that goes back to the early 1930s in the operations field). Whilst services were identified as an operations management concern in the early 1960s, service operations only started to take on a distinct identity in the 1970s.

Services as production

One of the early OM insights was that the design of production processes and the outputs of those processes needed to be closely linked, so that in services – as well as manufacturing – low volumes and high variety were linked (professional services, for example) as well as high volumes and low variety (mass services such as air transportation).

The early OM approach to service design is captured by Ted Levitt's (1972) "production-line approach to services"; that is, applying manufacturing principles in the service environment. Just as the production line maximised the output of cars, televisions and cans of Campbell's soup, and minimised the cost per unit produced, the service production line maximised the number of customers who could be served, whilst minimising the cost of serving each customer.

Levitt's "production-line approach" used the McDonald's hamburger chain as the epitome of service efficiency. Key principles illustrated by McDonald's included:

— Standardising and specialising services for narrow customer/ market segments
— Deskilling and division of labour in customer-facing roles
— Using customers as quasi-employees
— Substituting technology for human discretion and judgment
— Using self-service technology to substitute for employee labour

The McDonald's restaurant combined elements of Taylorism (work analysis and job specification for employees) and Fordism (standardisation of the inputs, processes and outputs). Unlike scientific management and mass production, McDonald's applied these principles to the customers as well. Customers carried their own trays to their tables and cleaned up afterwards. Every aspect of employee and customer behaviour was subjected to the same rigorous analysis and redesign as the French fries and hamburgers, and the deep fat fryer and hamburger grill. Every McDonald's, in every city, in every country, was more or less the same.

Operations management is concerned with the design, management, and improvement of the processes through which an organisation's products and services are delivered.

The production-line approach diffused across a vast array of mass services, as David Halberstam describes in his history of The Fifties, everything from the Holiday Inn chain of motels to Levittown and other vast tracts of standardised housing. Its success led to what sociologist George Ritzer called the McDonaldisation of everything: the standardisation not only of service concepts and service delivery systems, but also of every aspect of the service sector.

Sasser and colleagues (1978) at the Harvard Business School identified service design as designing, managing, and improving the service delivery system. The term service design was used to describe working out the details of people, technology, practices, and processes to achieve a certain level of service performance whilst minimising costs and maximising the use of scarce and expensive resources.

Service design combined Levitt's philosophy with Wickham Skinner's "focused factory" (1974), which argued that a single productive facility could not satisfy heterogeneous customer demands (e.g., low cost versus high quality), and that it should specialise in a particular homogenous customer segment. A classic example of extending the production line approach to professional services was Shouldice Hospital, which applied a mass service approach to hernia operations. Here, patients played important roles in their own well-being, and in the well-being of other patients. OM focused on achieving what Schmenner and Swink (1998) described as "swift, even flow" through both the front-room and the back-room service operations.

Bringing customers back in

Although many service activities could be designed and managed using principles derived from manufacturing, Dick Chase (1981) provided an important framework for service design by classifying servi

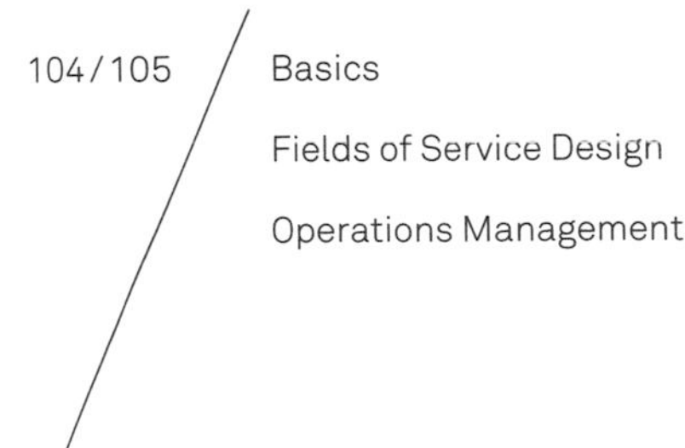

OPERATIONS PERSPECTIVE	DESIGN PERSPECTIVE
TECHNOLOGY-CENTRED	HUMAN-CENTRED
ARTEFACTS	NARRATIVES
STANDARDISATION	VARIATION
EFFICIENCY	EXPERIENCE

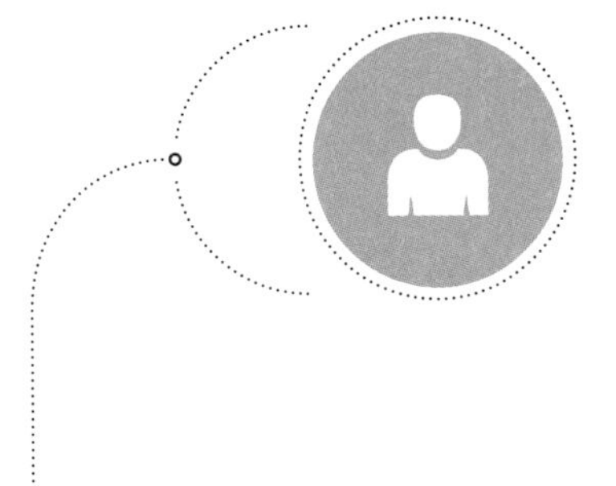

THIS IS USER-CENTRED.

The focus on the user is one of the main distinctions between the operation perspective and the design perspective.

es by the amount of customer contact present. Building on the sociologist Erving Goffman's insights into how people behaved differently depending on whether customers were present, activities that required customer contact were "front-room" activities, whilst activities that did not were "back-room" activities, with "pure services" (mostly front office), mixed-services (both front and back office), and quasi-manufacturing (mostly back office) having distinct design and operation characteristics. Chase's critical insight was that front-room activities ("high customer contact") were qualitatively different from manufacturing activities, and insights from service marketing and human resource management needed to be applied here.

Heskett and colleagues introduced the service-profit chain model, which emphasised the importance of the service encounter between the customer and employee.

Technology in service design

At McDonald's, technology was extensively used in the front office to guide, monitor and control employee behaviour. Purpose-built cooking equipment and various timers took the guesswork out of cooking; supporting technologies such as picture-coded tills simplified front-office roles; substitutes for automation such as roles and scripts were used to make employee-customer interactions more efficient; the physical facility was a machine designed to shape customer behaviour in countless ways. However, the McDonald's employee, no matter how callow, continued to be an important touchpoint for customers, just as he or she is today at Starbucks.

With the growth of computer and communications technology, service design took another leap forward in the pursuit of efficiency by substituting technology for direct customer-employee contact entirely. Of course, we can point to early examples of self-service technologies such as the vending machine (invented in the 1880s in England) or the cash machine (invented in the 1960s), but these required the customer to be physically present at a site designated by the service provider. However, the invention of the web, which popularised the use of the internet, revolution-

ised services, since the service provider, such as Amazon, could be located anywhere in the world.

Service design: the operations approach

As noted above, service design has been used since the 1970s to describe both the attributes of the service delivery system, and the process for determining these attributes. However, in its focus on efficiency and technology, the OM take on service design differs considerably from the design-led approach that is the norm today. Although the human elements of employees and customers are not ignored, they are seen as elements of the service to be controlled, standardised or even eliminated (as with e-services and other forms of technology mediation).

If we compare the traditional OM approach with the design-led approach, we can identify a number of critical differences between the two, as summarised in the earlier table. Although it may be in some ways the antithesis of service design in the design-led perspective, it is an established perspective with a definite dominant logic. The "production line approach to services" identified in 1972 still represents the "ideal" service design, whether fast food, customer service in a call centre, or surgical operations. In the abstract view, a service is a machine, which can be reduced to systems, machines, and employees and customers that can be treated "as if" they were machines too. The designing of the machine and its parts to be the most efficient, so that it is time- and cost-saving, is the most important task. And, if each machine can be "cloned" multiple times, such as the McDonalds and Starbucks that have become ubiquitous from Seattle to Beijing, so much the better.

DESIGN ETHNOGRAPHY: TAKING INSPIRATION FROM EVERYDAY LIFE

GEKE VAN DIJK

Design Ethnography is aimed at understanding the future users of a design, such as a certain service. It is a structured process for going into depth of the everyday lives and experiences of the people a design is for. The intention is to enable the design team to identify with these people, to build up an empathic understanding of their practices and routines and what they care about. This allows the team to work from the perspective of these users on new designs for relevant slices of their daily lives. Designers use this understanding to work on idea generation, concept development and implementation.

Ethnography is a research methodology developed and used in various social sciences such as anthropology and sociology. Its literal meaning is "description of people". The origin of the methodology lies in the late 19th century when academics ventured out into the colonies to study cultures, human behaviour and social relations. One of the founders of modern social anthropology, Bronislaw Malinowski, shook up the field by stating that ethnographers should see things from the point of view of their subjects, rather than imposing their own cultural and political prejudices on them. Many other influential researchers have followed along these lines and developed the field further. Important names in this respect are Max Weber, Émile Durkheim, Claude Lévi-Straus, Clifford Geertz and Margaret Mead. For a useful and concise introduction to ethnography, the book Social & Cultural Anthropology by John Monaghan and Peter Just (2000) is a good start. Nowadays ethnography is used to

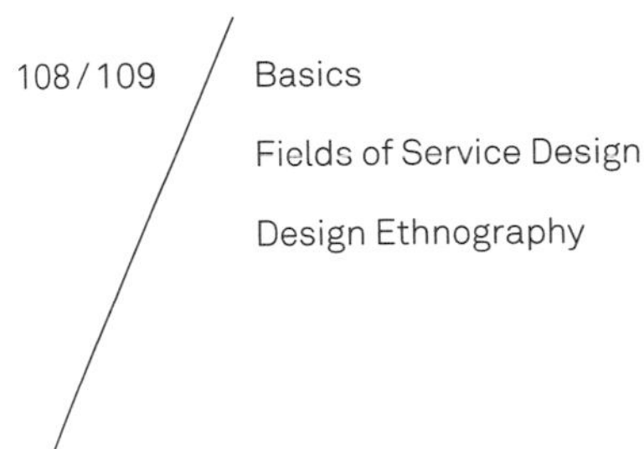

study both urban and industrial societies. And the research methods have evolved from participant observation to include more interaction, conversation and co-creation.

Firmly rooted in the design process

Design ethnography is ethnographic qualitative research set within a design context. It delivers results that inform and inspire design processes, for instance service design processes. It offers reference material on people's everyday lives; their practices, motivations, dreams and concerns. The results can also be used to communicate the results of the research to other people in the project team who may have different backgrounds

Design ethnography allows the team to work from the perspective of these users on new designs for relevant slices of their daily lives. Designers use this understanding to work on idea generation, concept development and implementation.

and represent different disciplines (e.g. technology, marketing, communication, management, customer services). Design Ethnography explicitly aims to generate materials that communicate the insights from the research to a wide group of stakeholders, to make sure that the foundations for the designs are well understood and accepted.

Design Ethnography is purposefully not an expertise outside of the creative process. It has a place right in the middle of it, just like the other specific expertises that exist within design (e.g. product design, interaction design, graphic design or design management). It is important that design ethnographers work in close collaboration with the rest of the design team. Being isolated from the overall design process, like traditional marketing research, does not make sense. Design ethnography is about facilitating empathic conversations between users, clients and designers, as well as other experts and stakeholders involved in the service design process.

Design ethnographers are design thinkers. They firmly understand the design process. They know what is needed at every stage of the process, and how this can best be explored, discussed and shared. Some design ethnographers are initially trained as designers, and have later specialised in doing design research based on ethnographic methodologies. Other design ethnographers may have been trained as anthropologists or social researchers, and specialised in applying this to design processes.

Key role in service design

Service design is a very wide field that encompasses many disciplines, not only the various expertises of design, but also other disciplines such as strategy and technology. The teamwork between these disciplines needs a shared focus and language. The results from design ethnography facilitate that focus and language by offering a firm reference point that connects all the disciplines involved – the people they are ultimately developing the services for. This is relevant not only during the design stage of services but also during implementation. Design ethnography helps to communicate concepts, guidelines, strategies, scenarios and the like to people throughout companies.

As services are intangible, difficult to standardise, and co-produced while they are delivered/consumed, the core starting point of the service design approach is to be human-focused. You must engage with the hearts and minds of people if you want to design successful and popular

services. You cannot really do service design without some form of design ethnography. The level of detail of the ethnographic research can vary greatly between projects (depending on time, budget and experience). In small-scale projects it might be just a few days, while in large-scale projects it can take several weeks.

Service design is an inter-discipline where T-shaped people collaborate. The concept of T-shaped people was introduced to the design and innovation field by the design consultancy IDEO (Kelley, 2000). The idea behind the metaphor is to indicate that most professionals have both a deep expertise in a given field and a broad understanding of other fields they encounter in their work. In strategic and innovative projects, as many service design projects are, various T-shaped people with different ba/

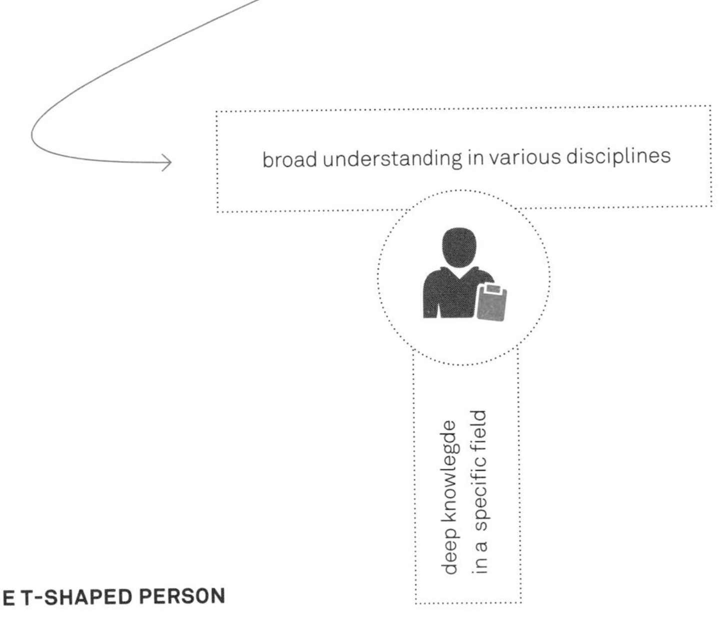

THE T-SHAPED PERSON

Who are these Service Designers?

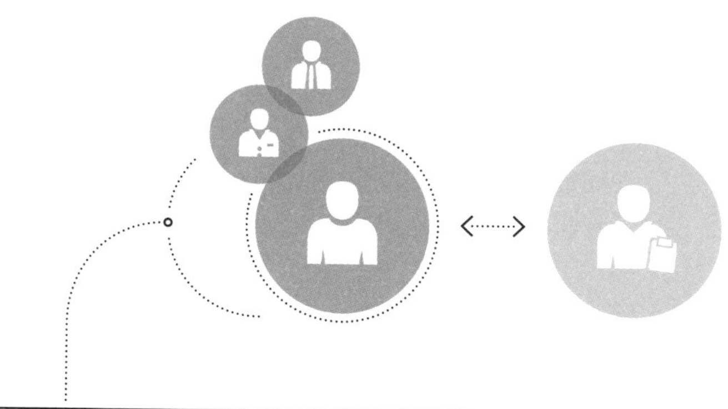

ckgrounds and roles are working together as part of the same team. This is both true for the age

THIS IS CO-CREATIVE.

A broad understanding in various disciplines and a deep knowledge in a specific field is crucial for co-creative work in interdisciplinary teams.

acies involved and the team members from the client organisation. There is usually a notable overlap between the various specialists. That is why and how they understand one another and are able to collaborate. Without the deep expertise of these various specialists, the knowledge and skills in the service design team would be very shallow. Generalists who know a bit of everything cannot make a real difference in service innovation. Design ethnography is one of the areas of deep expertise that contributes to the design discipline. The combination of a general understanding at the top ends of the Ts, and the additional deep expertise at the bottom ends of the Ts leads to valuable collaborations that trigger successful new service concepts and ensures their effective implementation.

Standing on the shoulders of giants

As explained in the introduction, ethnography is a research tradition with a long history. Design ethnography builds on this history. It is not a completely new or naive approach. Some key anthropologists were experimenting with co-creation and visualisation of ethnographic material as early as 1960. They not only observed and studied people, but empathically interacted with them to gradually discover the deeper motivations for certain social practices and preferences. Jean Rouch was one of these anthropologists. He expressed the results of his studies in books as well as photographs and films. His films were often made in close collaboration with his subjects. They would be involved not only as actors, but also as active members of the film crew. An example of such a film is "Chronicle of a Summer" (1960). Rouch's work has for instance been an important inspiration for the development of the more recent ethnographic method "Design Documentaries" by Bas Raijmakers (2007).

Design ethnography uses many proven tools and techniques and adapts them for specific contexts. Gradually we can see a set of methods evolving that are specifically suited and successful for use in service design projects. During the early stage of immersion in everyday life, these are typically methods to trigger and document empathic conversations with the people who will be ultimately using and delivering the services. During the analysis stage that follows, the methods focus on clustering and probing the research data to discover relevant and inspiring insights. The methods used during the development stage contribute to idea generation, concept development, co-creation, prototyping and validation. The Tools section in this book offers detailed descriptions of many of these methods. Throughout the research and development process, design ethnography offers a bridge between the service users, the service providers and the service designers.

Synergy between design and ethnographic research

A strong connection between design and ethnographic research is important for successful service design projects. The empathic conversations between the various people and parties involved require both a sensitive attitude and a strong, visually engaging approach. The research activi-

ties and materials need to be well designed in order to get people involved and elicit useful and inspiring results. And the subsequent new designs need to be researched again, to make sure that the final results will be further improved in an iterative process. In this way service design not only takes inspiration from everyday life, it puts it at the very heart of the design process.

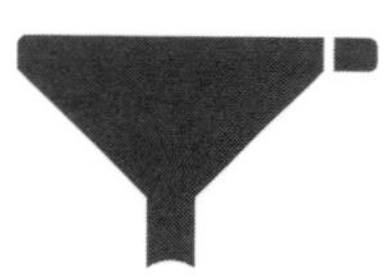

Lucy says: *What does matter is that understanding value and the nature of relations between people and other people, between people and organisations, and between organisations of different kinds are now understood to be central to designing services.*

Ralf says: *Whenever possible, try to integrate service design logic into management models and management thinking and create cases for integrative service design thinking.*

Marc says: *Service design thinking supports the cooperation between different disciplines towards the goal of corporate success through enhanced customer experiences, employee satisfaction, and integration of sophisticated technological processes in pursuing corporate objectives.*

Simon says: *To value your customer, you need to spend some time understanding the interactions they have with your service, and that means two things. First, viewing your service through the customers' eyes. And second, designing in such a way that customers receive consistent experiences over time that they consider valuable.*

Jakob says: *Visual design plays an important role in three ways. It pre-empts the actual service process, and it controls customer expectation. The so-called look and feel can evoke a positive prevailing mood, or even makes the service usable in the first place through visual aides. Lastly, the visual appearance acts as an anchor that links the user to the positive experience.*

Satu says: *Iterative design helps to solve problems found in user testing. There must be a cycle of design, test and measure, and redesign, repeated as often as necessary. This is a way to incorporate results of behavioural testing into the next version of the system.*

How does Service Design work?

Methods & Tools

TOOLS OF SERVICE DESIGN THINKING

IT IS AN ITERATIVE PROCESS

Marc Stickdorn outlines a reiterating four step approach for designing services.

AT-ONE

Simon Clatworthy presents an example of a service design workshop series.

THIS IS A TOOLBOX – NOT A MANUAL

With the help of the service design community, STBY describes a collection of service design tools.

This second part describes how service design actually works. The first text explains the service design process along four iterative stages and the difficulty to define a standardised procedure to design services. The subsequent article however introduces an example for a rather structured approach for the early phases of a service design process. In the following a toolbox of 25 service design methods and tools are illustrated and assigned to respective process stages.

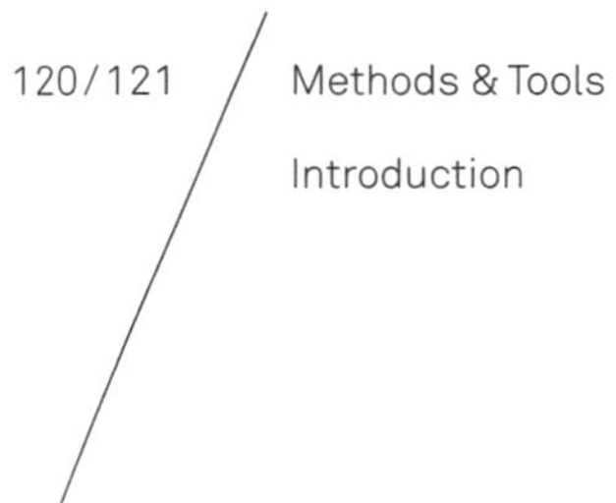

MARC STICKDORN, AUSTRIA
Iterative process

SIMON CLATWORTHY, NORWAY
AT-ONE process

THE COMMUNITY, ALL OVER THE WORLD
Tools

**GEKE VAN DIJK,
THE NETHERLANDS / UNITED KINGDOM**
Tools editing

LUKE KELLY, UNITED KINGDOM
Tools editing

**BAS RAIJMAKERS,
THE NETHERLANDS / UNITED KINGDOM**
Tools editing

IT IS AN ITERATIVE PROCESS

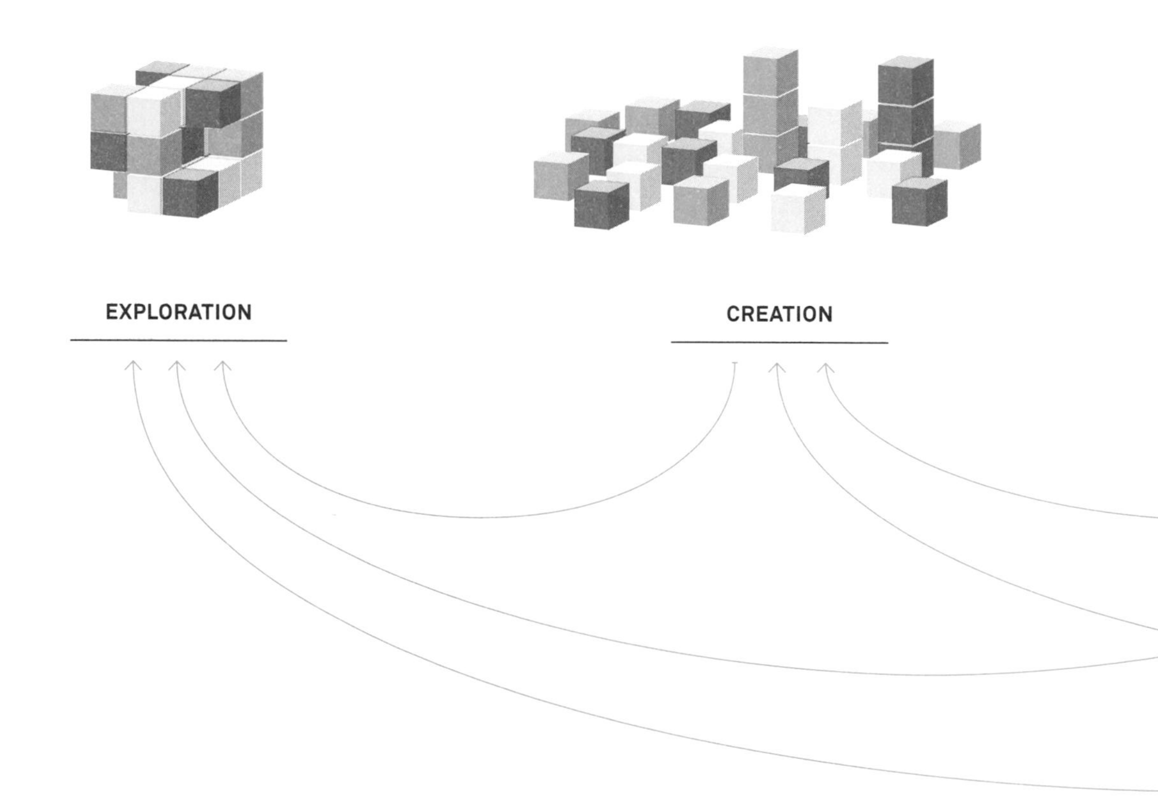

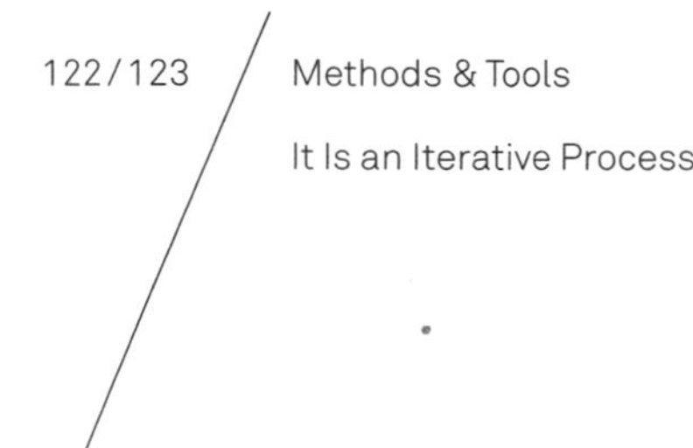

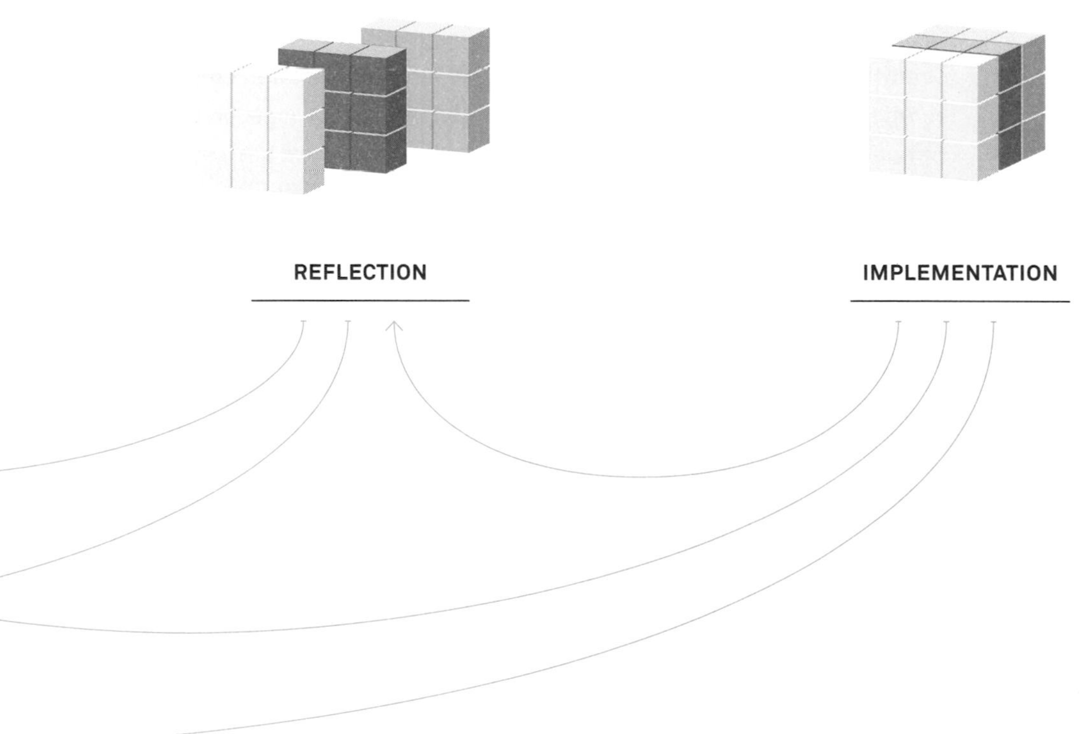
REFLECTION
IMPLEMENTATION

MARC STICKDORN

The iterative process of service design thinking

It is rather simple to imagine the process of designing a physical product such as a car. It might start with market research to discover what kind of car potential customers would prefer; which features, body, colour, interior design and what engine. Obviously, only if there is a market for a product such as this, is it worth designing. Based on these explorations, designers start creating ideas. Through various design sketches and later through virtual 3D or even tangible clay models, a fundamental idea takes form. Based on the creation of a first design concept, technical components need to be integrated and various aspects of the concept need to be re-modelled and improved. Prototypes are built and tested in terms of functionality, usability, production feasibility, cost and pricing, market response and so on. Only if these tests remain positive will the new car be produced and brought to market. Any mistakes during this process may result in enormous costs and possibly even damage to the image and reputation of the manufacturer. Such reputational damage can be witnessed in any recent callback situation by big automobile manufacturers. As this simple example of an exploration-creation-reflection design and implementation process illustrates, a well-thought-out approach to the design of a new product is crucial for its subsequent success. While the design processes for physical products such as this are well established, is it similarly possible to implement a structured approach to the design of services?

The following pages illustrate such a framework for service design processes. Although design processes are in reality nonlinear, it is possible to articulate an outline structure. It is important to understand that this structure is iterative in its approach. This means that at every stage of a service design process, it might be necessary to take a step back or

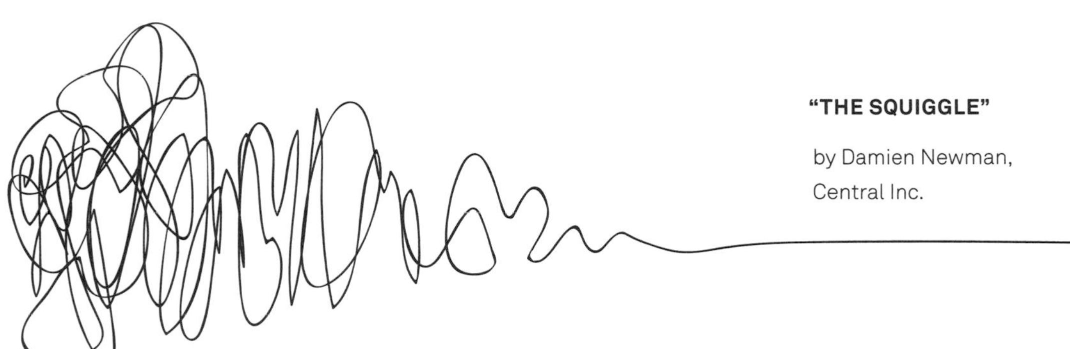

"THE SQUIGGLE"

by Damien Newman,
Central Inc.

Although design processes are in reality nonlinear, it is possible to articulate an outline structure. It is important to understand that this structure is iterative in its approach.

even start again from scratch. The single but very important difference is in ensuring that you learn from the mistakes of the previous iteration. Thus, the proposed process is just rough framework and should not be considered a prescriptive, linear how-to guide. In fact, the very first step of a service design process is to design the process itself, since the process ultimately depends on the context of the service being designed and thus varies from project to project.

The iterative four steps of exploration, creation, reflection and implementation are a very basic approach to structure such a complex design process.

"Designers need to be critical towards any theory or model of a design process" (Hegeman, 2008). With this acknowledgement it is perhaps also worth noting that whether the process is intentional or not, it will assume a significance upon the final design outcome. The benefit of clearly articulating the design process is that it enables a greater degree of reflection upon the influence that the designer has had on the designed outcome.

The iterative four steps of exploration, creation, reflection and implementation are a very basic approach to structure such a complex design process. Literature and practice refer to various other frameworks made up of three to seven or even more steps, but fundamentally they all share the same mindset (Best, 2006; Mager, 2009; Miettinen & Koivisto, 2009). The wording also varies: identify-build-measure (Engine, 2009), insight-idea-prototyping-delivery (live|work, 2009), discovering-concepting-designing-building-implementing (Designthinkers, 2009), to highlight just a few.

When considering the design process it is important to keep a few fundamental considerations in mind. It is necessary to make recurrent leaps between designing in detail and designing holistically. This means that whilst working on the details of a touchpoint you need to keep in mind where that touchpoint sits within the whole customer journey, or when working on redesigning employee interactions you need to consider the organisational structure as a whole. Furthermore, you will always have to cope with dilemmas and paradoxes. Since you cannot pay attention to every aspect, insight or point of view, you will have to make decisions according to your budget, resources and the views of your clients.

THE DOUBLE DIAMOND

as described by the British Design Council

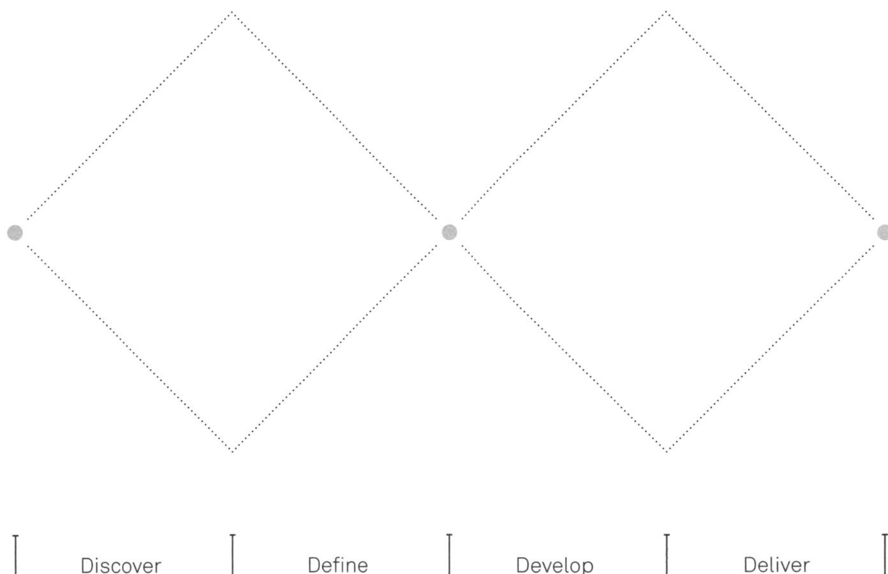

STAGE 1 – EXPLORATION

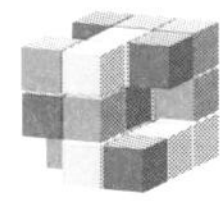

EXPLORATION

Discover

Although service design aims to put the customer at the centre of its process, the process seldom starts with the customer. The first task of a service designer is to understand the culture and goals of the company providing a service. Do they understand what service design thinking is? Is the company prepared for such a process? Since a service design process commonly involves co-creativity, it is important to agree on the extent to which the service designer has sovereignty within the creative process. Furthermore, the process starts by identifying the problem a service designer should work on; this problem is usually an organisational one or is initially viewed from the organisational perspective. It is important to understand the company's point of view on a certain problem, and in fact it could be argued that much of a service designer's role is in articulating the organisational problem from the perspective of the customer.

The second task is not finding a solution, but instead identifying the real problem. Gaining a clear understanding of the situation from the perspective of current and potential customers of a certain service is crucial for successful service design. Again, it is important to keep the big picture and as far as possible ascertain the true motivations behind customer behaviour. To this end, it is important to look for insights beyond simply gathering of empirical data. Service design uses a vast collection of methods

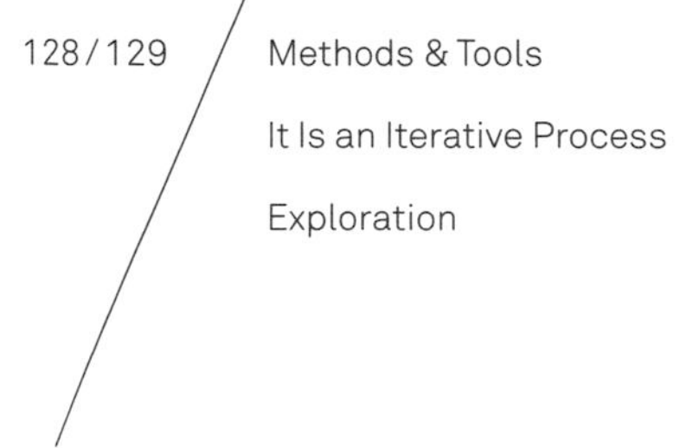

and tools from various disciplines to explore and understand the behaviour and mindset of all people involved. Ethnographic approaches from the social sciences have thus been adopted as one of the most commonly employed research approaches in the design of services. Put simply, it is not about trying to find the solution immediately – it is about finding the problem first!

Gaining a clear understanding of the situation from the perspective of current and potential customers of a certain service is crucial for successful service design.

The third task is to visualise these findings and as far as possible the underlying structure of the previously intangible services. This helps simplify complex and intangible processes and promotes a sense within the design team and amongst the service stakeholders that it is possible to change aspects of the service proposition that might not appear to be functioning appropriately. Again, there are numerous methods and tools from various disciplines that can be adopted to assist this.

STAGE 2 – CREATION

CREATION

Concept design

Creation represents the generative stage within this iterative process and is closely related to the proceeding stage of reflection. These are the two stages between which most iterations take place. It is all about testing and retesting ideas and concepts. One of the main features of service design thinking is that this approach is not about avoiding mistakes, but rather about exploring as many as possible mistakes. The crux is to make them as early as possible in the process and learn from these as much as possible before you implement or adopt the new concepts. The cost of an additional iteration during the concept design stage is marginal compared to the cost of failure with this concept after its launch.

If there is one prejudice against service design thinking it is that service designers share an obsession with sticky notes! There is a good reason for this; sticky-notes are a simple and quick tool to visualise processes, illustrate associations and relationships or provide mnemonics during co-creative ideation processes. Service design thinking is not only iterative during the process of the presented four stages, but also within each stage, within each workshop, within each brainstorming session.

Sticky-notes provide a visual support to keep track with this quick and iterative approach to development. The task is to generate and develop solutions based on the identified problems

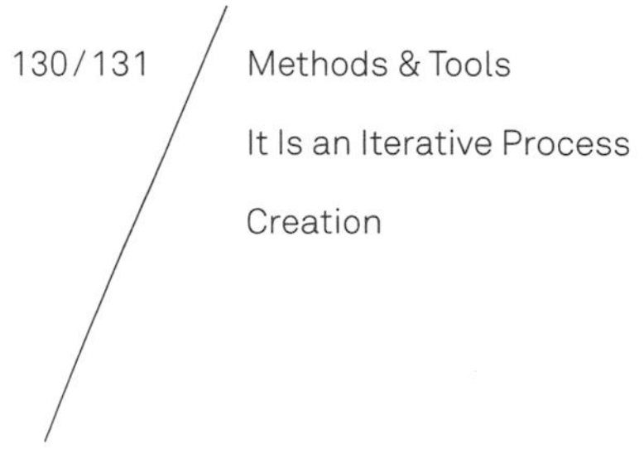

and in-depth insights generated in the exploratory stage; the identification of customers' needs, motivations, expectations, the service providers' processes and constraints, and the illustration of the customer journey, consisting of a sequence of touchpoints. In order to achieve holistic and sustainable solutions

> One of the main features of service design thinking is that this approach is not about avoiding mistakes, but rather to explore as many possible mistakes.

it is crucial to include all the main stakeholders and work with interdisciplinary teams that include customers, employees, and management as well as engineers, designers and other stakeholders involved in both the service design and service provision process. Achieving co-creativity among interdisciplinary teams is a key feature of a good service designer. Following the five principles it is important to work user-centred to co-create solutions which consider the whole touchpoint sequence, provide evidences and create holistic concepts. Again, there are a variety of methods and tools for doing this.

STAGE 3 – REFLECTION

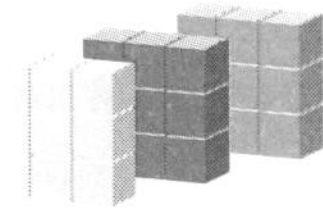

REFLECTION

Prototype

Building on the ideas and concepts from the previous creation stage, it is time to test them. As mentioned earlier, there are many iterations between these two stages of development. Testing physical products is rather easy and consists of building prototypes based on these previously visualised ideas and then testing these prototypes with a few customers or experts to gain feedback and consequently improve the prototypes and retest them until they match their expectations. Service design shares the same iterative approach of testing and retesting. However, applying prototyping techniques in the development of intangible services needs distinctive methods from those implemented in product design prototyping.

The main challenge at this stage in the process is dealing with the intangibility of services, since you cannot simply put a service on a table and ask customers what they think about it. Even using rather plain ways of gathering feedback through interviews and questionnaires is confronted by this problem. Customers need a good mental picture of the future service concept. Generating such a vision of a service concept in the mind of customers is the task at this stage. In this context it is important to consider the emotional aspects of a service. A mere description is seldom enough to create a clear vision. Providing a conceivable story through a comic strip, storyboards, videos or photo

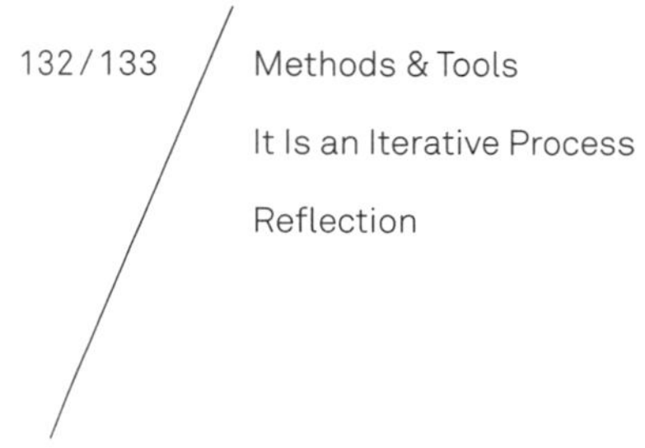

sequences helps generate the necessary emotional engagement but still lacks meaningful user interaction.

Therefore, it is important to prototype service concepts in reality or circumstances close to reality. Service design thinking uses different staging and roleplay approaches from theatre to play through certain service situations and helps incorporate the emotionally important aspects of personal interactions with the service proposition. Using such a playful approach not only elicits fun and emotional engagement for users, but also represents a strong method to test intangible service concepts at low cost and with the opportunity for quick interventions and testing of iterative improvements to these concepts. Since it is not always possible to prototype service moments in their real

It is important to prototype service concepts in reality or circumstances close to reality. Service design thinking uses different staging and roleplay approaches.

environment, the environment in which service situations take place needs to be constructed as a kind of scenery. Keeping the scenery simple and rough is not a disadvantage, but instead can result in increased imagination and creative response from the participants.

STAGE 4 – IMPLEMENTATION

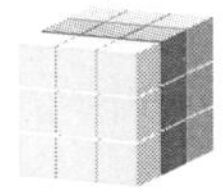

IMPLEMENTATION

Implement

The implementation of new service concepts by necessity demands a process of change. The management of change is an art in itself. Key to this art are a few basic principles of change management that need to be considered at this point. In this context the basic sequence of planning change, implementing change and reviewing change is a rough and easy guideline and is supported by many basic theories of change management (Cameron & Green 2009).

The change should be based on a consistent service concept formulated and tested during the previous stages. A clear communication of this concept is essential and needs to include the emotional aspects of a service – the desired customer experience. Besides customers, the employees are also important actors from now on in the process. Their motivation and engagement is crucial for a sustainable service implementation. For this reason it is important to involve employees from the beginning of a service design process. Making the mistake of disrespecting their input in these earlier stages can prove costly later. It is essential that the employees understand the concept and support it. Communication with them can be mediated by various tools from staff guidelines to comic-strip storyboards, photo sequences and videos. Ideally, employees should contribute to the prototyping of certain service moments and there-

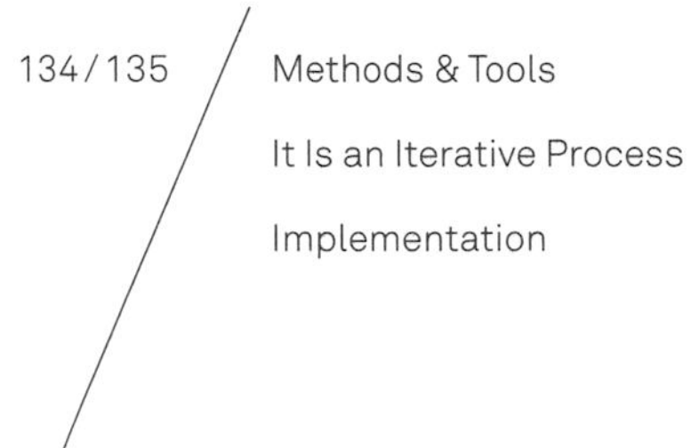

fore have a clear vision of the concept. At an organisational level, it is important to keep an overview of the improved processes and deliverables. Service blueprints are the standard method to illustrate these processes and evidence.

Ideally, employees should contribute to the prototyping of certain service moments and therefore have a clear vision of the concept.

Implementing change relies on the fact that the management is convinced of the service concept and does not flinch from any resulting problems while implementing the change. Employees need to be accompanied during the implementation process and problems need to be solved quickly and creatively. There will always be some unconsidered aspects that create friction, but the more resources that are invested in the earlier stages, the more likely a smooth transition will be.

Reviewing change refers to the control of its success. Ideally, the change implementation is followed by another exploration to evaluate its progress. This leads to the iterative process of service design thinking.

AT-ONE: BECOMING AT-ONE WITH YOUR CUSTOMERS

SIMON CLATWORTHY

AT-ONE is an approach to assist project teams during the early phases of the service design process. It focuses upon the differences between products and services, and has a clear user-experience focus. AT-ONE has been developed during the past four years as part of a research initiative to improve service innovation.

The AT-ONE process is run as a series of workshops, each with a focus upon the letters A, T, O, N, E, described below. The workshops can be run separately or can be combined, such that the method is easily scalable. Each of the letters of AT-ONE relates to a potential source of innovation within the service design process.

Each letter can be planned individually or in conjunction with one another. The metaphor for the workshops is that each is a different "innovation lens" used to view and explore the same design challenge. Thanks to the five different lenses, the goal is to stretch and explore the solution space as early in the design process as possible.

Each workshop has three phases, and is based upon commonly used creative processes (Isaksen et al 2000):

- Start: establishment of a common knowledge platform for all participants (1/5th of workshop)
- Divergence: exploration and generation of ideas and solutions
- Convergence: synthesis, prioritisation and decision-making

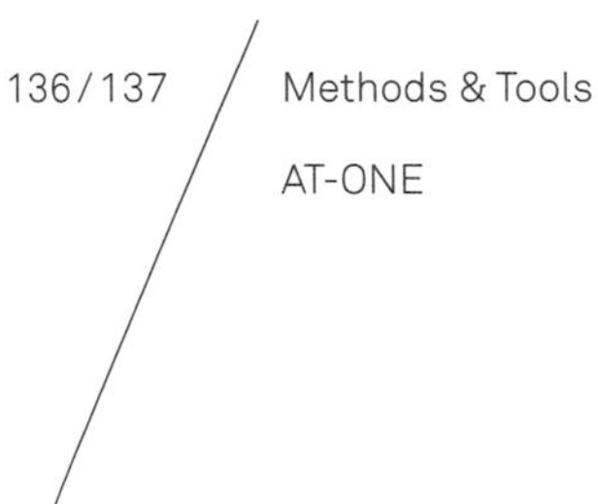

A key aspect to the workshops is the combination of participants representing stakeholders from the client organisation, their domain-specific expertise and the abilities of the service designers. As a designer, business expert or researcher reading this, you will probably be familiar with some of the elements utilised in AT-ONE. It does not introduce radically new tools to the development process. Instead, it combines best practice from business, design and research. Its relevance and novelty comes from the combination of the various elements in a customer-centric way and their introduction to the start of the design process.

A

A is for Actors, collaborating in value networks

One of the major changes in the past ten years has been a shift in understanding of how value is created. Value is created more and more in networks of collaboration rather than in traditional silos of expertise, so it is important to look at who needs to collaborate with whom to create the compelling experiences that will satisfy customers. Even though they are overused examples, the iPod and iPhone are examples that show the importance of integrating actors together when launching a service such as iTunes (payment, promotion, content, admin). The successful integration of an otherwise complex ecology of partners needed to satisfy customers was one of the contributors to this success. This is the core background for the letter A in AT-ONE – Actor networks.

The basis of the Actors part is a recent development in the area of value networks as an alternative to the value chain. Value networks are more prevalent in services. The key is to see the potential that lies in the reconfiguration of roles and relationships among the constellation of actors, to facilitate the creation of value in new forms and by new players. The underlying strategic goal is to create an ever improving fit between the network's competencies and its customers. The Actors section investigates users as co-creators of value and one key aspect here is to replace an organisation's company-centred mapping of actors to one in which the customer is at the centre of the network and to consider how a different actor set can give improved customer value.

T →

Making touchpoints work as a whole

Think through the different ways you can access your bank balance. You can probably do this by calling someone at your bank and asking them, calling an automated computer generated system, by sending an SMS, directly from your smart-phone or PC, by reading your last bank statement, going into a bank or even by using an ATM. Each of these is a touchpoint between you, the customer, and your bank.

There is considerable potential to innovate through careful consideration of touchpoints. For one, experience shows that within an organisation, different parts of the organisation are responsible for different touchpoints. Who formulates the bank statement, who designs and maintains the online system, who is responsible for the bank building and personnel behaviour? Most likely, the answer will be; different parts of the organisation, who use different terminology, different tones of voice, and probably different interaction styles. So, just playing the game of "whose touchpoint is it anyway" will probably unearth quite a potential for improvement.

Service design is about choosing the most relevant touchpoints for service delivery and designing a consistent customer experience across these many touchpoints. It looks for opportunities to introduce potentially new and more effective touchpoints, remove weak touchpoints and to coordinate the user-experience across touchpoints in relation to brand

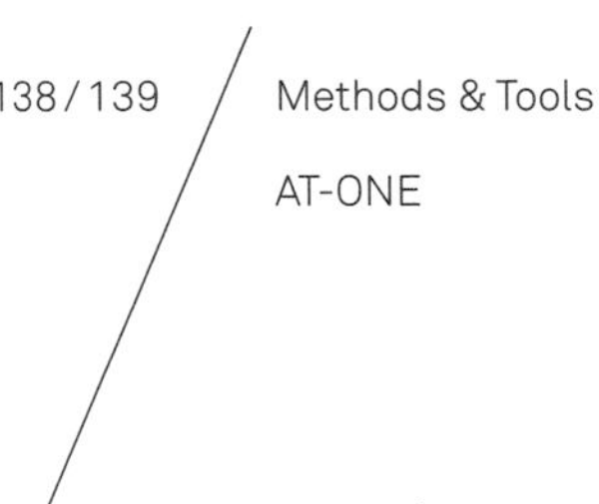

message and user needs. A major aspect of touchpoint innovation relates to the total experience that the service gives the customer upon completion of his journey through the service. Like a chain that will break at the weakest link, the customer experience will break at the weakest touchpoint.

O

The service offering is the brand

Service brands are unlike product brands. Often there is little brand differentiation and the service has a monolithic brand culture. This means that the service and the brand are very closely linked. If you consider a bank, even one with significant financial services, you will find that from a customer point of view, it offers a limited number of related services. Contrast that with an organisation such as Sony, and you will see that by comparison the bank has a limited diversification of services. It is only recently that service brands have begun to diversify. Virgin and Tesco (UK retailer) are good examples of organisations that offer a broad range of services under one brand. Common to both of these organisations is a clear understanding of what the company offers and that offering tends to be more of a philosophical orientation than closely related to physical products.

When brand and service are so closely linked, then service innovation will undoubtedly influence the brand in one way or another, and therefore as a result how your customers will perceive you. AT-ONE focuses upon understanding how the service offering is experienced at a functional level, an emotional level, and a self-expressive level. As part of the project we have developed a process model that helps to understand the brand DNA, and then use this to innovate the company offering. A central part of this is the creation of a service personality that describes the brand as if it were a person. Once the personality is described, it becomes easier to describe how the touchpoints should be designed, and the behaviours that each touchpoint should have. This process model is called the brand megaphone.

N

How do you know what customers want, need and desire?
Talking to your customers has become popular again. A few years ago, the focus for organisations was upon obtaining quantitative information (i.e. facts) about how customers viewed your service. This does of course give valuable data, nice graphs and a feeling of control, but it only answers what you want to know. It doesn't reveal what customers want to tell you, which might well be something quite different. Somehow, in terms of innovation, quantitative measures didn't give the answers that a project team needed. Talking to customers, observing customers and listening to customers can often reveal a different set of needs that escape traditional quantitative methods. Deep-seated or hidden needs and cultural trends can all be identified from dialogue with customers.

The Need part of the AT-ONE approach takes a user-centred design perspective from which to explore customer-needs. It uses personas as a vehicle for introducing a user perspective and adds input from a wide selection of user-centred methods, such as interviews, observation, participatory design sessions or observation. The main questions that the need tools attempt to address are those of whose needs the organisation should focus upon, how well do you as an organisation understand your customers' needs and to what extent are you as organisation satisfying them. Understanding, and involving customers at this stage, and ensuring that customers need, want and desire your service is probably one of the best ways to ensure the downstream success of your service.

E

Experiences that surprise and delight

Experiences are what customers have when they use your service, and when they recall it afterwards. The experience phase of the AT-ONE process builds upon recent developments in our understanding of the way people experience services. Customers in the western world today are not only looking for functional solutions to problems but also desire pleasurable solutions to our everyday problems. Apple became more desirable than Microsoft, Nokia more than Ericsson, Nike more than Adidas and Starbucks became the place to buy coffee. Why? Not because of their functional offering, but because of how they make us feel. Joseph Pine and James Gilmore describe this as "The Experience Economy" (Pine & Gilmore, 1999). Functionality and usability are not enough in our lives; they have become to be expected as a baseline. What customers are looking for are emotional bonds and experiences. Experiences are now a valuable differentiator and not only offer a pleasurable service experience, they help us create and express our identities.

Several tools have been developed to assist in using experiences as a starting point for design. Ideally we aim to design service experiences at the start, and then reverse engineer the offering, the touch-points, the service and even the organisation to be able to reliably produce the desired experience. This can be termed an experience "pull" approach.

How does Service Design work?

1 Choose the order of lenses that best suits your project.

2 Analyse and plan the workshop for each letter.

3 Conclude each workshop by choosing the 5 most promising ideas.

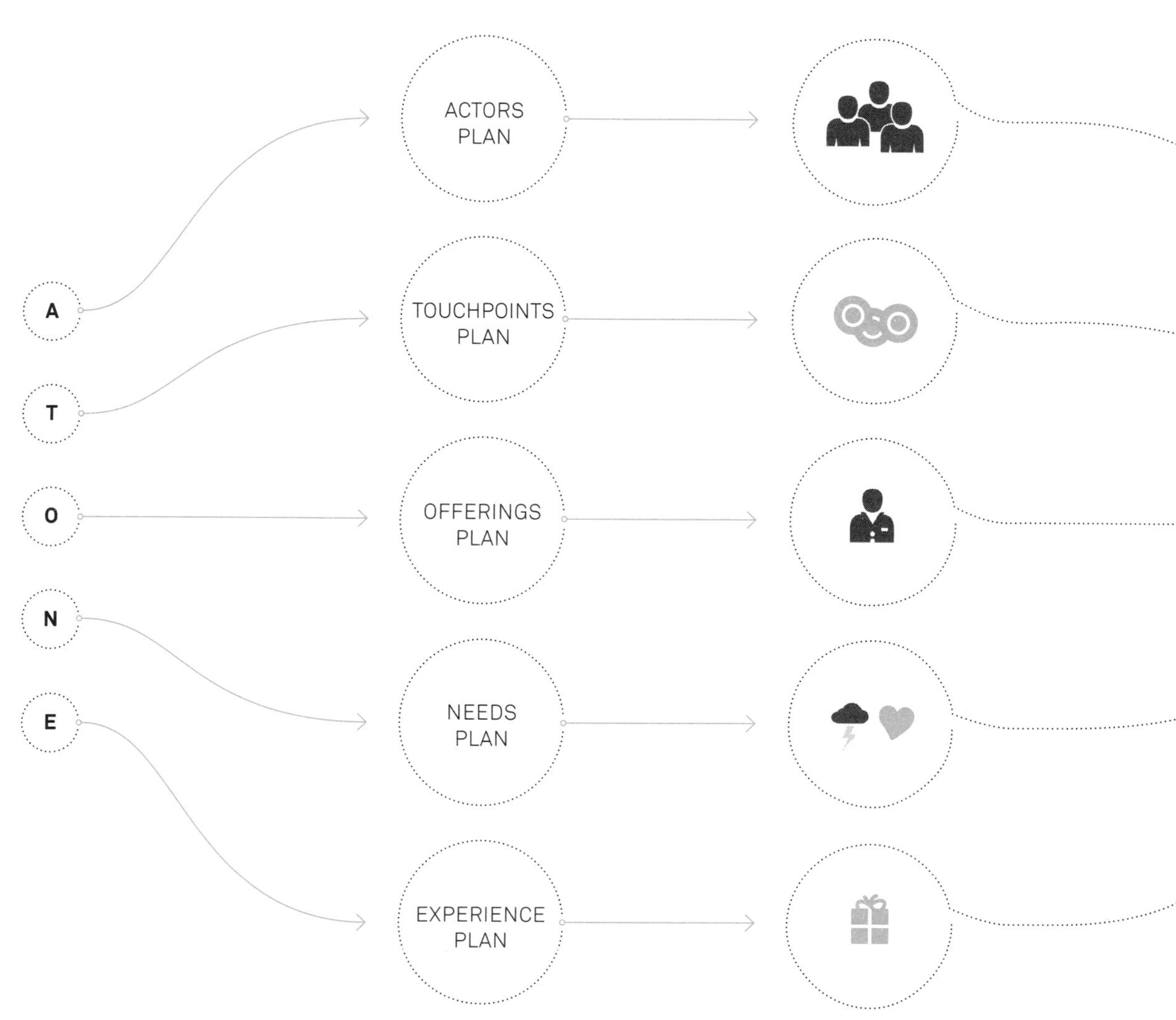

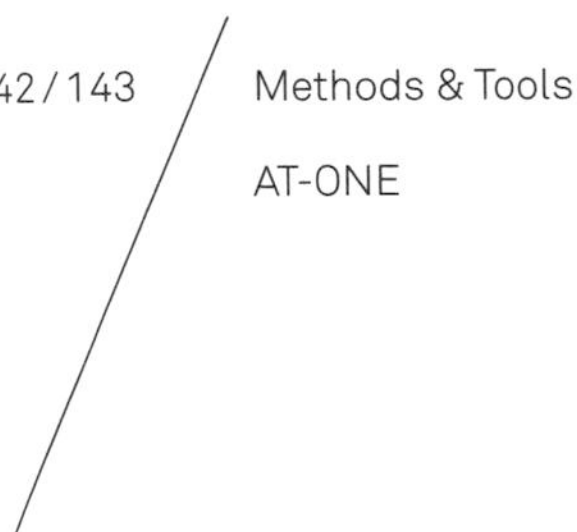

4 One workshop to combine and create 1–5 holistic concepts.

5 Visualise and communicate the final concepts to your leaders.

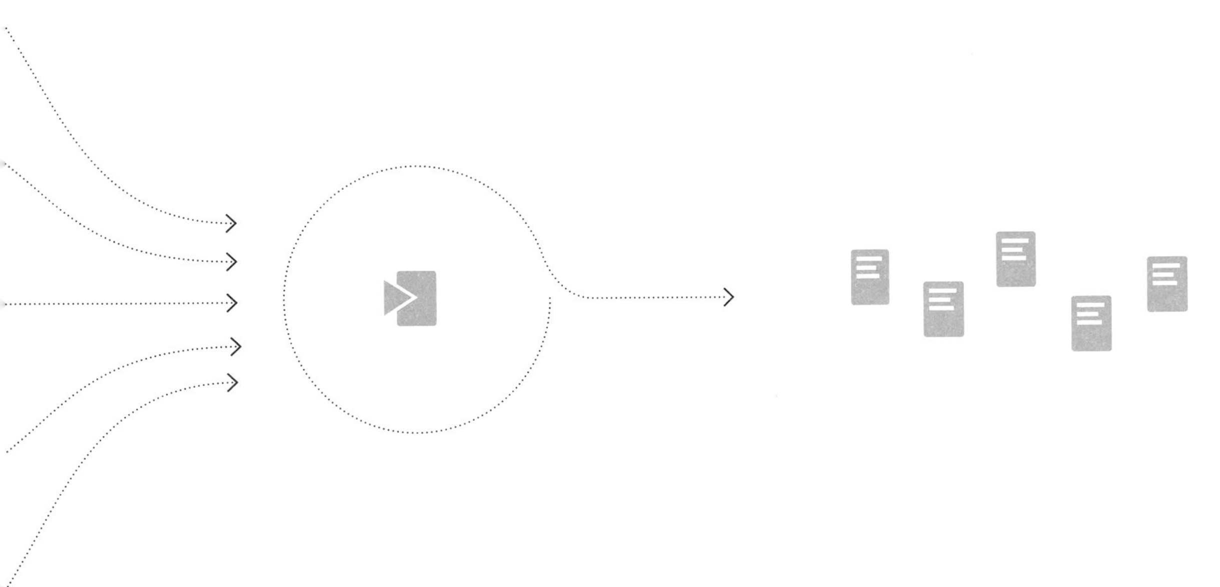

A — New combinations of ACTORS who together provide the service
T — Coordination and development of TOUCHPOINTS between customer and service
O — The design of what the service is actually OFFERING
N — The NEEDS that the service satisfies
E — The EXPERIENCE that the service gives the customer

What are the tools of Service Design?

Methods & Tools

THIS IS A TOOLBOX – NOT A MANUAL

THE COMMUNITY

To compile a set of the most widely-used and effective service design tools, we asked members of the community to contribute their thoughts and suggestions to an online forum. Where better to start than with the people who have been using and developing these tools in their everyday practice? The wide ranging collection of materials has been structured, edited and complemented by the editors. The endresult is a richly illustrated toolbox for service designers, offered here as an inspiration for anyone embarking on their own projects.

ONLINE CONTRIBUTORS IN ALPHABETICAL ORDER

Adam Lawrence / Ahmet Emre Acar / Aidan Kenny / Aleinad / Alexander Osterwalder / Alexis Goncalves / Anonymous / Arandag / Balulu / Bas Raijmakers / Ben Freundorfer / Bernard / Damian Kernahan / Daniel Christadoss / Darby / Dave / David Güiza Caicedo / D-LABS / Dolly Parikh / Eric Roscam Abbing / Esteban Kolsky / Fabian Segelström / Fergus Bisset / Geke van Dijk / Graham Hill / Jaap Frolich / Jakob Schneider / Jennylynnpie / Jo / John Coldwell / Josh Clarke / Julia Schaeper / Julian Sykes / Karine / Kirsty Joan Sinclair / Laura Pandelle / Lauren Currie / Luisalt / Luke Kelly / Luther Thie / Ly / Marc Stickdorn / Markus Hormess / Matt Currie / Melis Senova / minds & makers / Patrick Lerou / Qin / Rob Markey / Sachin /Saharald / Sarah Drummond / Satu Miettinen / Scott Rogers / Steve / Tennyson Pinheiro / Traci Lepore / Walter Aprile / Wim Rampen / Wjan

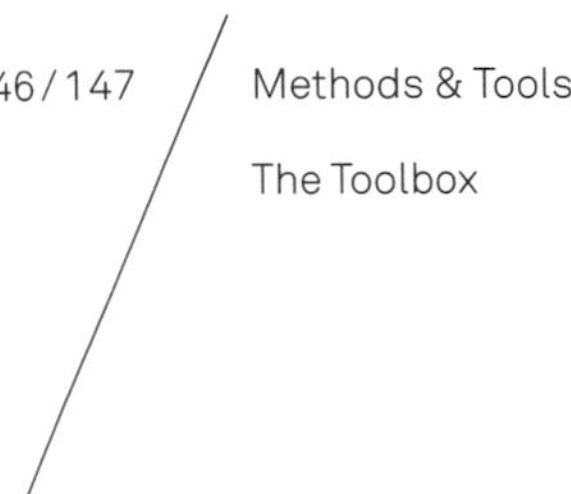

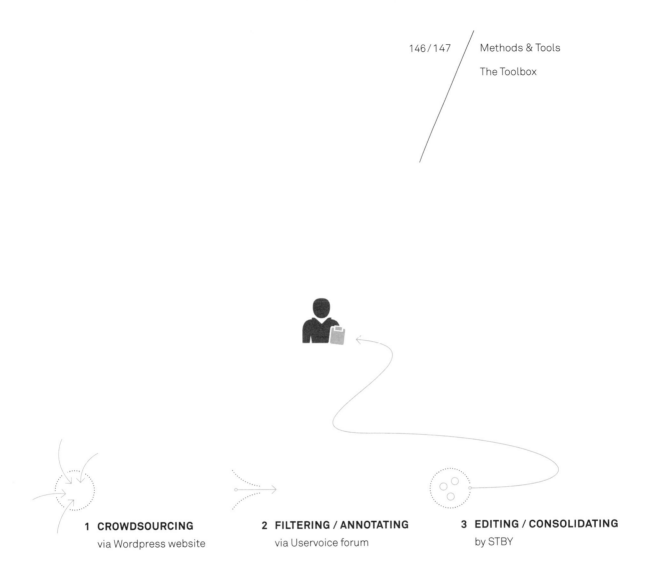

1 CROWDSOURCING
via Wordpress website

2 FILTERING / ANNOTATING
via Uservoice forum

3 EDITING / CONSOLIDATING
by STBY

THIS IS A TOOLBOX – NOT A MANUAL

GEKE VAN DIJK
BAS RAIJMAKERS
LUKE KELLY

This chapter brings together a wide range of service design methods and tools in an attempt to present a toolbox of effective and popular approaches to service design. It's not a manual detailing how a project should be conducted, as such a restrictive set of instructions would be at odds with the service design ethos. The methods and tools described here are resources from which bespoke, iterative projects can be constructed.

These tools can be used in almost any combination. Though they are presented here within the stages that most service design projects are likely to include, this isn't to say that there's only one way they can be used. Indeed, experimenting with existing approaches and new aims was how many of these tools came to be developed in the first place.

As in any other aspect of a service design project, there is no real right or wrong way to employ these tools. A successful project simply involves finding a workable combination, that can conceptualise, develop, and prototype ideas through an iterative process of gradual improvement.

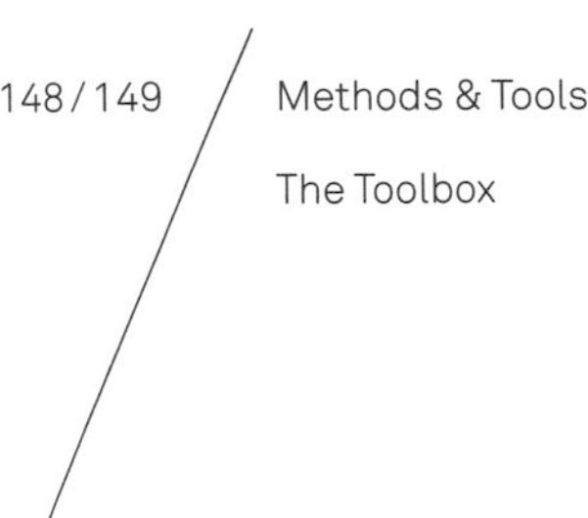

Explore
This stage is all about discovery. Service designers will be trying to discover new perspectives on a particular service. This could involve stepping into the shoes of customers, staff, managers, or even rivals, in order to develop new insights into the service experience. As this will form the foundation for the rest of the project, it is crucial that the tools used generate both intimate and engaging results.

Create & Reflect
Creation is where insights are visualised into new ideas and concepts, while reflection involves testing these ideas and concepts to find out how they can be further improved. Holistic solutions require the involvement of a wide range of stakeholders, and thus many of the creative tools here are designed around bringing as many people as possible into the creative process. The tools for reflection allow the ideas for solutions to be developed into prototypes, and tested against the insights generated in the exploratory phase.

Implement
The tools in the implementation stage provide ways to transfer the new or improved service designs to all sections of an organisation. They're about engaging new audiences, involving staff in the innovation process, and making a convincing and compelling case for change. Implementation means putting ideas into action.

EXPLORE

VISUALISING ALL ACTORS INVOLVED WITH A SERVICE

STAKEHOLDER MAPS

What is it?

A stakeholder map is a visual or physical representation of the various groups involved with a particular service. By representing staff, customers, partner organisations and other stakeholders in this way, the interplay between these various groups can be charted and analysed.

How is it made?

225 Firstly, a comprehensive list of stakeholders needs to be drawn up. Besides interviews, this will usually involve a fair amount of desk research,
240 as the aim of the map is also to highlight stakeholders that the service provider did not mention (or may not even be aware of). In addition, it is
270 important to reveal both the interests and the motivations of each stakeholder, with these also being incorporated into the map.

Once the list is complete the focus switches to how these groups are related to each other, and how they interact with each other. These connections should ideally be highlighted in a visually engaging way, as the aim throughout this process is to produce an easily accessible overview that can both identify pain points and explore areas of potential opportunity.

Why is it used?

The overview provided by stakeholder maps is a good way to highlight the issues concerning each stakeholder group. These groups can then be clustered together by their shared interests, allowing the service provider

to deploy their resources more effectively when responding to problems and expanding their service. In a similar vein, groups can be categorised according to their importance and influence, with previously neglected groups perhaps being reconsidered once the influence they exert on others is revealed. The maps thus visualise the complex situations surrounding most services, in which many actors have an effect on how well it is received and perceived. A comprehensive but accessible overview of stakeholders is integral to any attempts at improving engagement.

EXAMPLE →

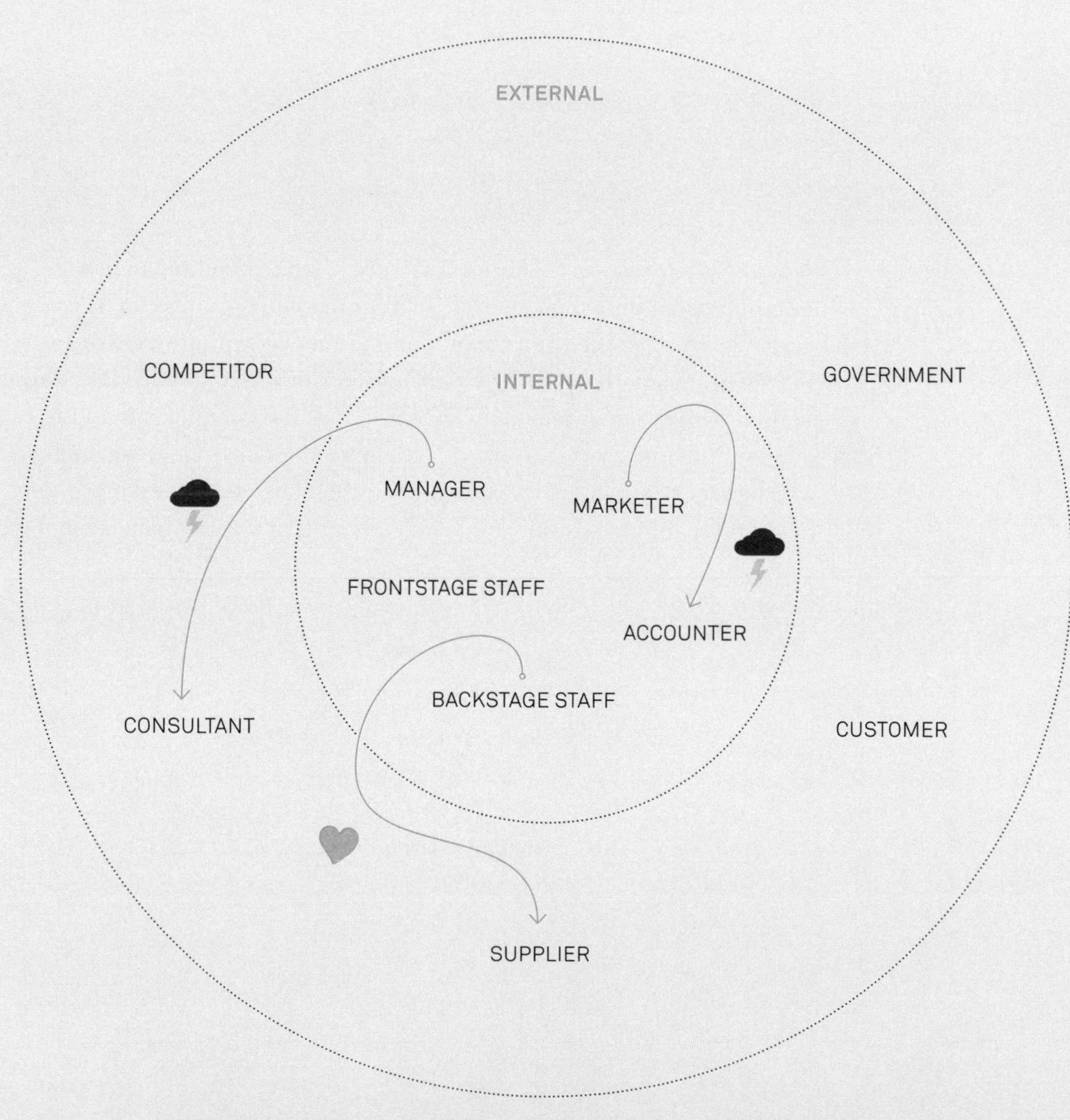
EXTERNAL
INTERNAL
COMPETITOR
GOVERNMENT
MANAGER
MARKETER
FRONTSTAGE STAFF
ACCOUNTER
BACKSTAGE STAFF
CONSULTANT
CUSTOMER
SUPPLIER

MARKETER — ACCOUNTER
The marketer feels overheard by the accounter.

MANAGER — CONSULTANT
The manager thinks that the consultant does not understand the company's culture.

BACKSTAGE STAFF — SUPPLIER
Backstage staff has a good relationship with the supplier.

A stakeholder map can have various formats. All of these should however identify both internal and external stakeholders, establish their relative importance to the project at hand, and also detail their relationship with each other.

EXPLORE

RAISING AWARENESS OF SERVICE QUALITY

SERVICE SAFARIS

What is it?
During a service safari, people are asked to go out "into the wild" and explore examples of what they think are good and bad service experiences.

How is it made?
Anyone can be invited to join in on a service safari. People from the client team often find it very revealing. To conduct the service safari, only the simplest set of tools is required. As people are being asked to record their experiences, they need to be provided with some method of doing so; a dictaphone, a small video camera, or even just a notebook and pen. When it comes to choosing some services to experience, people are often sent to explore services in the same sector as their own organisation. It is equally common, however, to ask people to explore each and every service they come across, in an attempt to define those factors common to any positive service experience.

Why is it used?
Safaris are one of the easiest ways to put people into the shoes of customers. Looking at a whole range of services allows people to develop an understanding of the common needs customers have, and the common problems that they encounter. These insights can then be developed into opportunities for service innovations, and are often all the more resonant due to people feeling like they have generated them themselves.

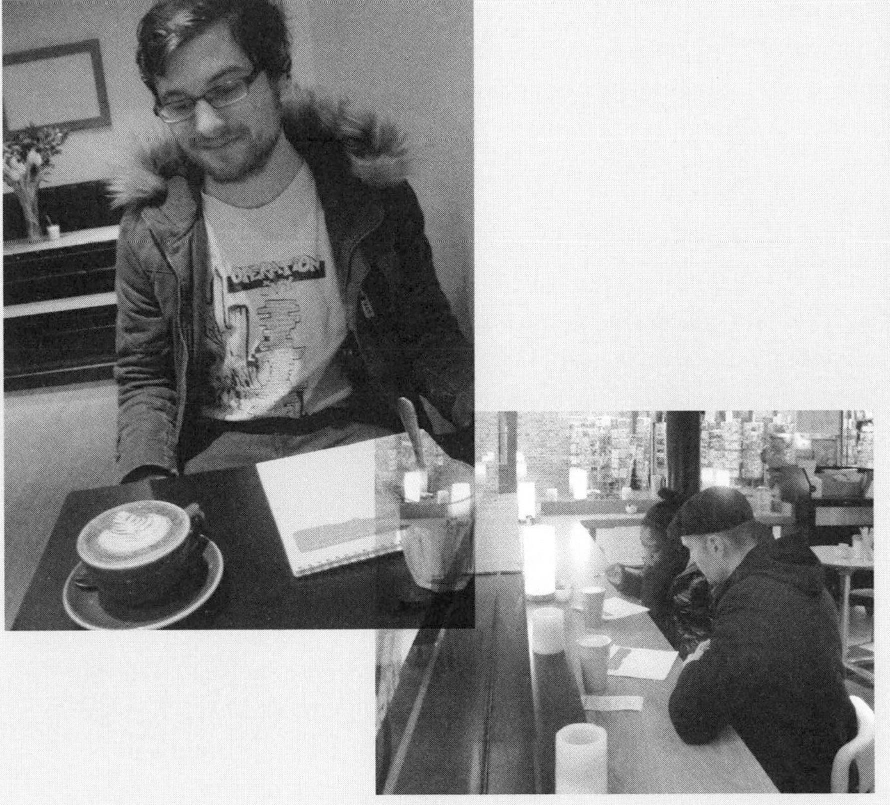

A safari allows a service to be observed and documented "in the wild". Pre-formatting a report sheet helps to structure notes for later processing.

EXPLORE

GAINING REAL-TIME SERVICE INSIGHTS

SHADOWING

What is it?

Shadowing involves researchers immersing themselves in the lives of customers, front-line staff, or people behind the scenes in order to observe their behaviour and experiences.

How is it done?

245 Though the researcher will often try and remain as unobtrusive as possible, they may still employ a range of different methods to document their
270 findings. Text, video, and photographs can all be used here, though a key consideration is always how to manage the "observer effect" – the in-
272 fluence the researcher may be exerting on the behaviour they're observing simply by being present.

287

Why is it used?

Shadowing allows researchers to spot the moments at which problems occur. By observing such moments at first-hand, they can document problems, which the staff or customers involved may not even recognise as such. Spending time within the service environment is often the only way to develop a truly holistic view of how the service is operating, as it provides an intimate understanding of the real-time interactions that take place between the various groups and touchpoints involved. Shadowing is also a useful technique for identifying those moments where people may say one thing, and yet do another.

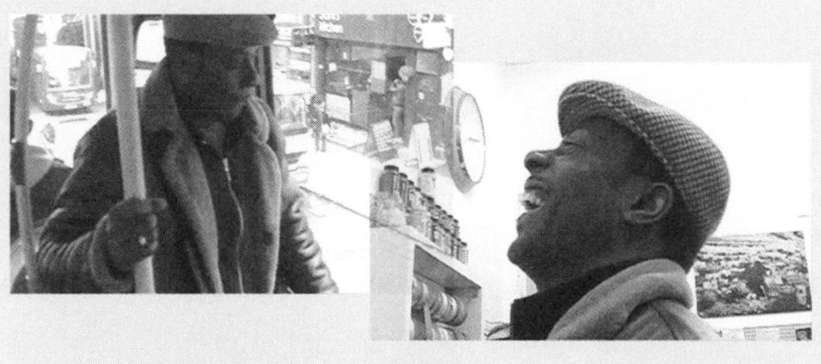

Video works well for shadowing, as it captures those details people may forget to convey during interviews. Successful shadowing often means keeping a low profile – high-heels are out, as the noise can be picked up on the microphone.

CUSTOMER JOURNEY MAPS

What is it?
A customer journey map provides a vivid but structured visualisation of a service user's experience. The touchpoints where users interact with the service are often used in order to construct a "journey" – an engaging story based upon their experience. This story details their service interactions and accompanying emotions in a highly accessible manner.

How is it made?
226 Identifying the touchpoints where users interact with the service is crucial. These can take many forms, from personal face to face contact between individuals, 272 to virtual interactions with a website or physical trips to a building. Constructing a customer journey map involves defining these touchpoints by generating user insights. Interviews work well here, but maps can also be documented by customers themselves – blogs and video diaries provide insights into the user's own language, which always makes for an engaging set of materials when constructing the map.

Once the touchpoints have been identified, they can be connected together in a visual representation of the overall experience. This overview should be visually engaging enough to make it easily accessible to all, but should also incorporate enough detail to provide real insights into the journeys being displayed. This might mean basing the map around personas, so that the customers doing the journeying become far more than just names on a page. Basing the map around materials customers themselves have produced also helps facilitate empathic engagement,

which is crucial for conveying the myriad emotions that most journeys are made up of.

Why are they used?
A customer journey map provides a high-level overview of the factors influencing user experience, constructed from the user's perspective. Basing the map on user insights allows it to chart both formal and informal touchpoints. "Personalising" the map – incorporating photographs along with personal quotes and commentary – can make it an even more immersive user-focused experience. The overview the map provides enables the identification of both problem areas and opportunities for innovation, whilst focusing on specific touchpoints allows the service experience to be broken down into individual stages for further analysis. This structured visual representation makes it possible to compare several experiences in the same visual language, and also facilitates quick and easy comparisons between a service and its competitors.

EXAMPLE →

What are the tools of Service Design?

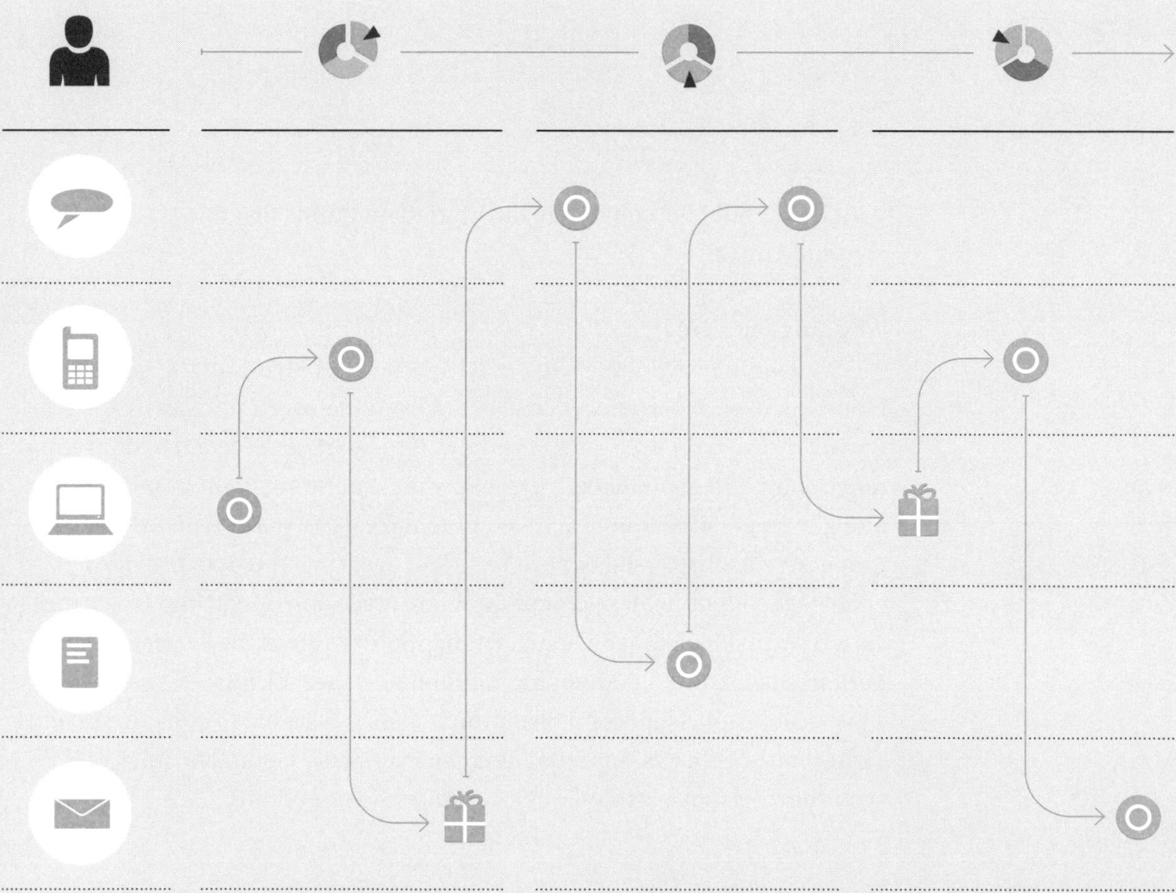

A typical customer journey is shown to be multi-channel and time-based. Customers get their information from various sources, some of which – like friends and family – are beyond a service provider's control.

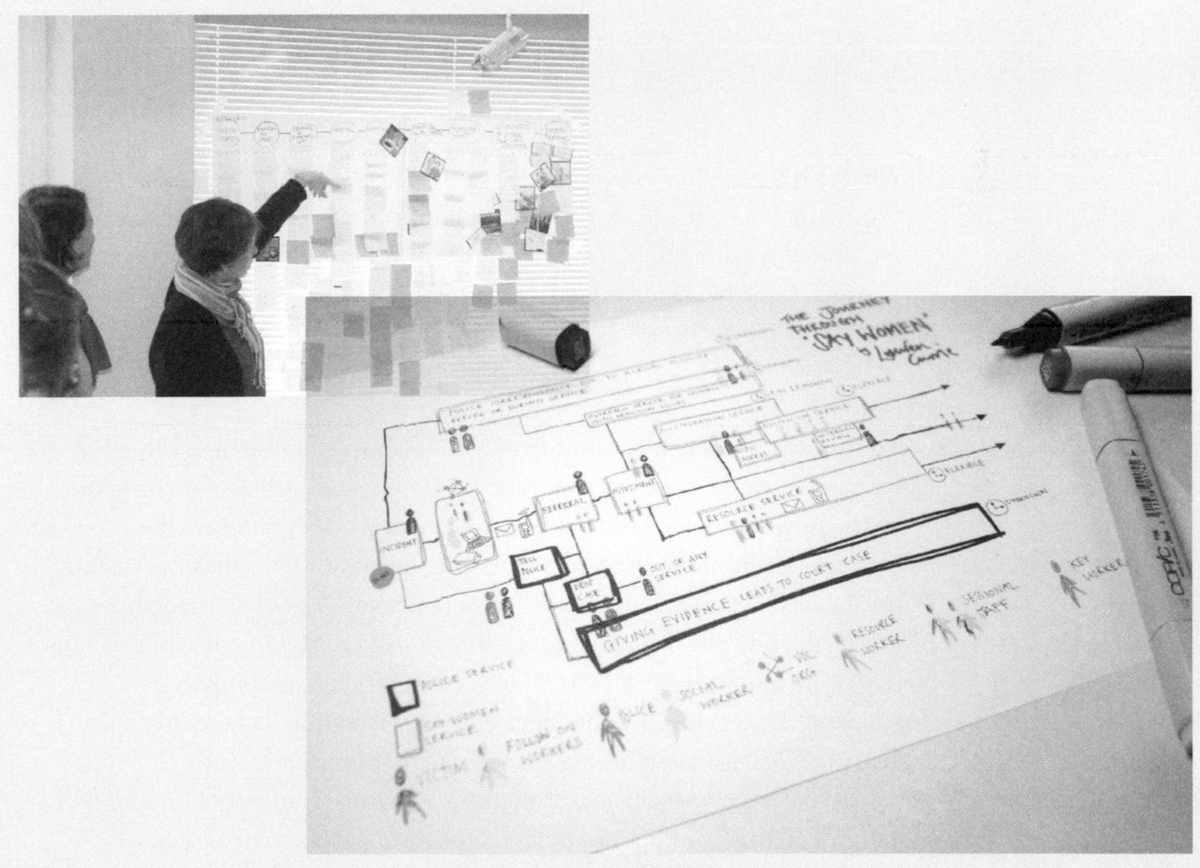

It's important to not only visualise the path of the customer journey – encapsulated via a series of touchpoints – but also to collect stories that explain why the journey happened as it did. What were the circumstances, motivations and experiences that resulted in this process?

EXPLORE

GAINING IN-DEPTH UNDERSTANDING OF STAKEHOLDERS

CONTEXTUAL INTERVIEWS

What is it?

Contextual Interviews are conducted in the environment, or context, in which the service process of interest occurs. This ethnographic technique allows interviewers to both observe and probe the behaviour they are interested in.

How is it done?

243 These interviews can be conducted with customers, staff, and other
relevant stakeholders. The interviewer visits the interviewee within the
255 environment in which they interact with the service under review,
and uses a combination of questions and observations in order to generate
257 the desired insights. Participants are usually selected via a specialised
recruiting process, which will take into consideration factors such as how
270 to put the interviewee at ease. This point is crucial, as conducting a
successful interview is dependent on making people feel comfortable
287 sharing what are often intimate insights into their lives.

The interviewer will also often be faced with a number of potential locations. Here, it's important to take into account the environmental prompts that might help provoke a more in-depth discussion – discussing work routines is always going to be easier when the conversation takes place in the office where those processes are defined.

The interview will usually be documented via audio recordings and photographs, and may even be filmed – a technique which often produces

richly engaging materials to present to the service provider and the wider project team.

Why is it used?

One of the key benefits of making an interview contextual is that it helps the interviewee to remember the kind of specific details that so often get lost in a traditional focus group setting. Most people are more comfortable providing insights into their thoughts and behaviour when discussing these from within a familiar environment, and these insights can be both validated and expanded upon by the observations of the interviewer – what people don't say is often just as valuable as what they do. Insights aren't just limited to the interviewee however. Contextual interviews allow researchers to also gain an understanding of the social and physical environment surrounding the service being examined. This helps generate a far more holistic understanding than is possible via traditional interviewing techniques.

EXAMPLE →

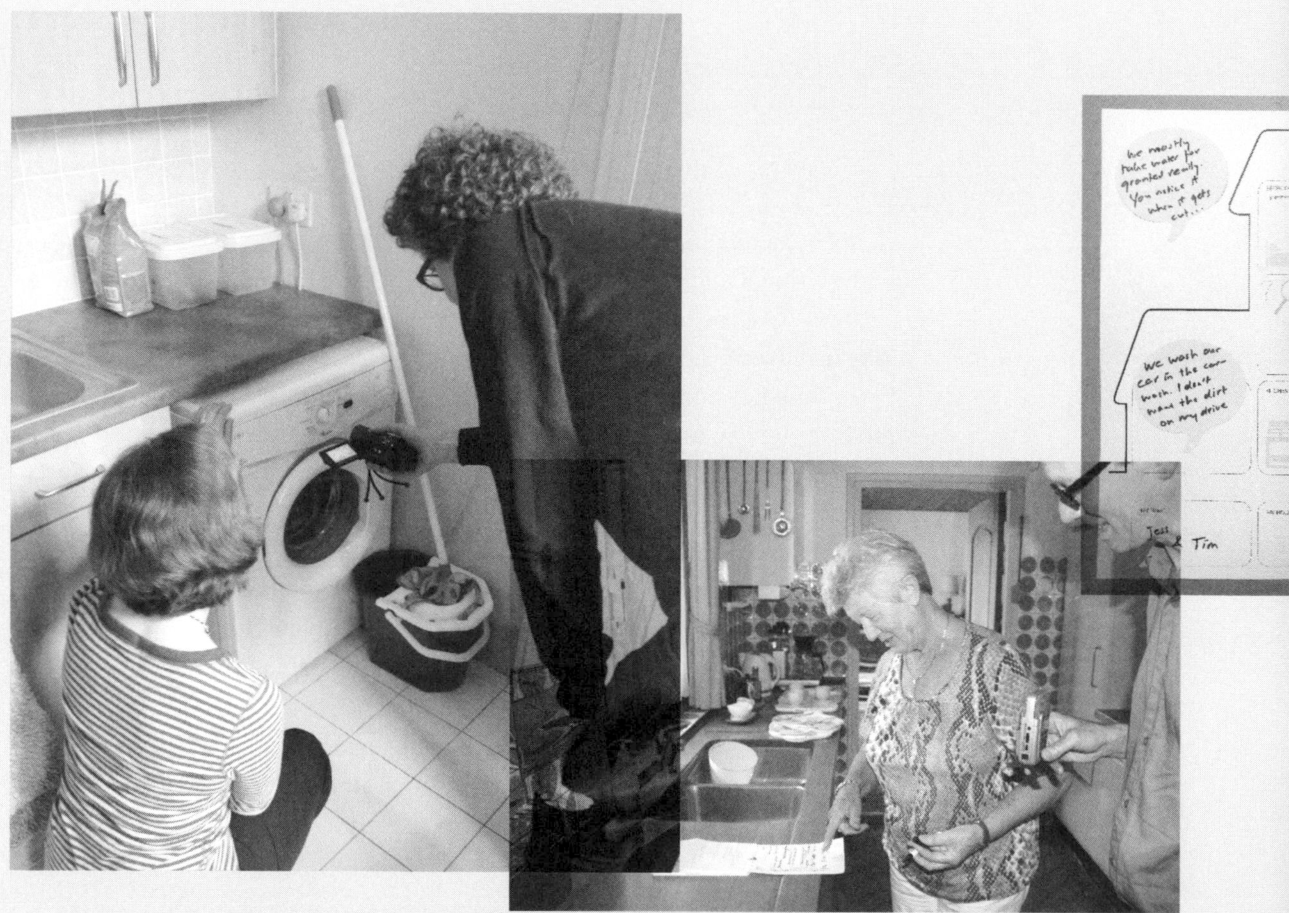

Conducting different parts of the interview in various places around the house (that are nevertheless relevant to the topic of the project) helps people tell a more lively story about their everyday practices.

1

2

1 Conducting interviews in the comfort of people's own homes helps them to convey their experiences and personal context in more detail. The researchers get a much richer notion of the person they are speaking with.

2 Using visual, tangible prompts to capture significant data during the interview is a useful way to document observations and comments for later analysis.

EXPLORE

REVEALING SUBCONSCIOUS STAKEHOLDER MOTIVATIONS

THE FIVE WHYS

What is it?

The 5 Whys are just those – a chain of questions used to dig below the outward symptoms of a user experience in order to uncover the motivations that are at its root cause.

How is it done?

The 5 Whys are usually addressed to explore a specific problem in greater depth. The person or team answering the questions has to produce a convincing explanation for each stage of the causal pathway leading back from the original experience or problem. Limiting this pathway to 5 stages prevents the process from losing relevance as it veers too far from the original question, but still provides insights into the underlying processes which may be exerting an influence.

Why is it used?

The 5 Whys are a simple, easy way to establish links between root causes and surface problems, and require very little preparation. This is useful for quickly gaining an understanding of complex issues, and in provoking those being questioned to go deeper when trying to explain common problems. The 5 Whys can be used in a wide range of circumstances. One benefit of defining causality by stages for example is that it may include steps in a service process that the customer doesn't see, which can be of great benefit for organisations trying to classify problems as either internal or external.

WHY DOES IT TAKE SO LONG TO SERVE A CUSTOMER?
Because we are so busy! There's always a queue of people waiting to be served at lunchtime.

WHY IS THERE ALWAYS A QUEUE OF PEOPLE AT LUNCHTIME?
It's the busiest time of the day, and we don't have enough staff to serve everyone.

WHY DO WE NOT HAVE ENOUGH STAFF TO COPE WITH BUSY PERIODS?
We don't have enough room to accommodate more staff – they would probably just get in the way.

WHY IS THERE NOT ENOUGH ROOM FOR MORE STAFF?
The service area is too cluttered, as the equipment we use is very large and bulky.

WHY IS THERE SO MUCH EQUIPMENT AROUND?
We purchase our equipment in bulk to save money. This usually results in cheap but bulky stuff, that we then need to navigate around.

The tactic behind the Five Whys is to keep delving deeper into the underlying motivations for a specific behaviour or opinion. Each new question is triggered by the answer to the previous question.

EXPLORE

GAINING PROFOUND INSIGHTS INTO USER PERSPECTIVES

CULTURAL PROBES

What is it?

Cultural probes are information gathering packages. Based around the principle of user-participation via self-documentation, the probes are usually given to research participants for a prolonged period of time, during which they can produce richly engaging material for design inspiration.

How is it made?

The possibilities for innovation in the design of cultural probes are almost endless. They may be something as simple as a diary that the participant is asked to complete over the course of a set period. This might be complemented with a disposable camera, or a set of instructions designed to elicit the kind of behavioural reflection the researchers are looking for. Video can also be incorporated within the probe, with the participants following a simple script in order to self-document insights that are unreachable using traditional techniques.

Once the probe is sent out, it can still be "directed" by researchers remotely. Regular instructions can be sent by email or text message for example, meaning that the material gathered by the probe can be tailored around the evolving aims of the project. Researchers can thus follow up on particularly rich insights without having to compromise the intimacy the probes achieve. The success of a probe is thus dependant not just on its original design, but on continually monitoring the insights it delivers in order to ensure it can adapt around new discoveries and changing priorities.

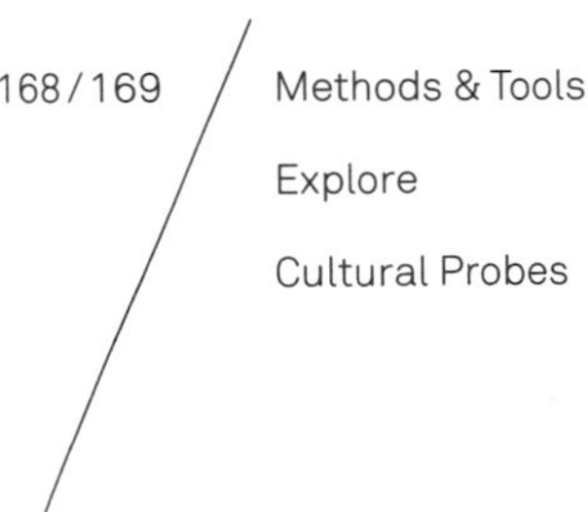

Why is it used?

In order to gain the most intimate insights, researchers need to be as unobtrusive as possible. Cultural probes allow insights to be generated without the researcher even being present. Simple scripts and instructions, often complimented by prompts such as text messaging, can structure the information that is gathered in order to deliver effective and consistent results. The intimacy of the insights generated also serves to build empathy with the participants. The probes often provide a highly impressionistic account of people's beliefs and desires, whilst producing a richly evocative set of research materials. They are thus hugely effective in overcoming cultural boundaries, and bringing a diverse range of people and perspectives into design processes.

EXAMPLE →

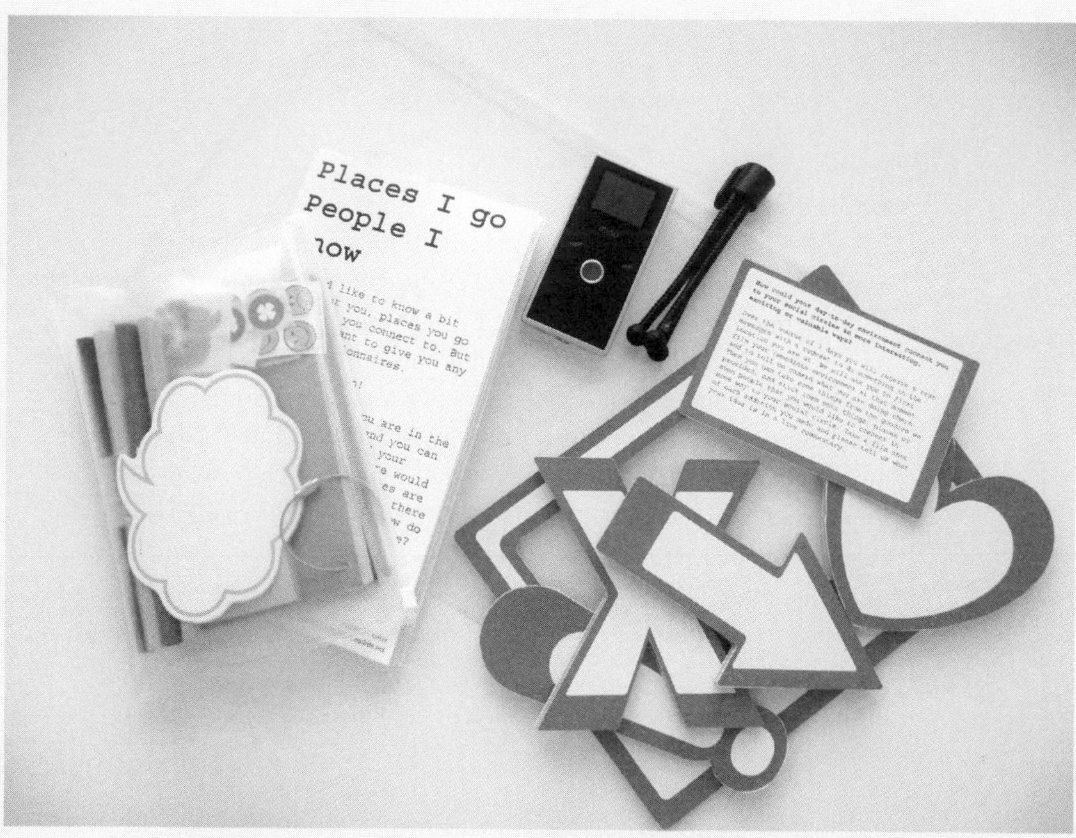

With a USB camera and a set of colourful tools participants can be invited to make video clips of service experiences – and even provide live commentary on them.

2

1

1 If a study requires people to keep a log of specific activities and experiences, provide them with a nicely structured notebook. This will also be useful during the analysis of the data.

2 Including postcards and maps in the probe pack, along with questions added on stickers, is an effective way of prompting people to note down daily activities and thoughts.

EXPLORE

GAINING USER-STRUCTURED DOCUMENTATION OF SERVICE PROCESSES

MOBILE ETHNOGRAPHY

What is it?
Mobile ethnography can be defined as ethnographic research that takes place independently of geography. This usually means that the researcher is not present in person, but the technique differs from cultural probes in that instead of participant's being directed, the insights generated revolve around how participants choose to structure the research themselves.

How is it done?
Recent advances in technology allow mobile ethnography to be conducted in practically any environment. Equipping participants with smartphones, for example, allows them to gather time- and location-independent user-centred information. This might include the touchpoints where they perceive themselves to be interacting with a particular service, which they can then document using a combination of audio, text, photo or video.

Why is it used?
Having participants define their own touchpoints – and even rate their effectiveness – provides a user-structured image of how a service is operating. The materials produced are in effect digital sticky notes, which can subsequently be clustered and analysed in order to chart and reflect upon the trends that may emerge. The technique is not limited to eliciting feedback from customers; internal mobile ethnography projects can deliver revealing insights about staff processes, experiences and opinions.

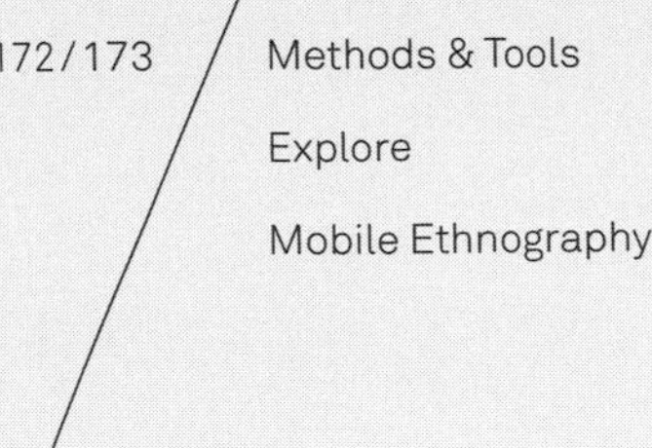

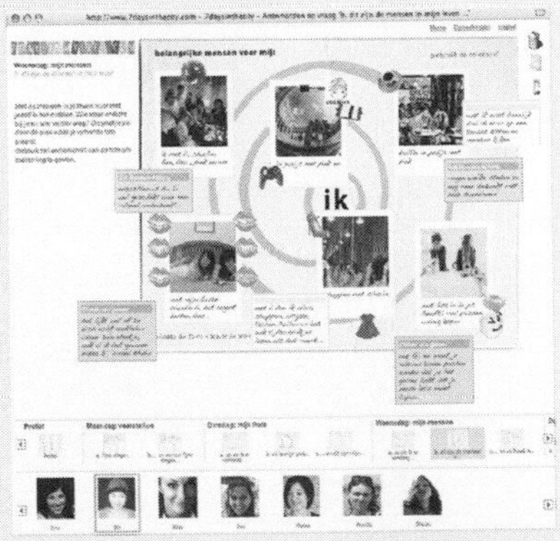

Mobile ethnography can be conducted anywhere and at any time. Keep it open; participants may need some guidance, but not too much structure – that would defeat the point!

EXPLORE

VISUALISING ROUTINES AND ACTIVITIES OF USERS

A DAY IN THE LIFE

What is it?
A Day in the Life collates the research material pertaining to a particular type of customer (which may have already been collated into a persona) in order to create a descriptive walkthrough of their typical daily activities.

How is it done?
A Day in the Life can be presented in several different formats; simple graphics or a comic-strip are quick and easy to produce, whilst using video or photography produces a rich depiction of a user's everyday environments and routines. Regardless of the format chosen, the Day in the Life should incorporate as many of the insights gathered as feasible – the purpose is to provide an overview of a typical day, including what a customer is thinking and doing outside of their service interactions.

Why is it used?
A Day in the Life contextualises a customer's service interactions, allowing a great deal of background information pertaining to their thoughts and feelings when interacting with a touchpoint to be conveyed. Simply focusing on those instances where customers come into direct contact with a service ignores these contextual insights, whilst uncovering people's everyday problems and solutions provides a far more holistic view of their drivers and motivations – something that's integral to tailoring services effectively.

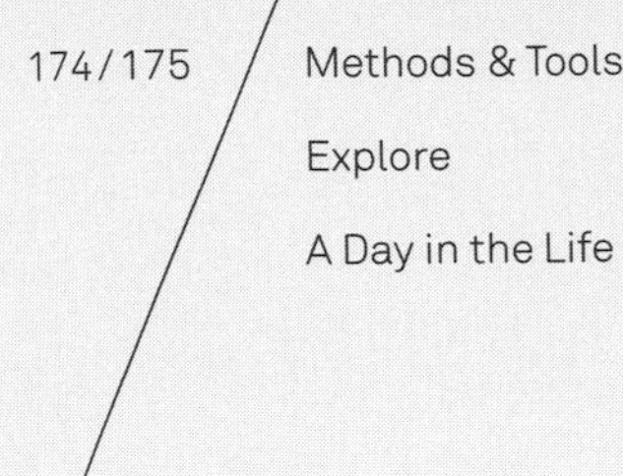

One effective way to collect data for a “Day in the Life” is to ask participants to note down their individual activities during a specific day in the previous week.

EXPLORE

REVEALING CUSTOMER EXPECTATIONS OF SERVICES

EXPECTATION MAPS

What is it?

Making an Expectation Map involves investigating and charting what customers expect when they interact with a service. The map can either focus on one specific service, or take the more generalised form of analysing a particular service category.

How is it made?

The material used to construct an expectation map can come from a variety of sources. A first draft of the map can be quickly and easily developed from sources such as media coverage for example, with this then serving as a general indication of how a company is being perceived "out in the wild". Conducting original research meanwhile – i.e. in-depth interviews with customers designed to gather their reflections – allows the map to be more detailed and targeted around a particular area.

Why is it used?

Expectation mapping often serves as a diagnosis tool, drawing out those areas of a service in need of attention from a customer-based perspective. Expectation maps that focus on a particular aspect of a service are a useful way to define and review those areas where customers are regularly experiencing problems. An expectation map might be created in relation to what customers expect when contacting the service provider, by the telephone for example, with this being contrasted with similar maps of in-person visits or email correspondence.

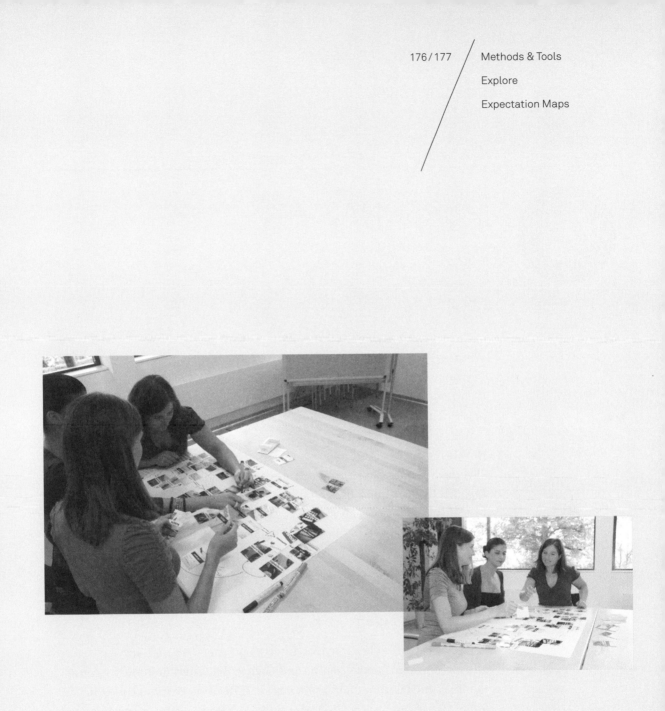

Producing expectation maps in an open, playful manner helps ensure the participants are relaxed enough to share their real feelings.

EXPLORE

VISUALISING CUSTOMER GROUPS AS RECOGNISABLE ARCHETYPES

PERSONAS

What is it?

Personas are fictional profiles, often developed as a way of representing a particular group based on their shared interests. They represent a "character" with which client and design teams can engage.

How is it made?

226 The most common way of developing personas is to collate research
insights into common-interest groupings, which can then be developed
244 into a workable "character". The key to a successful persona is how
engaging it proves to be, and thus a wide range of techniques – from visual
representations to detailed anecdotal profiles – can be used to bring these
characters to life. Most personas are developed from research insights
gathered from stakeholder maps, shadowing, interviews, and the like.

Why is it used?

Personas can provide a range of different perspectives on a service, allowing design teams to define and engage the different interest-groups that may exist within their target market. Effective personas can shift focus away from abstract demographics, and towards the wants and needs of real people. Even though the personas themselves may be fictional, the motivations and reactions they exhibit are real; personas are a collation of feedback elicited during the research stage of a project, and as such embody the real-world perceptions surrounding a company's service.

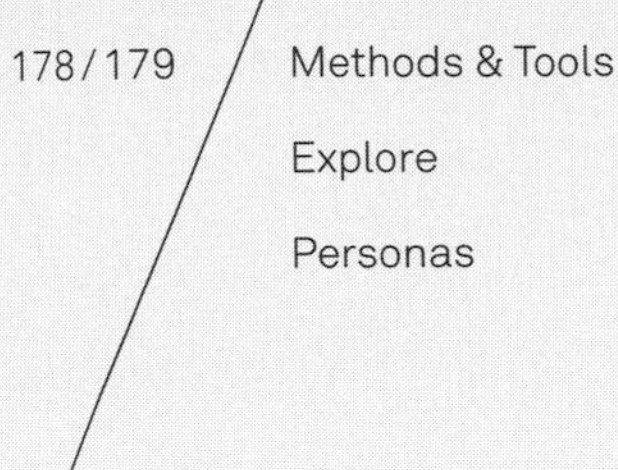

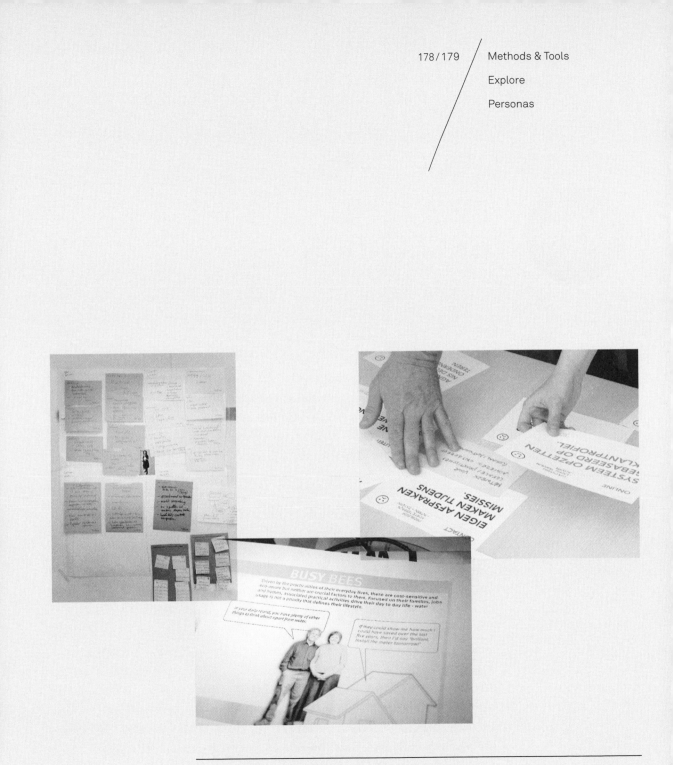

Personas can be constructed as a group activity in workshops. This facilitates discussions around specific customer segments. For more formal and sustainable use personas are usually visualised and further detailed in reports.

CREATE & REFLECT

STRUCTURING AND INSPIRING BRAINSTORMS

IDEA GENERATION

What is it?

Ideation techniques are what service designers use to structure and inspire group brainstorming sessions. They usually take the form of simple exercises which can be used to stimulate group discussions, whilst also providing a structure within which to work. Mind-mapping, S.W.O.T. analysis and Six Thinking Hats are all examples of ideation techniques.

How is it done?

Different methods will obviously be used in different ways, but all will be centred upon generating momentum or reflection during group discussion sessions. This is something the service designer will most likely incorporate into the programme of any given discussion, after giving thought to which technique is most suitable in relation to the session's goals. Choosing the right ideation technique for the situation at hand is a crucial skill for any service designer to learn – as is being able to abandon a technique that's not delivering results in order to try something else.

Why is it used?

The range of different techniques has a different set of motivations for their use. Some for instance may be deployed as "ice-breakers", relaxing the participants so that they can take part in the session more fully. Others will provide prompts to imagination, or simple pointers around which the discussion can be organised. All have the goal of stimulating idea generation by allowing group sessions to work more smoothly.

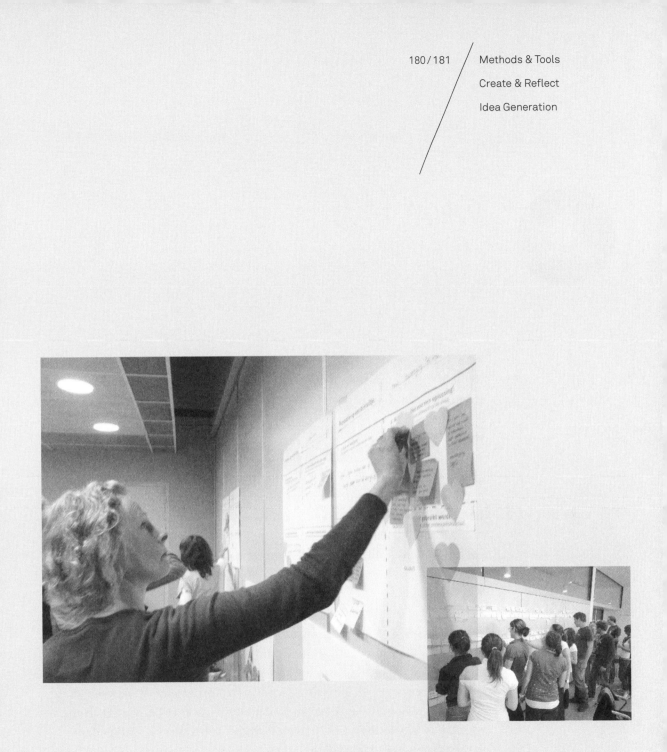

Exercises for idea generation during workshops need to stimulate and inspire people. Using visual materials and creating an active work dynamic is crucial.

CREATE & REFLECT

EXPLORING CHALLENGING FUTURE SERVICE SCENARIOS

WHAT IF …

What is it?

"What if …" is a question that service designers may pose in order to prompt exploration of even the most outlandish scenarios.

How is it done?

"What if …" differs from design scenarios in that it is generally used to explore wide-ranging changes rather than specific service experience situations. This often means presenting people with a challenging question on how their service would be affected by changes taking place at the technological, societal or cultural level. People are asked to explore such situations, and imagine the kinds of problems they would present.

Why is it used?

Asking "what would happen to your service if the internet went mobile?" at the start of the 21st century would have helped several service providers prepare for the problems they were about to encounter. Today, similar questions can be used to prepare companies for the wide range of changes likely to occur over the next few decades. Exploring such situations is often an effective way to isolate and analyse the key components from which a service is designed. Looking at how well a service could adapt to the potential problems of the future, helps focus attention on what it is doing right – and what could be done better – today.

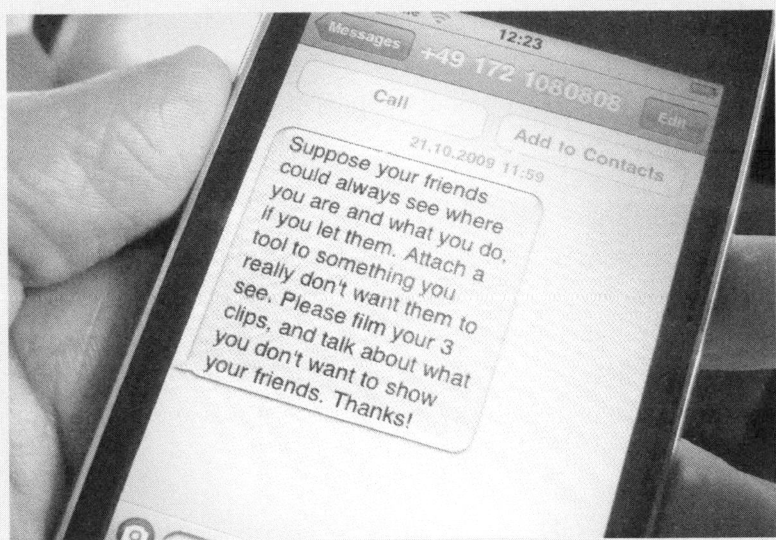

"What if ..." questions need to provoke participants to explore potential future situations, without drowning them in everyday concerns. They can be used in both field studies and workshops.

CREATE & REFLECT

EXPLAINING KEY ELEMENTS OF SERVICE IDEAS IN STORIES

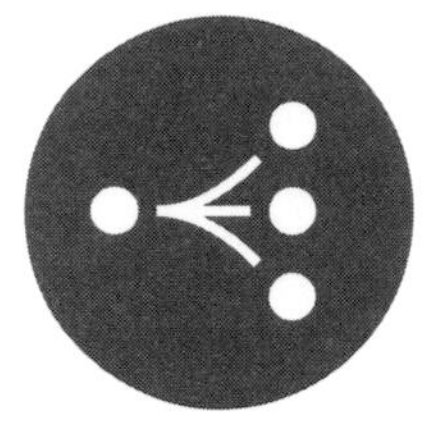

DESIGN SCENARIOS

What is it?

Design scenarios are essentially hypothetical stories, created with sufficient detail to meaningfully explore a particular aspect of a service offering.

How is it made?

229 Design scenarios can be presented using plain text, storyboards, or even
videos. Research data is used to construct a plausible situation around
241 which the scenario can be based. In order to lend added authenticity,
personas can be incorporated within the scenario in order to orientate the
258 situation being examined around a clearly defined character. Precisely
what this situation is depends on the objective of the scenario.

273

Why is it used?

Design scenarios can be used in almost any stage of a service design project. Problematic areas of a current service offering might be developed into scenarios in order to brainstorm solutions; prototype scenarios examine potential problems new service ideas might encounter; “negative” scenarios ask “How could things be made worse?” in order to provoke discussion on what’s actually working well. All of these scenarios are able to help review, analyse, and understand the driving factors that ultimately define a service experience. Creating them in a group setting meanwhile encourages knowledge exchange between the various stakeholders involved.

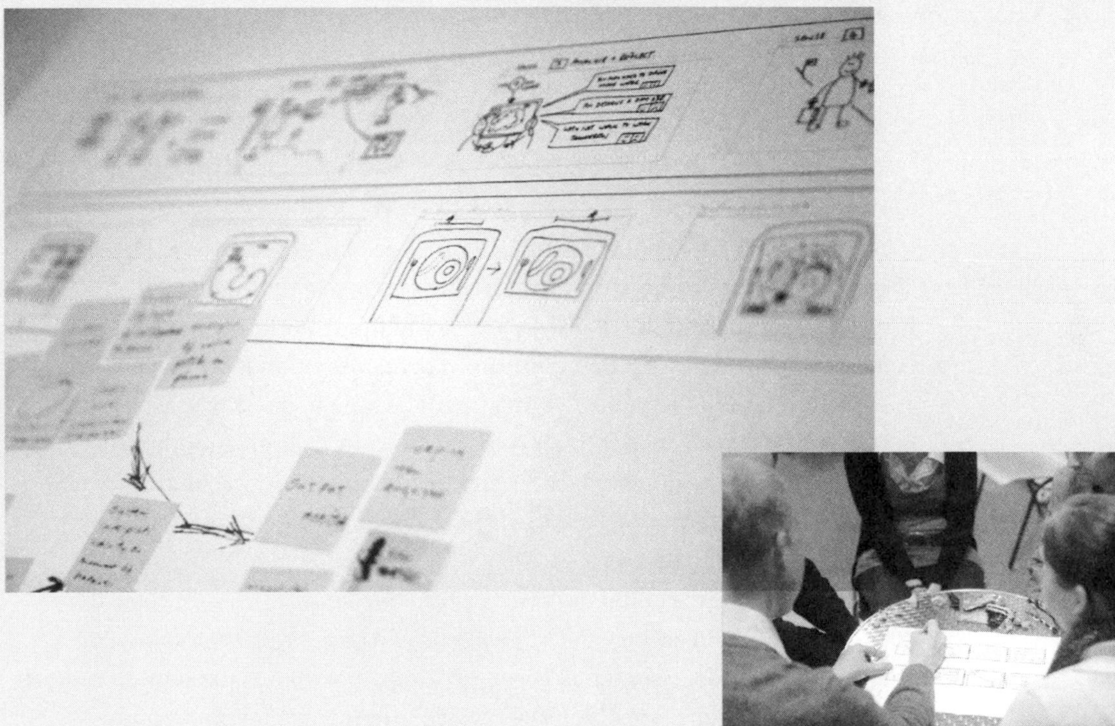

Scenarios make concepts and prototypes accessible and engaging by placing them in an easily relatable context. This helps facilitate discussions about how people will experience new services in the future.

CREATE & REFLECT

VISUALISING CONCEPTS AND IMAGINED USES OF NEW SERVICES

STORYBOARDS

What is it?

A storyboard is a series of drawings or pictures that visualise a particular sequence of events. This might include a common situation where a service is used, or the hypothetical implementation of a new service prototype.

How is it made?

245 Storyboards can be constructed in a number of different ways. The most
common is the comic-strip format, in which a designer will create
273 a series of illustrations that tell the story of the situation being examined.
The designer will try and include as many contextual details as pos-
274 sible here, so that anyone viewing it will be able to quickly grasp what it
is going on. The aim of the storyboard is to gain insights into the user
experience being depicted. Either real-life or imaginary scenarios can be
used, with the former occasionally being documented in photographs
as opposed to illustrations.

When used in a collaborative or workshop setting, the storyboard should be able to convey the key aspects of a service or prototype in as straightforward a manner as possible. This often means presenting a short illustrated scenario in which the service is being used, which might incorporate several contrasting outcomes. This can then be presented to a group of designers or potential customers, with the aim of provoking a discussion about what seems to work and what doesn't.

Why is it used?

Storyboards do exactly what the title implies – they allow stories about user experiences to be brought into the design process. The kinds of stories used are those that provide a perspective on a service or prototype – they're a way to encapsulate the experiences of people using the service. By putting a service situation in its proper context – even if it's still a prototype that doesn't physically exist yet – storyboards can be used to provoke meaningful analysis, sparking discussions about potential problems and areas of opportunity. The process of creating them meanwhile forces designers into the shoes of the people using a service, which again helps to bring that perspective into the design process.

EXAMPLE →

Storyboards visualised as comic-strips are a good way of communicating and reviewing future customer journeys. Organising them on separate cards makes it easy to adapt the story when new insights arise.

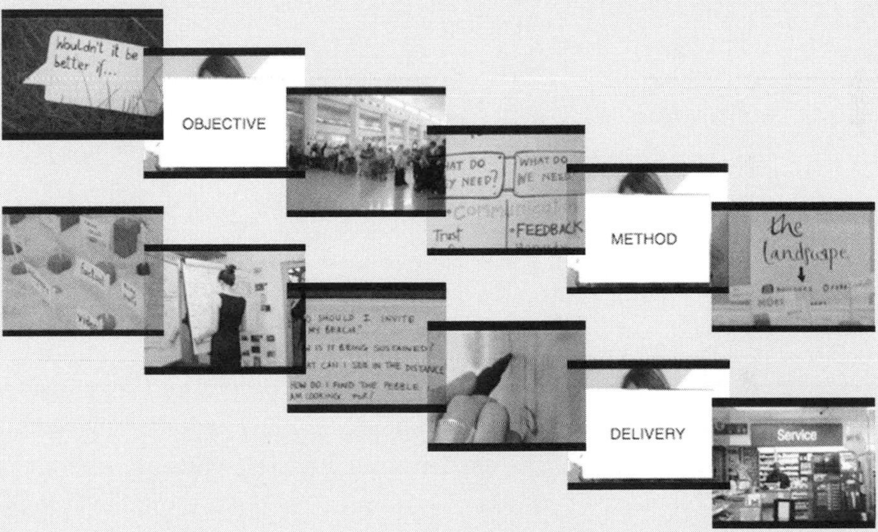

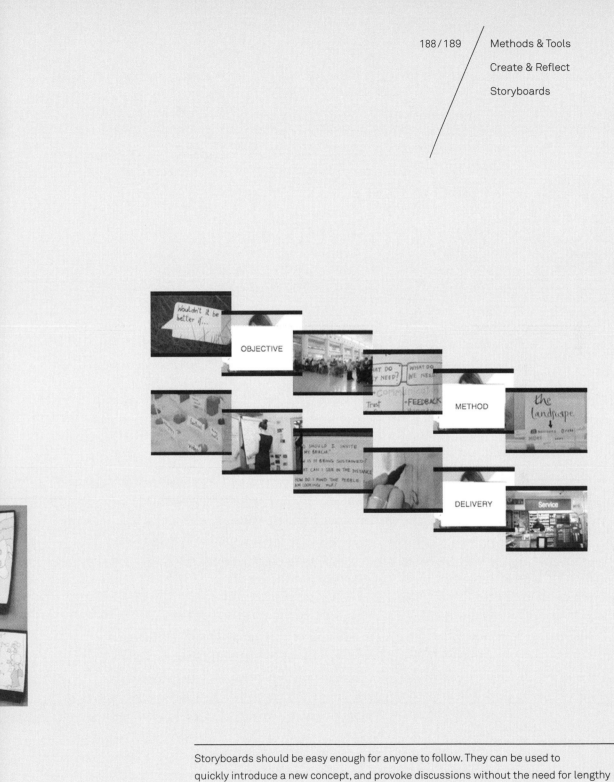

Storyboards should be easy enough for anyone to follow. They can be used to quickly introduce a new concept, and provoke discussions without the need for lengthy introductions.

CREATE & REFLECT

TESTING SERVICE CONCEPTS WITH SMALL SCALE PROTOTYPES

DESKTOP WALKTHROUGH

What is it?
A Desktop Walkthrough is a small-scale 3-D model of a service environment. Employing simple props like Lego figures lets designers bring a situation to life, acting out common scenarios and helping develop prototypes.

How is it made?
The models are usually kept fairly simple, and developed out of insights into the service environment. Simple Lego buildings with labels attached can be used to build the "set", whilst the characters inserted can be based on staff and customer personas. Common situations can then be acted out by moving the characters around the model and simulating the interactions they may have.

Why is it used?
Desktop walkthroughs allow an iterative analysis of the situations depicted. The same scene can be acted out multiple times, and in several locations, with new ideas and refinements constantly being introduced to the simulation. Prototypes can also be tested using this method, as they're "brought to life" in a highly engaging manner. Walkthrough models provide a common language in which various people can assess and co-develop a prototype, or analyse and restructure a problematic touchpoint.

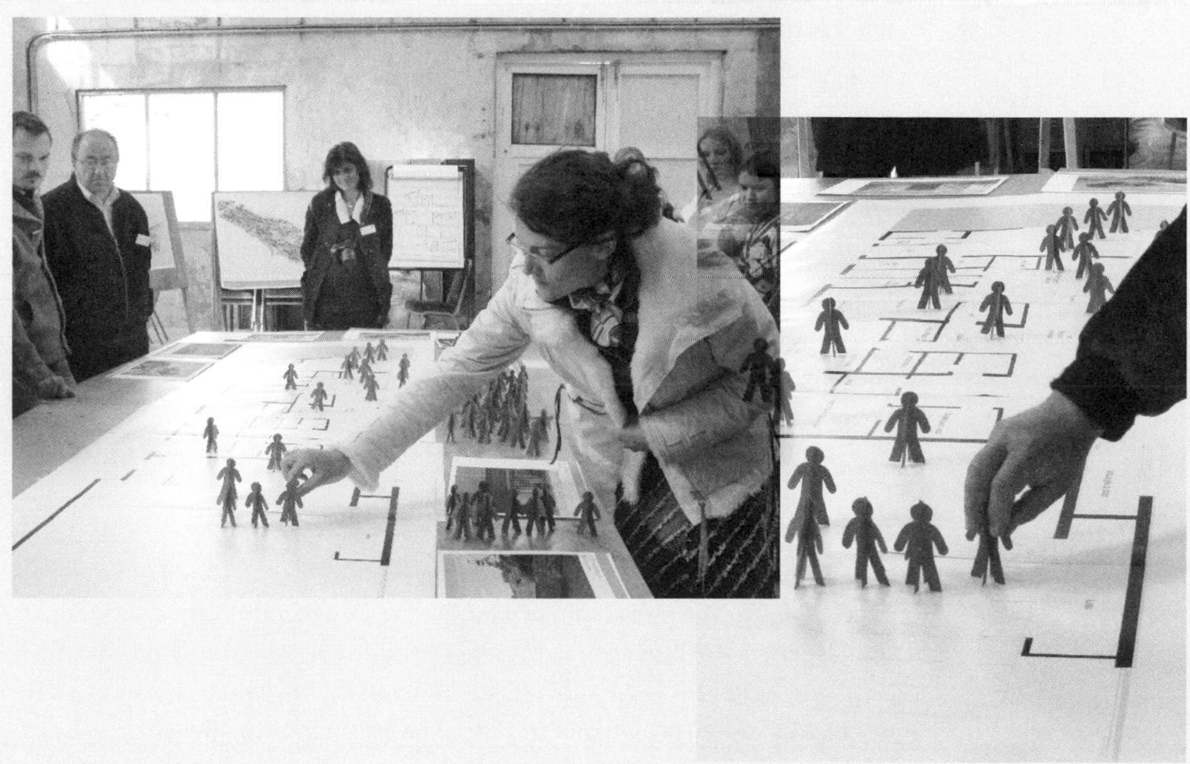

Desktop walkthroughs can take many different forms. The main aim is to have a tangible setup that enables people to exchange expectations on future usages. The more personal the setup is, the more lively discussions it will provoke.

CREATE & REFLECT

TESTING SERVICE CONCEPTS WITH LIFE-SIZE PROTOTYPES

SERVICE PROTOTYPES

What is it?

A service prototype is a simulation of a service experience. These simulations can range from being informal "roleplay" style conversations, to more detailed full scale recreations involving active user-participation, props, and physical touchpoints.

How is it made?

231 Usually some form of mock-up of the service system will be created.
The prototype can vary greatly in terms of tone and complexity, but the
242 common element will be the capacity to test the service solutions
being proposed in something approaching a "real-world" environment.
259 The prototype will generally be developed iteratively, with suggestions
and refinements being constantly incorporated.

274

Why is it used?

286 Service prototypes can generate a far deeper understanding of a service
than is possible with written or visual descriptions. The principle of
288 "learning by doing" is prevalent throughout, with the focus on user experience meaning the prototype can also generate tangible evidence on which solutions can be founded. Prototypes also help iterate design solutions, as they can quickly incorporate and test the ideas and refinements they may provoke.

Prototypes don't have to be confined to a studio setting or workshop – testing them out "in the wild" can also provoke insightful responses.

CREATE & REFLECT

TESTING SERVICE CONCEPTS WITH VARIOUS STAKEHOLDERS

SERVICE STAGING

●●●

What is it?

Service staging is the physical acting out of scenarios and prototypes by design teams, staff, or even customers in a situation that resembles a theatre rehearsal. Those participating will usually act out an encounter that one of the team has experienced, or explore a prototype situation.

How is it done?

When using service staging it is crucial to create a playful "safe space" environment to ensure that participants are comfortable and open enough to become fully involved with the exercise. After a storyboarding phase to record real experiences or develop new prototypes, people take on roles – such as customer or staff member – and act out the situation in an iterative cycle, moving from the starting storyboard to a new design. Group methods like "forum theatre" are used for idea generation and to keep everyone involved. Alternatively, one person may serve as the "director", making suggestions to solve the problems that are revealed.

Why is it used?

Service staging brings kinaesthetic learning and emotion into the design process. It allows people to focus on the minutiae of subtext and body language, both of which are crucial to understanding the real-world situations in which a service is delivered. Playing different characters in a reality-based scenario allows designers to empathise with the personas on which they are based.

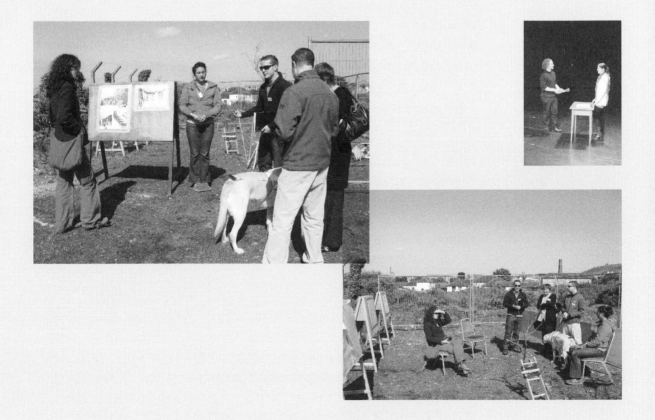

Service staging can be used for the design of services in and around a new building by creating a part of the space "on-site" and asking people to try it out.

CREATE & REFLECT

ADAPTING THE SERVICE DEVELOPMENT IN ITERATIVE STEPS

AGILE DEVELOPMENT

What is it?

Agile Development is an iterative methodology that allows projects to grow and develop over time, adapting around both the evolving needs of the client, and the research materials the project may generate.

How is it done?

Derived from the world of software engineering, the approach is centred on several key principles. An agile project places emphasis on individuals and interactions over processes and tools, for example. This means that formalised methodologies are abandoned in favour of iterative approaches that can accommodate the input of a wide range of stakeholders. This allows a project to adapt and evolve as it progresses, instead of constraining it within a rigidly formalised methodology.

Why is it used?

Agile projects are able to remain in tune with a project's key objectives, even when the situations, environments, or personnel involved change. They can adapt around the responses and ideas provoked by the material gathered in the initial research stage. The materials that service design projects create aren't limited to a single, "correct" method of application; the key to a successful project is often working closely with client and design teams in order to develop a long-term framework for innovation. Agile projects actively adapt in order to assist with implementation and innovation.

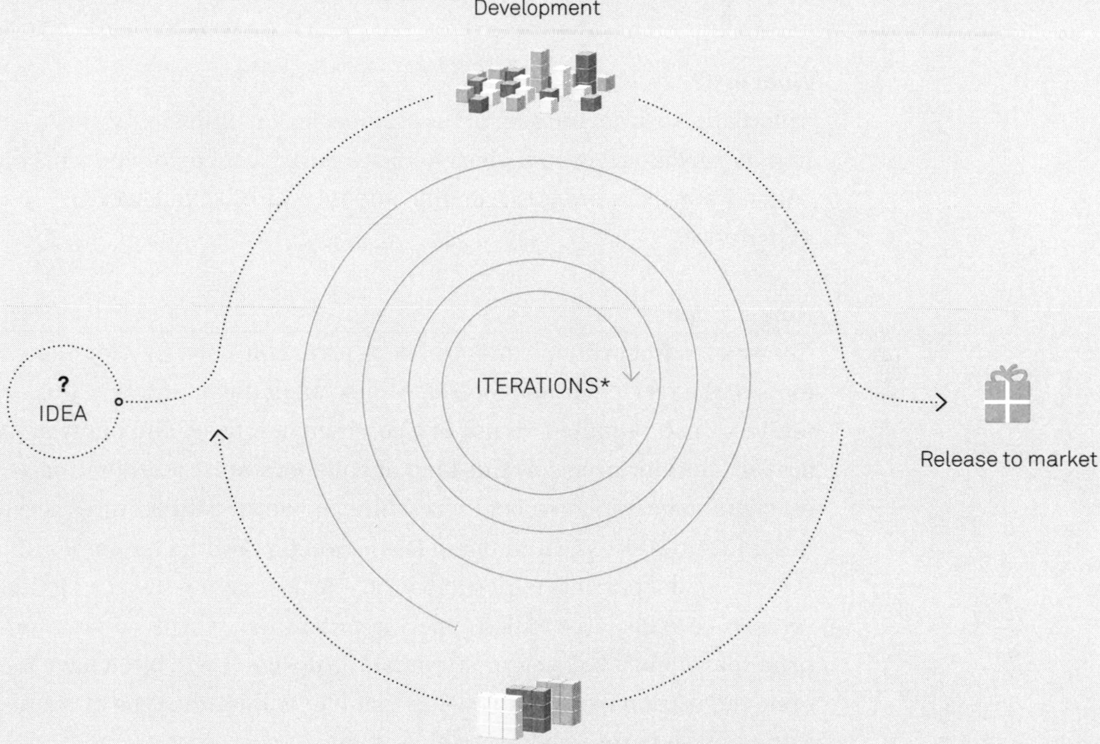

* Loschelder's heuristic spiral

Agile development involves frequent "scrum meetings" where the project team discusses the ongoing development of the service. This iterative process of developing and reflection goes on until the service is ready for release.

CREATE & REFLECT

INVOLVING STAKEHOLDERS IN THE CREATION PROCESS

CO-CREATION

●●●

What is it?

Co-creation is a core aspect of the service design philosophy. It can involve anyone from staff, designers, executives or customers working collaboratively in order to examine and innovate a given service experience.

How is it done?

229 Co-creation is a principle that can be used in conjunction with many other
tools in the service design toolset. Almost all of the methods in this
246 toolbox can be adapted for use in a co-creative setting, and many of them
are designed for precisely this kind of collaboration. Incorporating
257 co-creation into an exercise successfully, however, still requires service
designers to address a number of issues when planning the session.
260 Various initial barriers to participation – fear of saying the wrong thing,
reluctance to disagree with a superior, unfamiliarity with co-creation
271 principles – must be overcome, whilst the designer will often have to moderate the session in order to ensure that it generates the type of results that can be incorporated in the next stage of the process.

This moderation can be achieved at least in part by structuring a co-creation session effectively. The focus here should be on producing materials that can set the boundaries for a discussion, without constraining the possible responses of the participants. Knowing when to ask a generalised question in order to open up a discussion, and when to

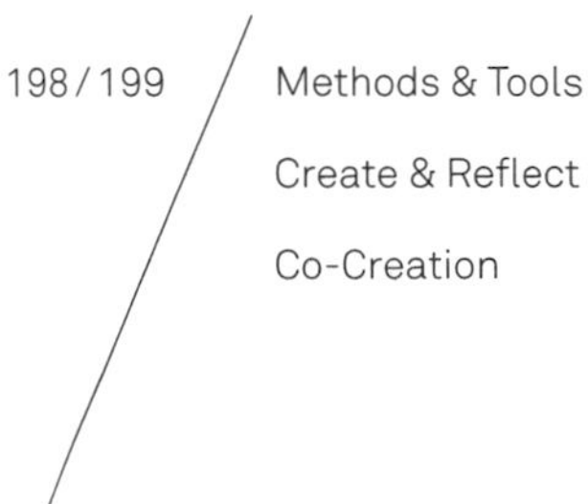

press a specific point in order to bring the focus back to the service under review, is essential in ensuring that co-creation sessions run smoothly.

Why is it used?

In one sense, co-creative exercises are a way to incorporate an open-source development philosophy. This does not mean, however, that the design of a service becomes a "group decision", as the ideas and solutions proposed will always be iteratively filtered so that only the strongest, most resonant themes are developed into new prototypes and innovations. The co-creation session aims to explore potential directions and gathers a wide range of perspectives in the process. The results of the session will then be used as inspiration for the core design team, who need to develop and refine it further in the next stages of the design process. An additional benefit of co-creation is that it facilitates future collaboration, as it brings groups together and thus creates a feeling of shared ownership over the concepts and innovations that are being developed.

EXAMPLE →

Co-creation sessions usually involve a mix of people working in small groups, who then present their work to the larger group for feedback and discussion.

The materials used during a co-creation session can vary from 3D desktop models to 2D mood boards and drawings. The most important thing is that people feel free to express their ideas – it's crucial to keep things simple and open.

IMPLEMENT

COMMUNICATING SERVICE CONCEPTS THROUGHOUT ORGANISATIONS

STORYTELLING

What is it?

Storytelling is a method for sharing insights and new service concepts. Compelling narratives can be constructed for all aspects of a company's service, from the lives of its customers, to staff experiences and the service experience it provides.

How is it done?

Storytelling situates new or improved services within a narrative context, using key insights and ideas to tell compelling stories from a variety of perspectives. Storytelling is often paired with personas in order to convey deeply resonant insights into user experiences. Narrative techniques can also effectively show how new service innovations affect all departments within a service provider.

Why is it used?

Telling a story makes a service proposition more compelling. Insights and ideas divorced from the context in which they were generated often lose their resonance as they filter through an organisation. When situated within effective and accessible narratives, by contrast, they are able to maintain their relevance, even when presented to people unfamiliar with how the project was conducted. Indeed, presenting the project itself in a narrative context allows people to follow much more closely the processes, which can help companies re-orientate their business and organisation around service design principles.

GEOFFREY WANTS to join a gym to get fit and build muscle. He's intimidated by the other gym users however, who all seem much larger and fitter than him. How can his service experience be improved?

GEOFFREY TELLS the interviewer that he wants to try exercising at home, so that he can build up his fitness – and his confidence – before exercising in public. A service that helps Geoffrey keep track of his progress therefore would be very appealing to him.

GEOFFREY USES the tracking service to compare his progress with other gym users. He's doing very well! He's gained the confidence he needed to return to the gym, but will continue using the service at home as well.

Stories can be communicated in many different ways. Depending on the nature of the project text, visuals, video, roleplay, or a combination thereof might be employed in order to tell the stories involved.

IMPLEMENT

VISUALISING ALL ASPECTS AND ACTORS RELATED TO THE SERVICE DELIVERY

SERVICE BLUEPRINTS

What is it?

Service blueprints are a way to specify and detail each individual aspect of a service. This usually involves creating a visual schematic incorporating the perspectives of both the user, the service provider and other relevant parties that may be involved, detailing everything from the points of customer contact to behind-the-scenes processes.

How is it made?

230 Service blueprints are often produced collaboratively, as this is a great
way to bring together the various departments or teams which may
242 exist within the organisation of the service provider. As several different
teams often have some influence upon service delivery, bringing
270 them together to create a blueprint creates a shared awareness of each
team's responsibilities. A collaborative workshop is a very effective forum for this kind of co-creation, which is often aimed at constructing a "living" document that the teams of the service provider feel they own.

This notion of a "living" document relates to the idea that a blueprint should ideally be periodically revised. This can help ensure it remains consistently in touch with both the environment the service provider operates in, and the preferences of the users it caters for. Continually refocusing the blueprint around inevitable changes in people's lifestyle and motivations refines and improves companies' research activities, whilst reinforcing the need for the service provider to remain agile enough to respond to an evolving environment.

Why is it used?

By describing and outlining all of the elements contained within a service, the blueprint allows the most crucial areas to be identified, whilst also revealing areas of overlap or duplication. Producing such a document collaboratively promotes co-operation and teamwork, and also helps to co-ordinate the people and resources the service provider has at its disposal. Service blueprints are able to show the processes that lie behind the critical service elements around which user experience is defined. They're often produced in draft form at the start of a service design project, in order to explore those aspects of the service that can be reviewed and refined. Once ideas and innovations have been formulated, the blueprint is further detailed and expanded at the implementation stage. This helps provide a clear roadmap for the actual service delivery.

EXAMPLE →

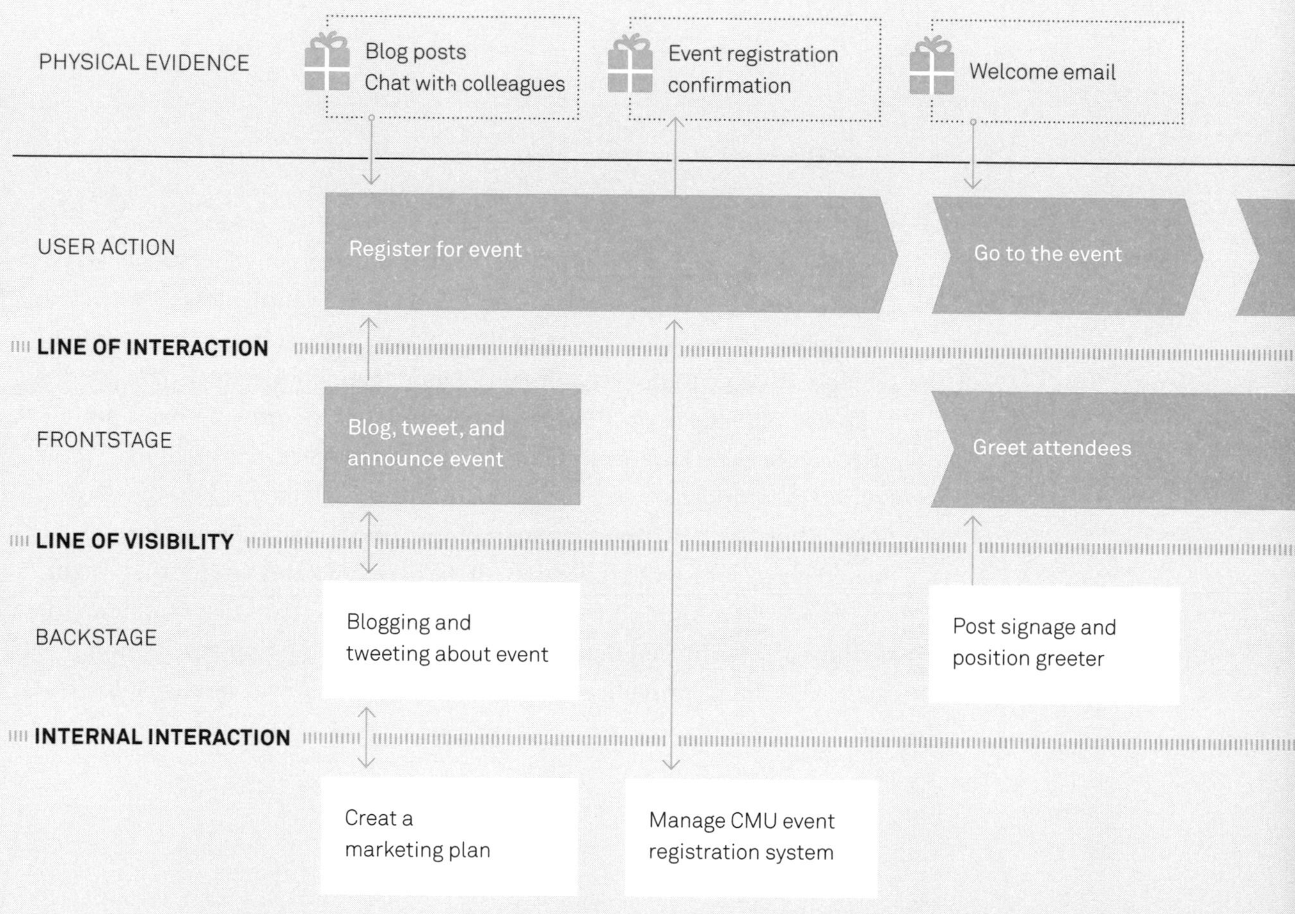

The "line of interaction" represents the touch points between the user and the service provider. The "line of visibility" represents the distinction between visible front-office staff (or systems), and the back-office workers and processes that are invisible to the user.

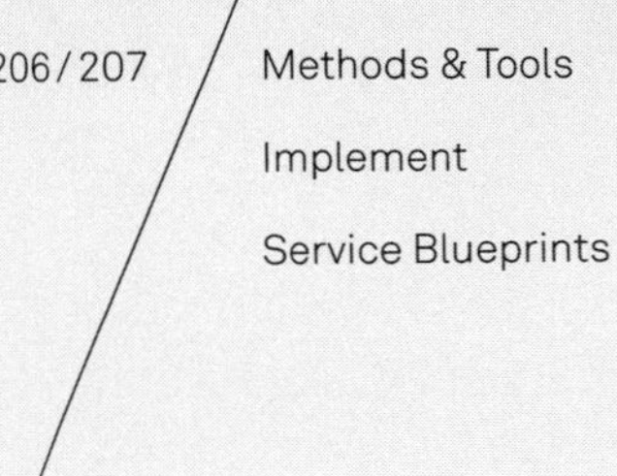

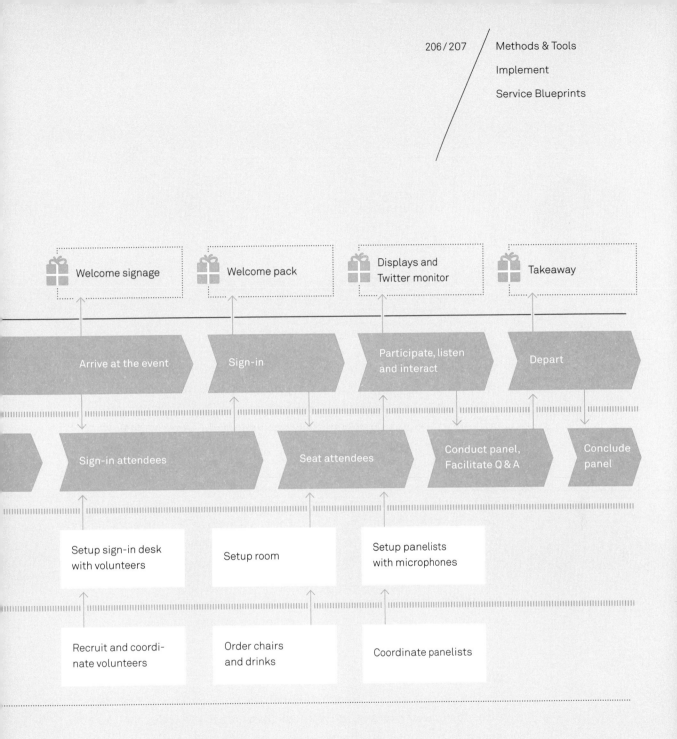

Welcome signage

Welcome pack

Displays and Twitter monitor

Takeaway

Arrive at the event

Sign-in

Participate, listen and interact

Depart

Sign-in attendees

Seat attendees

Conduct panel, Facilitate Q & A

Conclude panel

Setup sign-in desk with volunteers

Setup room

Setup panelists with microphones

Recruit and coordi-nate volunteers

Order chairs and drinks

Coordinate panelists

Exemplary service blueprint inspired by Brandon Schauer, Adaptive Path

IMPLEMENT

SUPPORTING STAFF TO UNDERSTAND, EMBRACE AND IMPROVE SERVICES

SERVICE ROLEPLAY

What is it?
Just like theatrical rehearsal methods can be used to explore and generate ideas (see Service Staging), other drama techniques can be used to assist with their implementation. This generally involves interactive training experiences that help staff contribute to the improvement of the service experience.

How is it done?
Staff members are asked to enact several situations where they might come into contact with a customer. The roles in these exercises are highly interchangeable, with each participant switching between customer, staff, or manager as new ideas come up and are immediately tested. Prompt cards detailing a specific persona, problem, mood, or personal characteristic focus the exercises around specific insights, whilst recording them on video allows the participants to review and analyse each situation at a later date.

Why is it used?
Service Roleplay helps provide staff with the tools and training needed to meet customers' needs effectively. The insights underpinning tools like personas are translated directly to service touchpoints, building empathy with customers throughout the entire organisation. They also help staff members build up ownership over the innovations they're being asked to implement, as their feedback fine-tunes the introduction of new ideas.

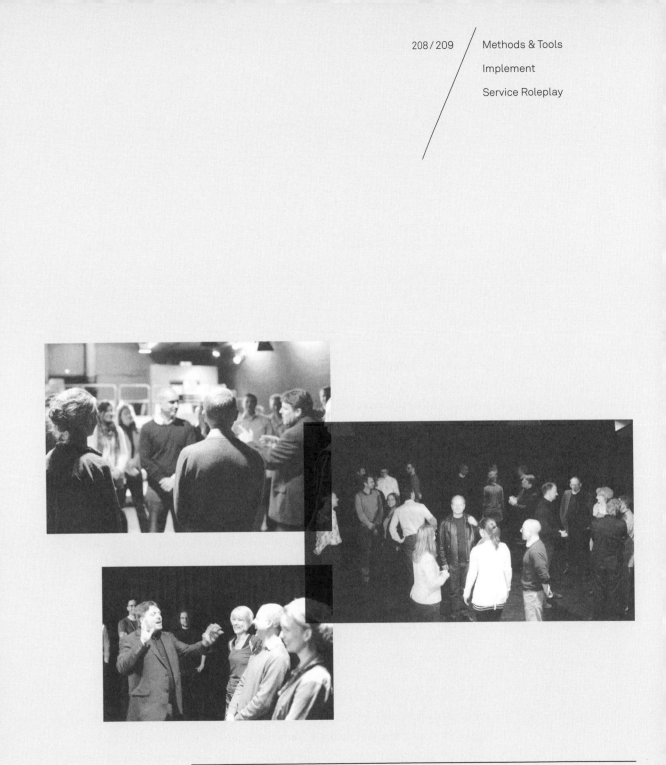

Recording roleplay sessions on video allows the participants to analyse their actions in a follow-up workshop.

IMPLEMENT

VISUALISING CUSTOMERS OVERALL RELATIONSHIPS WITH SERVICE PROVIDERS

CUSTOMER LIFECYCLE MAPS

What is it?

A Customer Lifecycle Map is a holistic visualisation of a customer's overall relationship with a service provider. This may include a series of customer journeys over time; from the customer's initial contact with a service, right through to the point where they eventually stop using it altogether.

How is it made?

Known data about customers is visualised into a series of key events relating to their service usage. These represent the stages a typical customer will pass through when using a service. At each of these stages research material is incorporated into the map to provide insights into customers' drives and motivations.

Why is it used?

Generating this detailed overview of a customer's series of service journeys allows companies to make more complete and balanced business cases, and develop more effective marketing strategies. The maps allow service providers to present their customers with a holistic offering, as the lifecycles of several services can be synchronised around customers' evolving wants and needs; by understanding why their interaction with one service might cease, providers can develop and market new services which intuitively serve customers' changing desires.

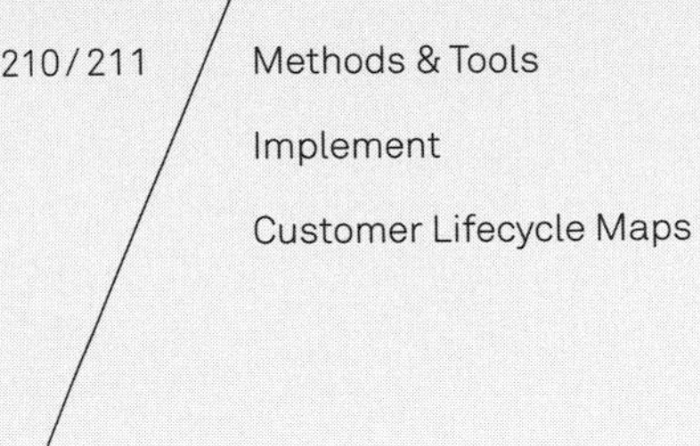

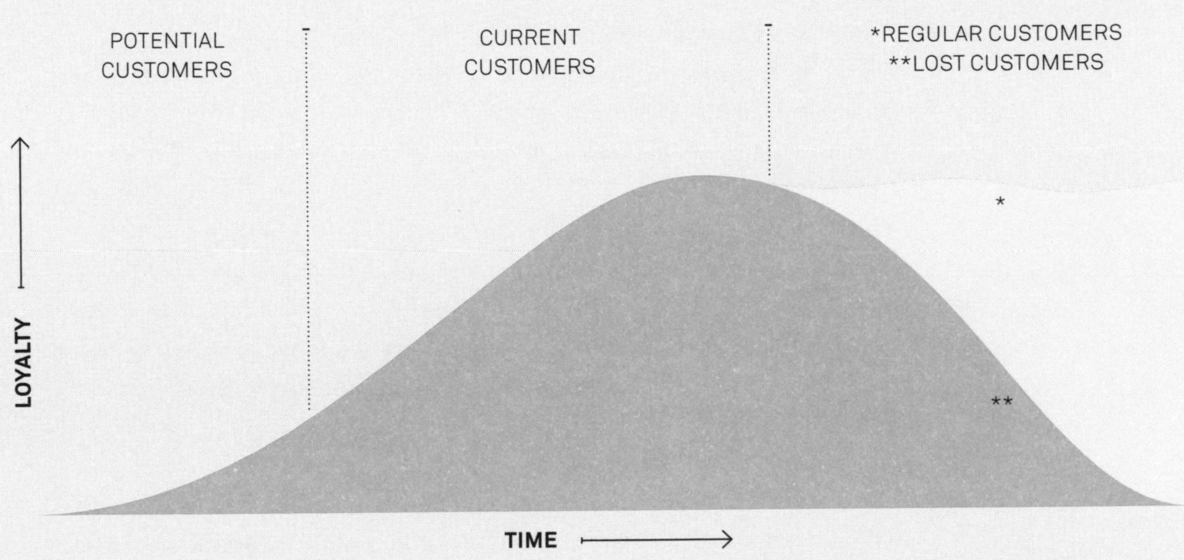

Lifecycle maps are often used to highlight the points where people may abandon a service – something that's of crucial importance when planning new service offerings.

IMPLEMENT

CLARIFYING THE MATCH BETWEEN BUSINESS STRATEGY AND SERVICE DESIGN

BUSINESS MODEL CANVAS

What is it?

A Business Model Canvas is a useful tool for describing, analysing, and designing business models. It was developed and popularised by the book Business Model Generation.

How is it made?

The canvas usually takes the form of a large table printed onto a writable surface. This table is split into nine sections, each of which is said to represent one of the "blocks" of a successful business model. The table can then be filled in collaboratively, with groups of people using sticky notes to sketch and model the various aspects of their business model.

Why is it used?

Increasingly popular, the canvas can be used in almost any sector, and can benefit service providers in a number of ways. Public sector organisations, for example, have used the canvas to help departments view themselves as service-focused businesses, whilst those organisations providing a range of different service offerings often use it as a focusing tool. Its key benefits – bringing clarity to an organisation's core aims whilst identifying its strengths, weaknesses, and priorities – allow it to provide an up-to-date "snapshot" of any organisation attempting to implement the results of a service design project.

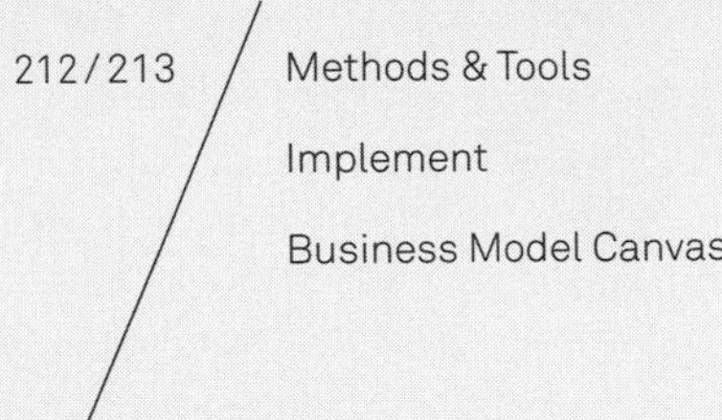

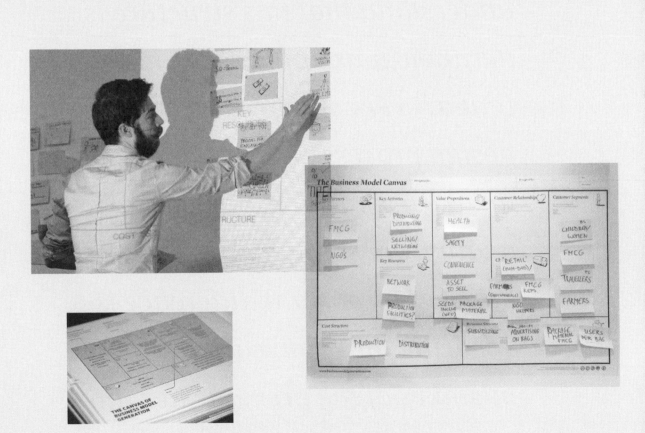

Using the Business Model Canvas as a template or visual reminder of the various factors a business model needs to incorporate helps manage the scope of discussions.

Marc says: *It is important to understand that this structure is iterative in its approach. This means that at every stage of a service design process, it might be necessary to take a step back or even start again from scratch. The single but very important difference is ensuring that you learn from the mistakes of the previous iteration.*

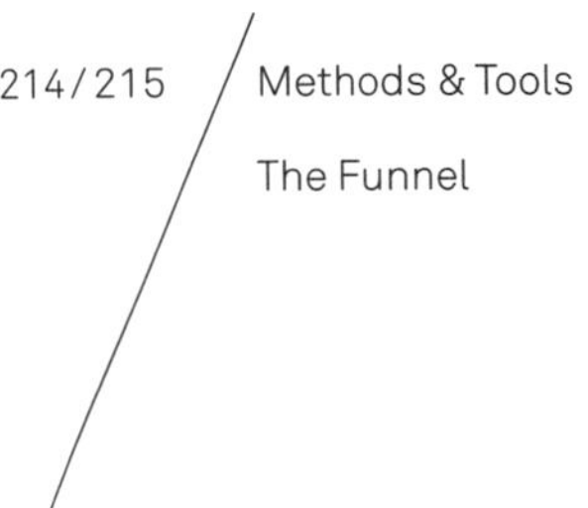

Simon says: *Service design is about choosing the most relevant touchpoints for service delivery and designing a consistent customer experience across these many touchpoints. It looks for opportunities to introduce potentially new and more effective touchpoints, remove weak touchpoints, and coordinate the user-experience across touchpoints in relation to brand message and user needs.*

Geke says: *As in any other aspect of a service design project, there is no absolute right or wrong way to employ service design tools. A successful project involves finding a relevant and workable combination that can conceptualise, develop, and prototype ideas through an iterative process of gradual improvement.*

Applied Service Design

Cases

SERVICE DESIGN THINKING IN PRACTICE

This second part describes how service design actually works. The first text explains the service design process along four iterative stages and the difficulty to define a standardised procedure to design services. However, the subsequent article exemplifies an approach for a rather structured process of the early phases of a service design process. In the following 25 service design tools are described and assigned to respective process stages.

ARNE VAN OOSTEROM, THE NETHERLANDS
NL Agency and DesignThinkers

SARAH DRUMMOND AND LAUREN CURRIE, UNITED KINGDOM
MyPolice and Snook

BEATRIZ BELMONTE AND ASIER PÉREZ, SPAIN
Hello Change and Funky Projects

JAMIN HEGEMAN, UNITED STATES
UPMC and Carnegie Mellon University

ERIK WIDMARK, SWEDEN
SEB and Transformator

NL Agency
Ministry of Economic Affairs

designthinkers

NL AGENCY AND DESIGNTHINKERS

NL Agency (Dutch Ministry of Economic Affairs)
NL Agency is a department of the Dutch Ministry of Economic Affairs that implements government policy for sustainability, innovation, and international business and cooperation. It is the contact point for businesses, (knowledge) institutions and government bodies for information and advice, financing, networking and regulatory matters.

NL Agency strives to achieve a strong innovative business community in a safe and supportive, sustainable society and promotes sustainable economic growth by building a bridge between the market and government, at both national and international levels. NL Agency provides companies, (knowledge) institutions and government authorities with advice, knowledge and financial support.

DesignThinkers
DesignThinkers is a co-operative organisation consisting of several associates. We build our organisation on the basis of freedom, trust and equality. These principles infuse a great sense of responsibility and entrepreneurship among all the people working at DesignThinkers.

DesignThinkers believes in the importance of creative thinking, facilitating ongoing conversation and learning by doing. We are a new marketing agency for a new era. We build communities, develop strategies and campaigns, design and implement innovative products and services.

Businesses, (knowledge) institutions and government bodies

NL Agency's primary target groups are businesses, (knowledge) institutions and government bodies. Private individuals are therefore not a primary target group of NL Agency.

The target groups of NL Agency and related services that were investigated in these series of Customer Journey LAB Workshops are small- and medium-sized companies in the Netherlands – either companies that are looking for opportunities to export their services or products abroad, or companies that are looking for funds to speed up their innovation process, or companies that want to protect the product or service they have developed.

How to create a client oriented service organisation

The different divisions that together make up NL Agency all deliver different services to different kinds of organisations in the Netherlands. Municipalities, small, medium and large companies, and all kinds of other organisations make use of the services provided by NL Agency.

The different divisions, however, are mainly set up around the services they deliver and not so much around the customers they provide their services to. To stay competitive and survive the changes that organisations like NL Agency are presently facing, they need to reassess the way they are structured, function and build relationships with customers. Closing the "reality gap" between the organisation and people (employees and customers alike) should be the number one priority. And for this they need a new set of skills, methods and tools.

NL Agency Services lack the focus on the customer.

DISCOVERED USERS' PROBLEM

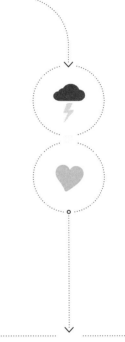

Main goal of NL Agency is to become a client-oriented service organisation.

COMPANY'S PROBLEM

Service delivery is continuously being improved and renewed based on true customer experience through the customer journey LAB.

SERVICE VISION

ARNE VAN OOSTEROM EXPLAINS

DESIGNTHINKERS' PROCESS

NL Agency needs to design and implement systems that will allow their organisation to have meaningful and ongoing conversations with customers, using the insight they gain to improve and innovate in an on-going iteration. And this all starts by taking a good look at the organisation from the outside. There are no magic tricks. But it seems common sense to start with the people you work with and your customers. To facilitate this ongoing conversation, DesignThinkers developed the Customer Journey LAB.

The Customer Journey LAB is an ongoing iterative method, developed by DesignThinkers using service design and design thinking methodologies, to build a culture of trust and adaptability, which is the most important step to building a relationship with your customer and maintaining a strong, long-term, almost irreplaceable competitive edge. It is an effective way to gain insights and improve your customers' experiences.

Exploration: discovering the customer's emotions

Service design methodologies and in this case the Customer Journey LAB tools made NL Agency look from a customer perspective at the services they provide. The "emotional journey" of a customer making use of the different services provided key indicators where services needed to be improved or completely renewed.

The objective for this LAB environment was to generate ideas that would improve the experience customers have when using NL Agency services. The focus has been on the front-end channels and touchpoints the customers encounter when working or getting in contact with NL

Agency. This way you'll discover the landscape you are in from the customer perspective.

In order to make this article more of a guide into the application of scientific methodologies to design and in order to respect our client's privacy we focus in this article on giving you a comprehensive description of the tools we used in this Customer Journey LAB environment for NL Agency.

Context and stakeholder mapping: "The Bullseye"

Context or stakeholder mapping is a tool DesignThinkers use as a first step in setting up the Customer Journey LAB environment. Getting a complete picture of what is going on in the mind of customers is of vital importance to understand their behaviour.

We list all stakeholders and we order the hierarchy in circles of influence around the centre, where you are: "The Bullseye". When working with customers you'll have the customer in the centre. We describe all relationships on the map by answering the questions: What do we do for them? What do they do for us? This map shows you the landscape or force field you are dealing with. And you can discuss how this influences the quality of your work and how a customer benefits or suffers from it.

The insights we gained from the Customer Journey LAB setting with NL Agency – e.g. customers were not always put in the centre of the map (proof of non-customer centric thinking within the organisation). The environment of NL Agency is very complex with sometimes too many stakeholders. Employees are directed by both internal policy makers and external customers, which results in conflicting drives for service delivery. As a result, a lot of time is spent on managing internal affairs instead of focusing on the main purpose: the customer.

Persona "Hans"

A good way to simulate the presence of customers is to create Personas, or Customer Profiles. Participants of the LAB are "forced" to step into the life of a typical customer and investigate and describe his/her personal and business situation now (present situation) and in the future (ambitions).

Emotional Customer Journey

An Emotional Customer Journey Map is built up layer by layer. We start "above water", with the customer and slowly dive deeper and deeper into the organisational structures and context. The tool can be used with customers or management, employees and other stakeholders or, even better, in a mix. It lets us be submerged in their world, their reality, to get a deeper insight into customer needs, perceptions, experiences and motivations. It will answer questions like: What are people really trying to achieve? How are they trying to achieve this? What do they use and in what order? Why do they make a choice? What are they experiencing, feeling, while trying to reach the desired outcome?

We list all actions that (as far as possible) the customer has to take to reach an outcome (placed in a horizontal line) and rate the touchpoints on a scale from one to ten and an Emotional Journey Graph emerges. Don't start listing actions when the customer uses your service the first time. Start before the moment he/she decides to use your product or service. This way we visualize behavioural patterns.

As a dedicated entrepreneur, our NL Agency Persona Hans is positive about a lot of services provided by NL Agency. However, filling out all kinds of forms, sometimes with the same information, diminishes his enthusiasm.

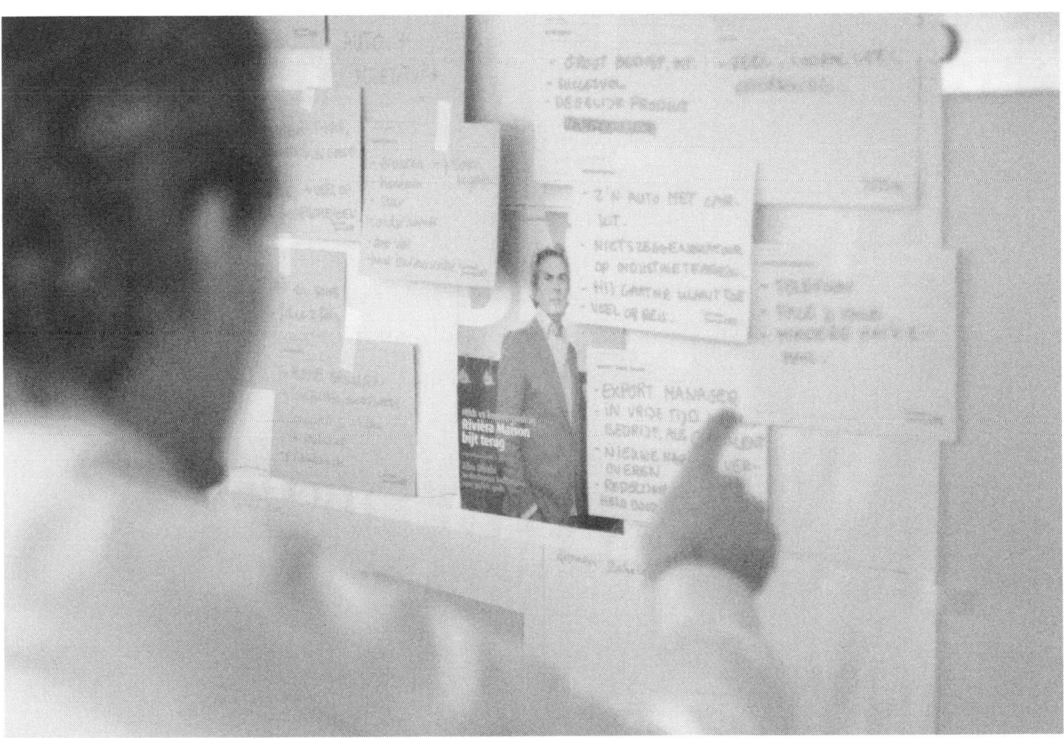

In the LAB sessions for NL Agency **Persona Hans** was developed. Hans turned out to be an experienced entrepreneur, who enjoys networking and meeting other entrepreneurs. He is bound to "cash out" early and enjoy his retirement. He appreciates the NL Agency services, but is always bogged down by the administrative activities (filling out forms, evaluation questionnaires).

Creation: the moment people have the most fun

The next phase is to use creative, brainstorming and any other ideation techniques to innovate the service opportunities you identified (low grades) and/or design complete new and ideal journeys or services. This is usually the moment people have the most fun. You will be surprised by the talent and eagerness of people to engage in this creative process. People are usually a lot more creative than you might think, the challenge is creating the right situation and mood.

Introducing the priority grid

Using the Emotional Customer Journey Graph, the "lows" customers are experiencing while making use of the services of NL Agency can easily be collected. This is the starting point to find proper (business) solutions for improving or renewing services.

The "lows" in customers' experience are put on "Issue Cards" and well debated in the LAB environment. With the help of these Issue Cards the issues are indexed in order of priority, taking the customers' point of view into account. This makes it possible for NL Agency to decide where to start improving their services. The prioritised issues are plotted on a chart where short and long term feasibility are added. As a result a Priority Grid emerges. The Priority Grid shows in the left upper corner issues with higher priority that can be solved quickly. In the right lower corner one can find issues that need hardly any attention as they have low priority and are very difficult to solve.

For NL Agency online content-related issues were listed in the upper left corner. NL Agency felt these specific online issues could be solved

quickly with little effort and high impact on Customer Experience. These kinds of Quick Wins make an organisation like NL Agency understand the impact of a Customer Journey LAB environment.

Co-creation: developing solutions with customers

True co-creation is based on developing valuable solutions together with customers. Taking the Priority Grid as a starting point, co-creation in the LAB environment is an exercise that focuses on developing solutions for the issues found during the Emotional Customer Journey.

The customers of NL Agency that participated in the Customer Journey LAB sessions needed to describe at least four strategic directions for scenarios, starting with: doing "nothing". The idea is to both take extreme scenarios as well as scenarios which can be described as "middle of the road". Presenting these scenarios always evokes strong feedback and stimulates a good debate.

Reflection: Solution Service Blueprint

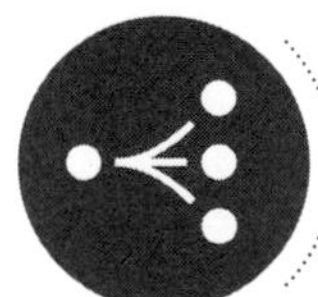

Now, to make a long story a bit shorter, we can go on listing the organisation underneath, writing down who supports the people delivering the service (back-office), and in turn who influences the back-office (we link back to the Stakeholders Map), until we have a complete organisational blueprint, a complete picture of the working of an organisation and the emotional journey, from the outside in.

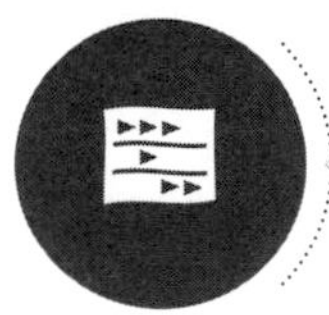

Instead of making a full Service Blueprint of the NL Agency organisation, we focused on what we at DesignThinkers call a Solution Service Blueprint. The Solution Service Blueprint needs to consist of the following elements: objective of the proposed solution in terms of impact on customers' experience and a blueprint of the service both from a functional perspective as well as from a look and feel perspective. Furthermore, the skills and character traits of the people working in the service process that need to be implemented or adjusted, need to be described.

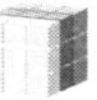

Implementation: The real moment of truth

Only those who are adaptable survive. That's just one of those inconvenient evolutionary truths! Generally speaking, companies and governmental organisations are not designed for adaptability. They are organised in static, pyramid-shaped, top-down broadcasting models and not organised to receive feedback from the outside or the bottom of the pyramid or to use this information for change and continuous improvement. Most organisations are incapable of having real and meaningful (two-way-street) conversations with their customers. With these series of Customer Journey LAB Pilots, NL Agency took the first step towards an ongoing conversation with their customers. The real moment of truth was presenting the outcome of the LAB environment to the management of NL Agency.

The final result of a typical Customer Journey LAB environment ranges from an Emotional Customer Journey Map, Service Blueprint, Roadmap or Marketing Proposition. To convince top management within NL Agency of the need for implementation of the newly developed Solution Service Blueprint we used Visual Prototyping exercises in the final Customer Journey LAB sessions. Together with specialists from within the organisation (IT, HRM, Project Management, Product Management) the

participants of the final LAB sessions were asked to create ads and marketing propositions for the different solutions. Developing an ad needs focus on the core message (objective) of the solution and stimulates creative thinking about the issues to be solved and the desired solution. This resulted in an impressive campaign that was presented to the top management.

Final statement

The Customer Journey LAB environment builds a mirror and enables us to question why we do the things we do. It makes things visible, which might have been right in front of us, but were so familiar we did not notice them or question them. It never occurred to us we could change them. It brings knowledge, already embedded in the organisation, to the surface and makes explicit what is implicitly already there.

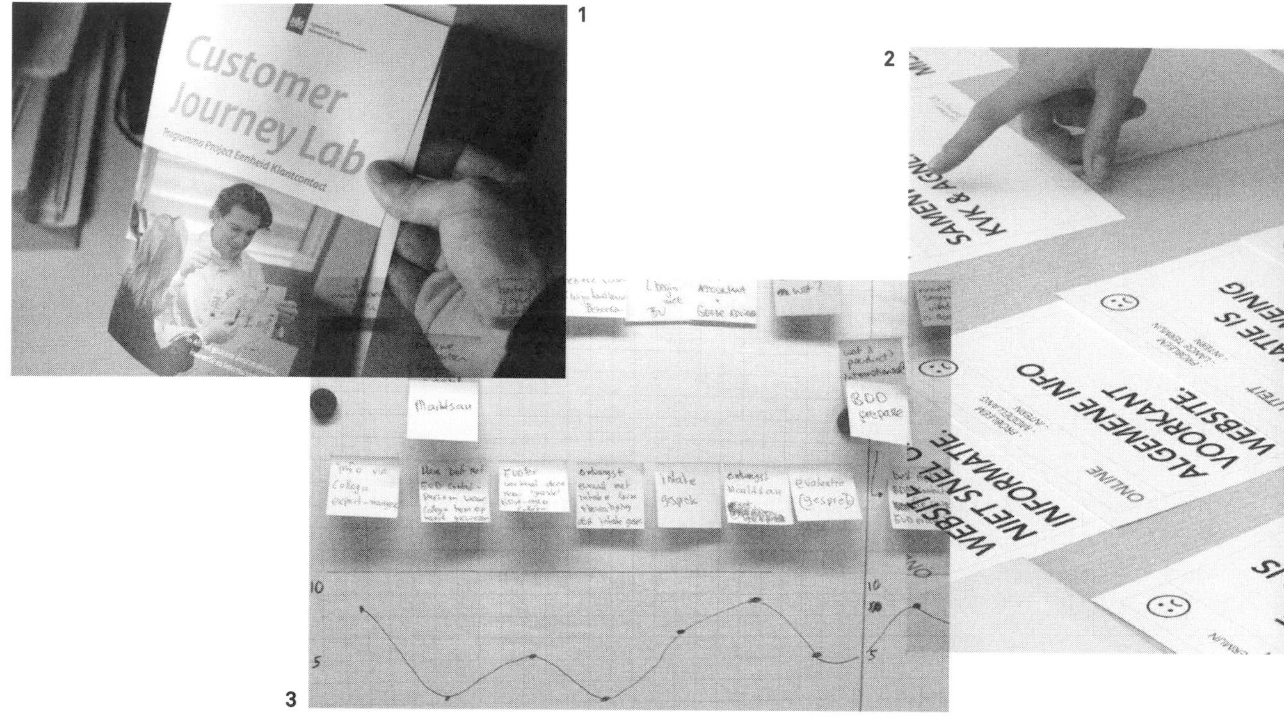

1 Customized invitation to the Customer Journey LAB

2 Indexing the Priority Grid

3 Emotional customer journey

4 Solution mapping

5 Stakeholder mapping

KWALITEIT
ONDUIDELIJKHEID
OVER VOUCHERS.
BRUIKBAAR
ONLINE
VERDWAALD OP
WEBSITE.

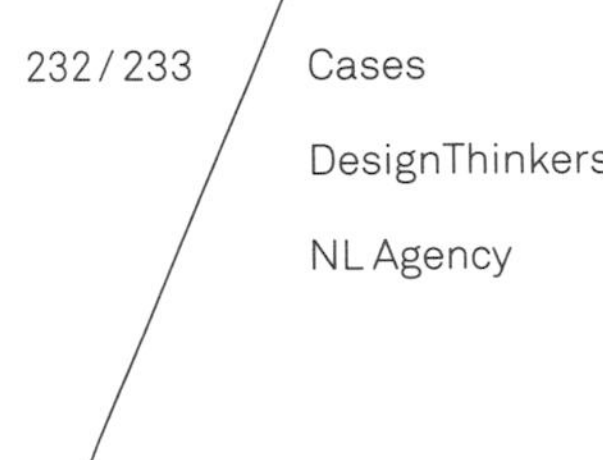

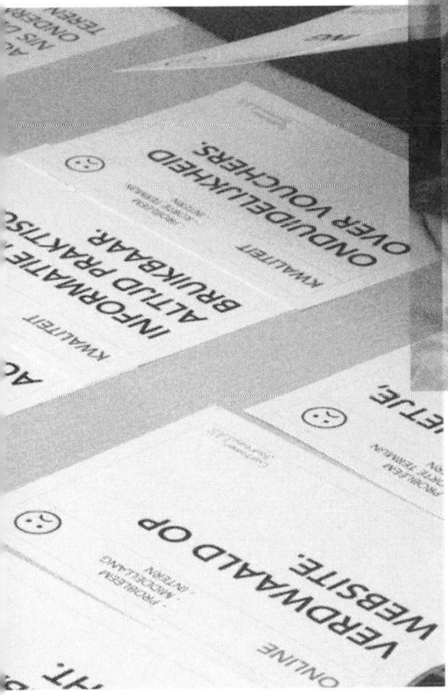

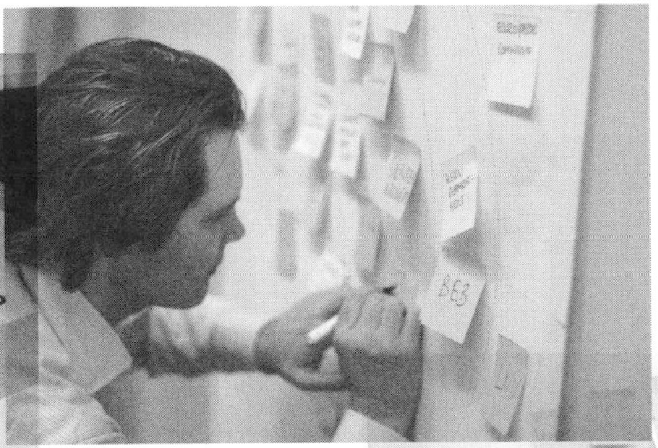

5

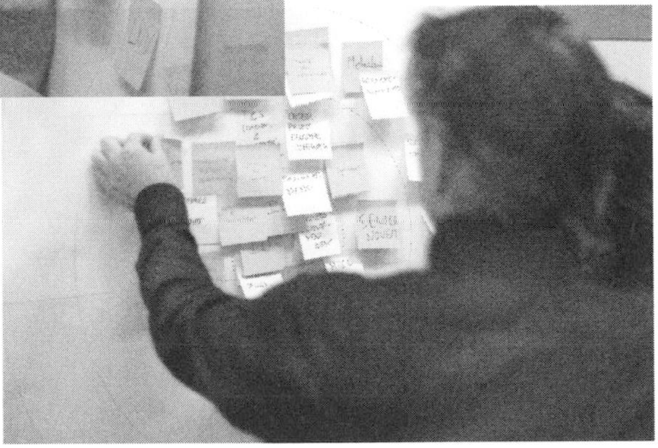

5

4

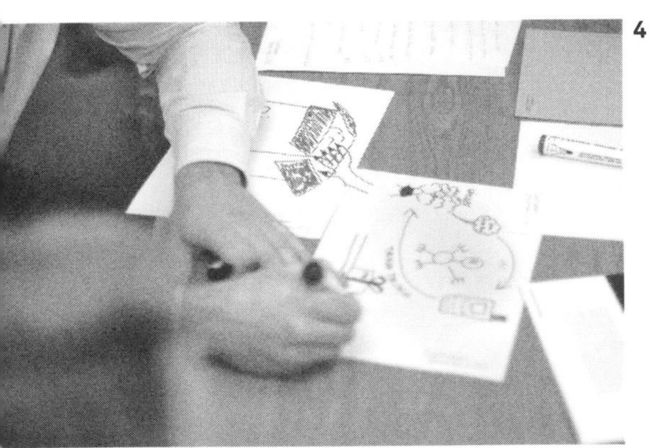

(my)
police

SNOOK™
transforming people

MYPOLICE AND SNOOK

Mypolice

Mypolice is a limited company that provides qualitative information about user experiences to the police, encouraging a more empathic understanding of the problematic areas within their service delivery. Established in October 2009, it has roots that stretch back to May the same year when the idea was entered into Scotland's first Social Innovation Camp. Mypolice interacts with a wide range of organisations from the public, private and third sector that operate within the field of crime and justice.

Clients of Mypolice include the 53 police forces across the United Kingdom, special forces including the Scottish Crime and Drug Enforcement Agency, independent strategic bodies including the Association of Chief Police Officers, and various third-sector organisations that deal with victims of crime and other associated issues.

Snook

Based in Scotland, Snook works within the field of social innovation and the public sector. Founded by two service designers, the company uses design thinking and creative methods to develop solutions based on empathic user insights. Snook works with organisations to co-create these solutions, ensuring that senior-level policy makers, frontline staff and users are all involved in this process to drive visible changes and transform their thinking. Founded in 2009, Snook has worked with a wide range of different sectors including health, crime, social services and the arts to co-create solutions for our future world and ensure that people are always at the heart of service delivery.

The Police and the public

Aimed currently at the UK, the website is used by the public to give feedback on their experiences with police, comment on local policing and view other user stories and site statistics. The police use the product to respond to concerns and reach new audiences in terms of visibility.

Lack of confidence in the police

There has been a breakdown in communication and trust between the public and the police. In the past ten years, recorded crime rates have fallen considerably; however, according to British Crime Survey Statistics, the public have not felt the impact of this and believe crime is rising. (Kershaw et al., 2008)

Confidence in the police has fallen dramatically. With a broadcast mentality, deeply rooted in tradition, the police find it hard to engage with the public, especially since a large proportion of this audience spend their time online. Police organisations themselves have admitted setting the agenda in traditional forms of consultation and with a risk adverse culture, fear of social media and a lack of understanding the digital world, the police are finding it difficult to join "the conversation online".

"Writing to the police feels so unfamiliar and formal, wish I could just tweet via @mypolice" / "Probably the most impenetrable public service to give feedback to."

Further to this, many interviewees in the design research phase of the project described the current police feedback system as "dated", "closed", "biased", that it had made them feel "pressurised to say the 'right' thing" and "uncomfortable".

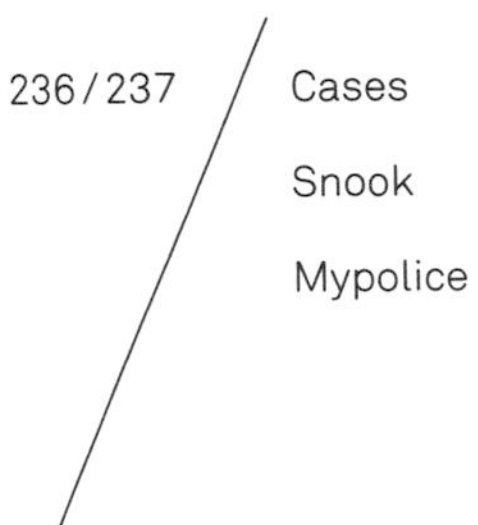

Citizens of the UK do not feel listened to by the police.

DISCOVERED USERS' PROBLEM

The police have in many cases lost the confidence of the British public.

COMPANY'S PROBLEM

Creating an independent and neutral space where the police and public can come together. A platform that closes the feedback loop, fostering constructive and collaborative conversations between the public and the police.

SERVICE VISION

SARAH DRUMMOND AND LAUREN CURRIE EXPLAIN

SNOOK'S PROCESS

"... it is often not known whether the deliverable of the design process will be a product, a service, an interface, or something else. The goal of this exploration is to define the fundamental problems and opportunities and to determine what is to be, or should not be, designed and manufactured." (Sanders & Simons, 2009)

In the case of Mypolice, Snook started with an idea and worked their way back. Based on a simple idea, the project team needed to explore the landscape and potential user base, to ask questions like who will use it, when, where, how and why? Moving from the creation stage to the exploration stage, the idea was reframed and a service was built around it to add value to the product. Additions to the Mypolice concept were drawn from first-hand research and based on insights gathered from interactions of the designers with the police and public. In essence, the company started with a light bulb moment and used a service design mindset and research techniques to grow and validate it.

It was Scotland's first Social Innovation Camp opening a call for ideas, when suddenly a friend's experience of feeding back to the police and the fact she spent hours on the internet daily made sense. And so Mypolice was born. Two days of intense development ensued between coders, designers and business experts, with the result becoming the winning idea in the early summer of 2009.

The idea for Mypolice came from different events all happening in parallel. Public confidence in the police had plummeted to an all-time low after the events of the G20 protests when Ian Tomlinson, a newspaper seller, was knocked to the ground by a police officer and died later that day.

This was in addition to a first-hand observation that provided the original stimulus for entering the idea into Social Innovation Camp.

After witnessing a friend feeding back to the police and complaining about having to phone them when they were part of the large demographic who prefer to use computers as a communication method, it was clear there was an opportunity to develop something to fill this gap. Looking at statistics released this year, Nielsen claimed that 80% of online UK users spend around six hours a day on social networking sites and platforms (Nielsen 2010). The idea for Mypolice was a recognition of these facts and a synergy of multiple insights.

Having two days to develop something, in a closed environment, certainly presents challenges in terms of being able to adopt a user-centred design approach. Here is where the backwards work began. The first newspaper headline had been something of a dampener on the experience of winning. With the title "Shop a cop website", the Sunday Times visited the head of the Scottish Police Federation, and painted a blurry picture of the Mypolice concept (Macaskill, 2009). In an attempt to remedy this, the Mypolice team visited Calum Steele, the head of the Scottish Police Federation, and showed him screenshots that had been mocked up during Social Innovation Camp. Calum saw potential and added some helpful comments on what functions it would need to make it work for the police. This was still a case of working backwards from a solution, but represented the first example of where it would be possible to find useful user insights to help successfully reverse-engineer the user centred development of the Mypolice concept.

THE PROCESS →

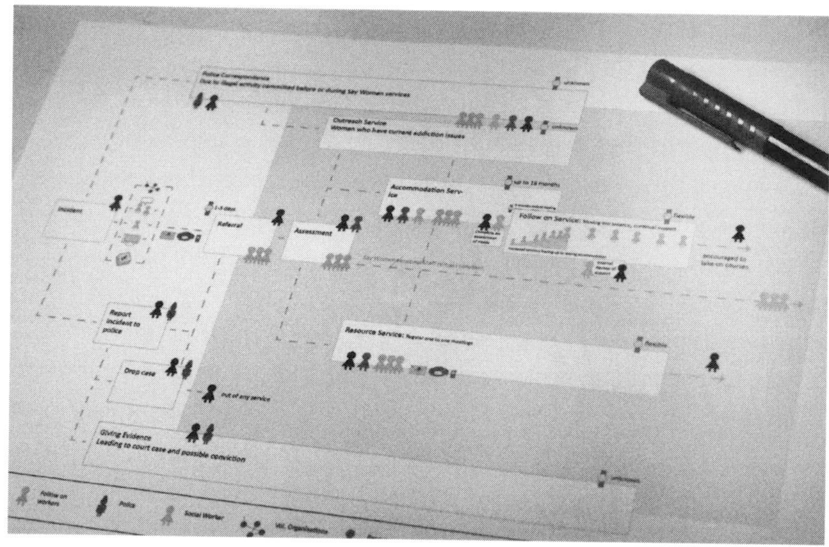

Stakeholder mapping through user journeys of a victim support service in Glasgow

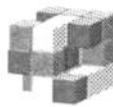

Exploration: mapping the crime and justice landscape

The development of Mypolice was not simply about developing the product, but also about marketing it and selling it. What must be remembered is that, as much as Mypolice is a product, a website (http://mypolice.org), it is also a service that it provides to the police and the public.

The process began by mapping the crime and justice landscape. This was useful in determining who Mypolice's clients were, what their needs were and how Mypolice would fit into and alongside existing systems. This began by charting police forces, building up a more holistic view of the landscape to include third-sector organisations, local government and national government. Placing these organisations around the concept

of MyPolice made apparent the constraints of who would interact with the service and for whom the service would be useful. This mapping process also helped reveal some of the qualitative and quantitative data that would have to be integrated into the service to make it obvious to users the benefits and utility the service provides. Media organisations sat close to the centre of the circle whilst government sat on the outside. This helped to define what types of functions the service needed to offer to have the most impact in a short period of time and who to target when talking about the concept.

Visually mapping the organisations and how they fit together was beneficial to encourage reflection about what the goals for Mypolice are. Straightforwardly, they are about producing a conversation between the public and the police and introducing social media as a vehicle to do so, but in terms of the bigger picture, the mission is to improve the police's service delivery, put users at the heart of this and eventually inform policy in a more empathic way.

Creation: design as business

During the summer of 2009, Mypolice contacted a local online enthusiast who is part of the community council in Garnethill in Glasgow and worked with him to develop a use-case scenario for how Mypolice could work in a community by setting in a real location and tapping into this potential user's local knowledge to help refine the concept.

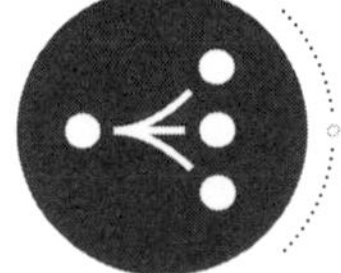

"As a discipline, service design should not be viewed in isolation, but as complement to service development, management, operations, and marketing" (Evenson & Dubberly, 2010).

At the time Mypolice was completing funding proposals to get some capital behind the idea and it was interesting to notice the parallels between the questions service designers ask when using certain tools and how funding proposals and early business plans are organised and worded. For example, using the standard categories behind a service blueprint, it was possible to categorise and organise the Mypolice concept into its constituent business components. The first question of a blueprint is how does a user become aware of the service? In a business plan, this is labelled as marketing and broken into two sections: corporate and public facing. More questions from a standard blueprint, like how will someone join the service, use it, grow with it and leave it, allowed the Mypolice team to create a plan of how to answer all these questions using the creative, and most importantly, low-cost techniques that service design offers.

Reflection: prototyping Mypolice

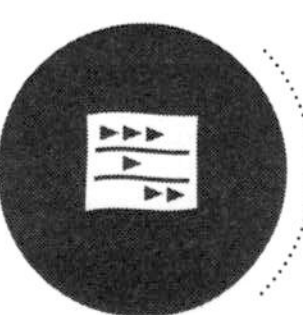

To answer the questions of who will use the MyPolice service and how they will use it, the team began in the local ... community cafe with a "Mypolice installation", using a paper prototype method to record people's stories and "tag" them to understand the kinds of things people might want to say on the site.

This involved sitting down with members of the public and openly allowing them to tell of their experiences, then asking them certain questions about what parts of it they would share online and what they wouldn't. These notes were then attached to a wall or placed in a box, depending on whether they chose to be anonymous or not.

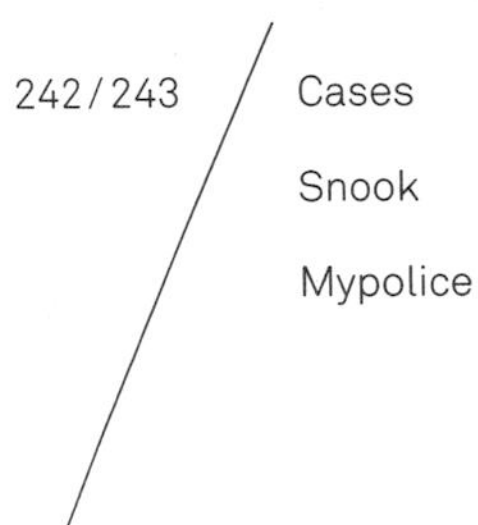

This session allowed questioning of people's internet habits and considering other options for accessing the site, including post and satellite TV options. Listening was crucial as asking direct questions about using the internet would have provided negative or quick answers. Users' stories and details about their lives allowed the gathering of insights about how people communicate with public services and the touchpoints they may prefer to use.

A common mistake, and possibly a reason why public sector websites cost the taxpayer large sums of money, is often that an idea conceived high up in the organisational hierarchy, is often untested and taken straight into implementation (BBC News, 2010). The benefit of prototyping with paper is that it costs nothing and it allows us to understand what will and what won't work at a very early stage. Service design and its process is a great money saver!

Exploration: understanding users

In the research stage, to further knowledge and understanding of users, time was spent in locals' homes, interviewing them and finding out how they felt about openly sharing their experiences with and comments on policing. Tours of locally run websites by active members of communities were useful for understanding when it was that people used these sites and, more importantly, gain understanding of why they did. Asking why and understanding the motivation for someone's actions is important to designers. Using the why question presents a designer with insights into people's lives and a deep level of understanding of the choices people make, allowing us to produce more relevant and valuable propositions as an outcome, in this case, why would someone become motivated to involve themselves in local community issues?

Building from this research and the people I had met, it was possible to construct personas, which enabled design in a people-centred way. Physically making the persona cards is useful as a constant reminder later in the design process, when engulfed in wireframes and technical details of the website, of what people want from it, and how they are likely to use it.

Exploration: marketing, growing awareness

Having answered the standard business questions through the method of a blueprint, the project team was able to figure out all the touchpoints of the service. A large part of this comes through our "marketing department" and involves consideration of how to make people aware of the service. In terms of mass marketing, radio and billboard advertising is a given, but there is a need to think deeper than this. Where are the interactions, with what types of users are you interacting?

As part of the landscape mapping, a big emphasis had been placed on third sector organisations, especially those who deal with victims of crime. During the research phase, time was spent with managers. The focus was mapping their service offerings, looking for interaction points with the police from an organisational and victim point of view and at what time someone would feel ready, emotionally, to submit a story to the Mypolice service or who else might do this.

It was also important to get inside the police networks. Due to some great people, Nick Keane for one from the National Policing Improvement

Agency, it was possible to keynote at conferences and be consulted on the use of social media in the police force.

Being immersed in police culture was interesting. Designers picked up huge amounts just through observation. Visiting police stations, being out on the beat with officers, attending conferences, meeting with both the heads and the frontline staff of the police proved significant for building up an understanding and empathy with the organisations to which Mypolice would relate.

Considering how to reach out to all these people was tough, but by using research (systems maps/personas/shadowing) it was possible to create a brand ethos that would work across all touchpoints. For the Mypolice service, everything needs to be designed, down to the last detail. The wording you choose in an email to thank someone for submitting a story, the card a policeman hands over when they've interacted with a member of the public, a radio advertisement's wording, a poster on a charity's wall, all this and more, needs to be designed. Importantly, the user's journey through the site and through the service and what they get out of it is crucial. To communicate this with police and the public, storyboards were generated to show how users might use the site and what happens after they "leave" it.

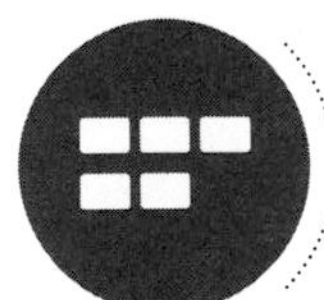

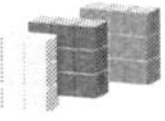 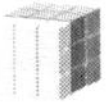 Reflection and implementation: planning the build

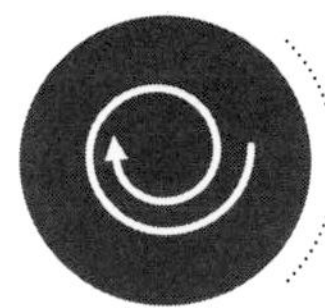

Once the team behind Mypolice had a clear understanding of what needed to be built and a bit of money behind the project, Mypolice recruited a developer and planning of the building and testing of the product began. In terms of software development, an agile methodology was adopted.

Developing the software iteratively through alpha, beta and gamma stages to establish what works and what doesn't. This gives space to uncover latent user needs and develop functions as the process progresses. Working in this way to develop software is similar to service design methods of rapid prototyping to assess and measure reaction to ideas and service concepts. Regular testing is part of the plan as well as having face-to-face user testing in our schedule and soft launches to see how users move around our website and what types of stories they submit.

Developing this in stages and pitching this to the police is co-creating a solution that works for them. This entails designing it at a basic level and then going and piloting it with a local police force to see how Mypolice can fit with their system. The pilot is designed to allow tolerance for change in how the service operates and the service design team will be sitting there with police when the first story comes through. To a certain extent, the police's process of response needs to be designed but this is very much an open innovation process of discovery, reflection and response to ensure the development of a product and service that work for both the public and the police.

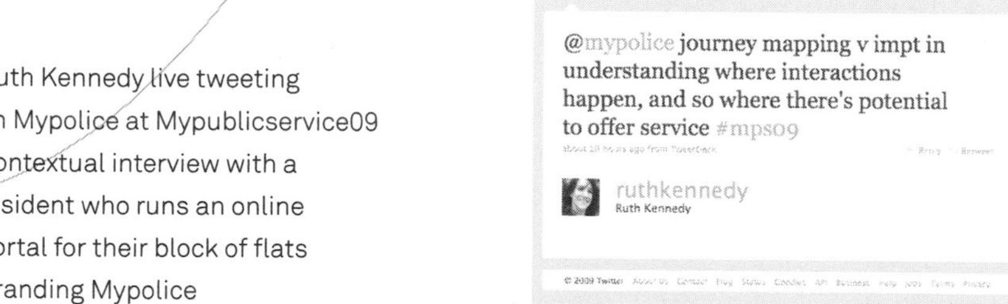
1
twitter
@mypolice journey mapping v impt in understanding where interactions happen, and so where there's potential to offer service #mps09
ruthkennedy
Ruth Kennedy

1 Ruth Kennedy live tweeting on Mypolice at Mypublicservice09
2 Contextual interview with a resident who runs an online portal for their block of flats
3 Branding Mypolice

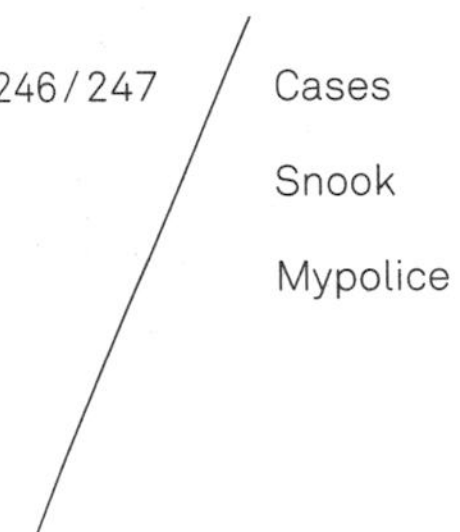

Final statement

Mypolice is about taking what service designers do on a regular basis to a higher level. Specifically, listening, as part of the service design process, becoming a part of what the police do and, in so doing, helping them by positioning ourselves in the middle, between them and the user to quantify qualitative data to make it easier for police to understand. This will help the police empathically respond to user needs, target important areas for development, and close the feedback loop by responding and altering their service both with incremental and radical change where needed.

3

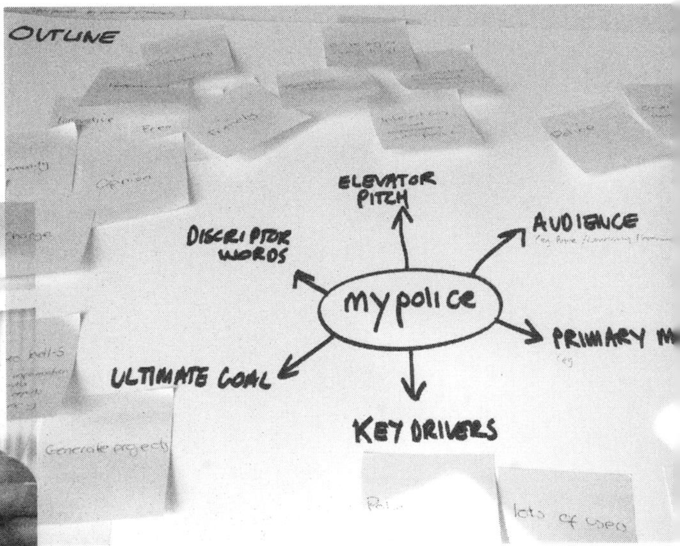

2

Applied Service Design

1

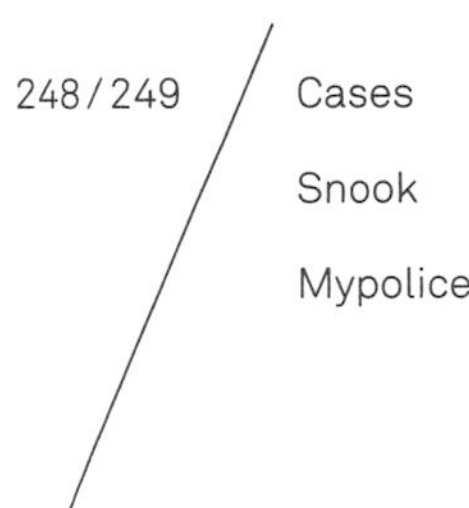

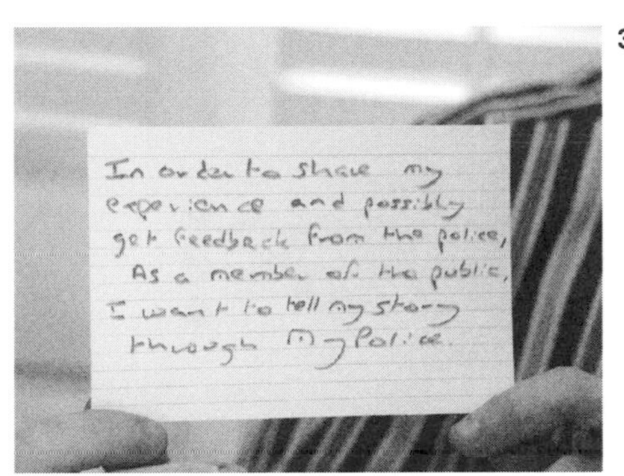

3

2

4

1 Planning the pilot along a timeline
2 Rapid prototyping the submit a story function at Mypublicservice09
3 Working with Unboxed consultancy to build Use Case scenarios
4 Lauren Currie talking to the public about police feedback

hello change!

FUNKY PROJECTS

HELLO CHANGE AND FUNKY PROJECTS

Hello Change

Hello Change is a recruitment service based on the mutual allurement of the job candidate and the employer. Initiated as an internal project at Funky Projects, Hello Change has ultimately emerged as a spin-off. It aims at companies that believe they are made up of people, not resources, and who look for the best fit when they need to add new people to their team as well as companies that believe that personnel selection is a key part of the development of an organisation, and who are looking for talented people.

Funky Projects

Funky Projects is a service design company that is constantly researching how to bring about innovation and design new businesses; we are entrepreneurial and want to be one step ahead of the client's specified project. We work from a process of reflection in action in order to design new types of transformational business. Funky Projects is a company that designs services and strategic creativity for companies, administrations and organisations with a focus on sustainable change. We currently have offices in Madrid and Bilbao, are working on international projects, and have been a member of the Service Design Network since 2009. The project Hello Change is a start-up promoted by Funky Projects and has involved the whole Funky Projects' team at different times and we have enjoyed the cooperation of clients and Hello Change's participants. We are sincerely grateful to all of them.

Companies and job candidates

Companies use the service because they want to add talent to their teams. Individuals use the system because they want to develop professionally.

How to attract and hire great people

There is a need for a new recruitment process for the times we live in. The task was to develop a process that moves from the recruitment systems of the industrial era to a recruitment system of the information era, where the identification of talent and attitudes are essential for companies that are looking for people-centred innovation and competitive differentiation. Classic recruitment processes often disregarded certain qualities, such as empathy, creativity, charisma and attitude, since these cannot be detected simply by reading a CV. An innovative recruitment process needs to take into account the fact that happiness at work makes employees more productive and a good fit is essential for building a mutually sustainable relationship. To achieve such aims, companies need new systems to spot people talent quickly by looking beyond their CVs and computer transcript. This enables employers to efficiently get people on board who will add value to the organisation's activities, wherever they are.

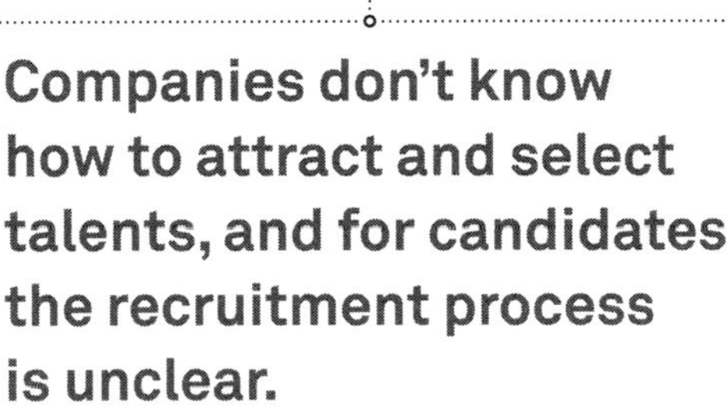

Companies don't know how to attract and select talents, and for candidates the recruitment process is unclear.

DISCOVERED USERS' PROBLEM

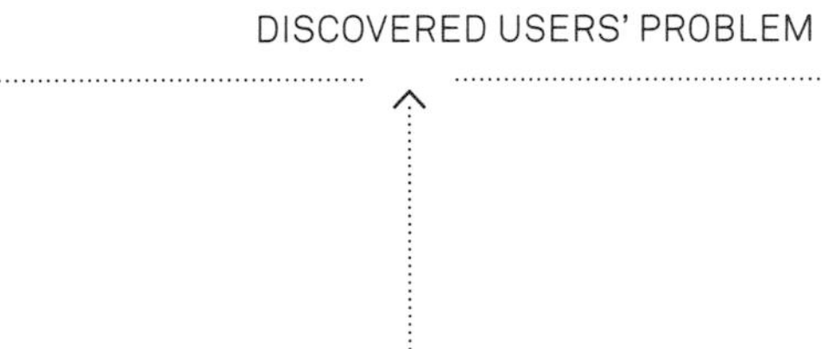

Current recruitment processes block companies' growth because they focus on outdated values and methods.

COMPANY'S PROBLEM

A recruitment process where both companies and candidates benefit from the gained experiences and imparted knowledge during the process.

SERVICE VISION

BEATRIZ BELMONTE AND ASIER PÉREZ EXPLAIN

FUNKY PROJECTS' PROCESS

The background: select people, not CVs

Hello Change has arisen from the need to design a new recruitment process for the times we live in. Hello Change prioritises people and their transformative capabilities, and is a process that acknowledges the fact that happiness at work makes us more productive, and a good fit is essential for building a mutually sustainable relationship. In developing Hello Change the design team prioritised explicit parameters that had previously been subjective within the recruitment process, such as empathy, creativity, charisma and attitude. These are qualities that cannot be detected simply by reading a CV.

The candidates can be in any part of the world and organisations have to be able to identify them, get to know them and attract them. Geographical dispersion and attractive opportunities in other places mean that companies have to find alternatives to face-to-face systems. Some services on the Internet aimed at finding a partner such as meetic.com or match.com also attempt to address these issues, although their approach is slightly different to that of Hello Change.

Hello Change is a system that quickly allows a new member of staff to incorporate and become an asset to the organisation. Companies need these people to add value from the first day of a recruitment process. Therefore, parts of the contents that usually form the process of "onboarding" of a company have been added to the Hello Change service. The onboarding process involves helping new employees become productive members of an organisation. In this context, Hello Change has been inspired by a process of identifying needs, which reflect new social realities and a number of negative experiences attempting to use existing solutions.

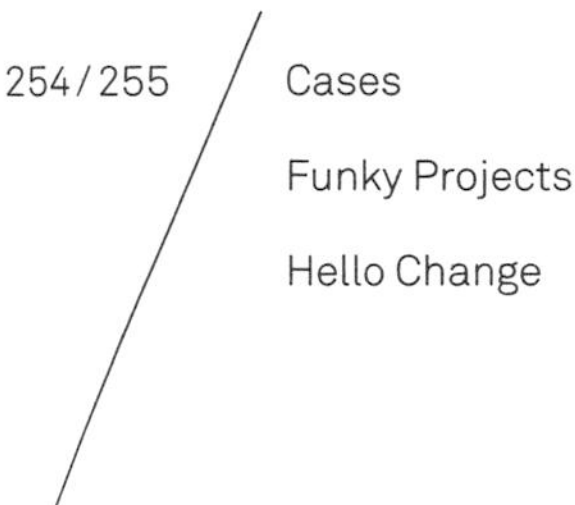

Exploration: recruitment processes that make an impact on companies

Through desk research and interviews Funky Projects found that in the knowledge and empathy era, where each company claims that their people are its most important asset, we continue to see industrialist ideas in the recruitment of staff with forms and standardised processes. A recruitment process is never cheap, but if bad hiring decisions are added to this, the growth of the company may be held back, people can be fired, and a lot of frustration might occur at both ends. Small- and medium-sized companies in the United Kingdom lose more than seventy million pounds every year as a result of bad recruitment processes (Jobsite, 2008).

The current economic climate and a change in social paradigm has put many companies in a difficult situation and forced them to reinvent themselves and the things they do. They have had to look carefully at the values of the people they employ, beyond their academic qualifications and the professional experience on their CVs. This is where the design of a recruitment process that focuses on the talent and attitude of a person becomes particularly valuable for a company's competitiveness.

"Organisations typically neglect to incorporate characteristics and behaviours for innovative working into recruitment and selection criteria." *—NESTA Report on Everyday Innovation, 2009*

Moreover, people have changed their demands and priorities when looking for jobs to beyond simply the offered salary; they know that the job may completely determine their personal development, their growth, their future and their happiness. The desire to work in a company that offers professional career development, an enriching work experience and a philosophy or spirit makes high added-value candidates much more

selective when they choose where they are going to invest their energy and time. They want to see the effect of their efforts in the world that surrounds them.

"A company that applies a recruitment process like this is not just any [old] company" —Candidate user of Hello Change

The internet and its social networks are going to set the pace for recruitment processes; they have also caused a key paradigm shift; that it is not about the people you know, but meeting people who know people who might interest you when it comes to finding your future employment. However, for many businesses talent hunting via these networks is still complex because they lack tools and options that go beyond profile management.

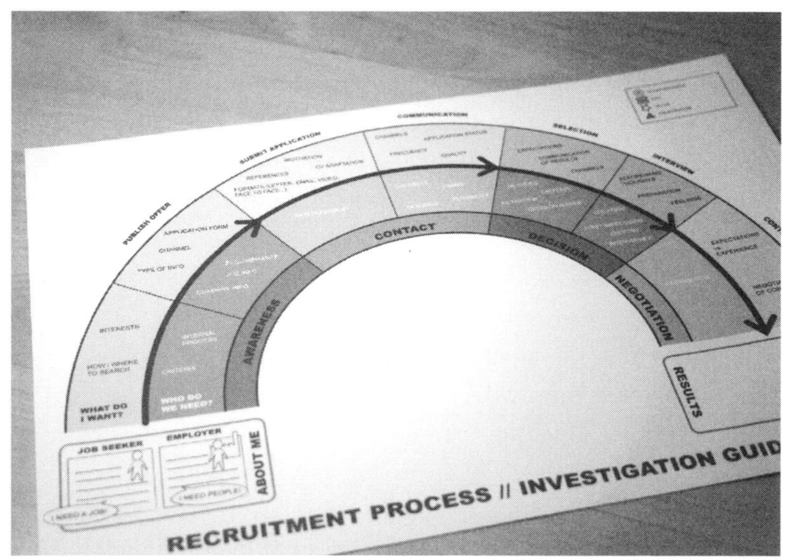

Investigation tracks the recuitment process experience on both sides: job seeker and employer.

Against this background, Funky Projects has designed a personnel selection system that goes further than the CV before getting to the interview stage, that allows you to select personnel online, with an open business logic that eliminates traditional opacity and from a win-win point of view in which both the participants and the company get to participate in a mutually beneficial constructive experience.

Creation & reflection: experience before processes and technology

The ideation process started with work sessions in which the spirit of the project was defined. In these sessions, participants were people from different backgrounds (engineers, journalists, researchers, scientists, interaction designers and creative designers) to put together a framework for flexible, polysemic work. The spirit of the project is the philosophy that inspires all later developments, whether for the experience design, applications design or the touchpoints. In the case of Hello Change, this spirit sought to create a recruitment process that would not only identify and filter but also empower and innovate.

As this is a service designed for people by people, the identification of interests, desires and worries of the people involved marked the beginning of the experience design. Through interviews with candidates and companies the research team started locating on the work map the expectations that the service would have to meet. By applying the logic of "reflection in action" (Donald Schön, 1983) the research became part of the design process. As the Hello Change team progressed with the interviews, the main lines of the service started to appear. During the research

other personnel selection services at international level were also studied as well as success stories in large companies that have created their own hiring processes, such as DELL or IBM.

The experience ideation focussed on a time line that included the moment prior to the recruitment process, the development of actions to identify potential candidates, and the final choice. For this, the research team used "design scenarios", to get a full vision of the experience beyond the sequential ideas that are usually part of a recruitment process. This process of projection into the future was refined by taking a real recruitment process as an example, and using its needs as the starting point for the first prototype for the service.

Once the service experience had been designed, the research team at Hello Change started with the design of the processes and technological requirements that would be needed in the service. This way of "focusing the technical ideation process based on the designed experience" worked to give the project tools the flexibility to be used in different contexts whilst at the same time maintaining a holistic view of the service design process. Taken as a whole, the Hello Change experience includes the following aspects:

- Experience of the employer company that involves a new personnel recruitment logic
- Experience of the candidates that gives them greater control over the recruitment process and allows them to access an experience that gives them a qualification
- Communication of the job offer that attracts the type of profile that the company wants
- Pre-web casting selection system (first selection of candidates)

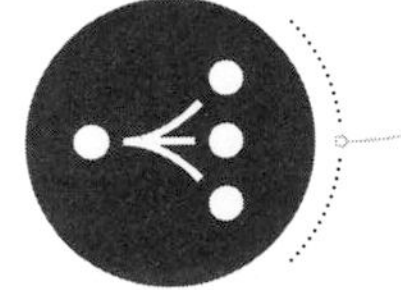

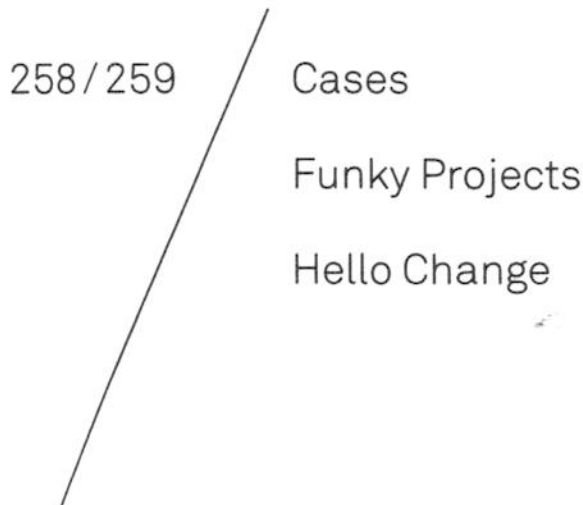

- Dynamic implementation of web casting and design of communication and welcome (candidates' selection in action space)
- Design of different tests to evaluate the attitudes of the participants in the online platform
- System for evaluating the activity on the platform and the actions of the participants
- Final casting workshop (workshop attended by the company and the candidates)
- Design of the communication of the process results to all the participants in Hello Change
- Design of the company onboarding process for the people chosen to become part of the employer company.

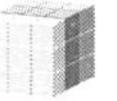

Implementation: direct implementation as prototyping

The prototyping of the Hello Change service was carried out with a recruitment process that Funky Projects had started up to extend its activities by opening a new office in Madrid. One of the first aspects to emerge in the implementation was the need to find a language and a tone of communication that would transmit the character of the company in the job offer. In this way it was possible to minimise the number of irrelevant candidatures and attract talented candidates from amongst the people interested. Together with the job advertisement, the pre-web casting selection system was created to generate reflection and knowledge amongst the candidates at the same time as offering the company their first impressions of the candidates' characters through their choices and answers.

From the beginning, Funky Projects designated a team that would participate in all the phases of the process, although with differing intensity. The team included people with various posts so that the hiring process of new staff would be an event that would involve the majority of the organisation, beyond their departmental responsibilities. The tests facilitated through the online platform were designed to detect the desired attitudes and capabilities in the candidates. To communicate the tests on the platform, the Hello Change team used videos made by the company itself. This approach to the work opened the doors of the organisation to the first round of candidates in exchange for all of the information they had offered during the process.

During the web casting process the Hello Change research team detected different needs with respect to the platform about the confidentiality of the information and the relationships between the participants. The former aspect required clear information from the company about what would happen with the material that was created by the candidates during the web casting and a greater number of options to choose the degree of privacy of the data submitted to the platform. The latter aspect meant that one person on the team took charge of making the activity on the platform more dynamic and doing a follow-up. To increase the number of voices and interactions, other people from the company were asked to participate on the platform occasionally. Bit by bit the Hello Change system extended throughout the company at different moments, meaning that everyone knew about the recruitment process and could share their individual opinions and perspectives.

During the web casting, it was necessary from the beginning to tell people the phases of the activities, the planning and the estimated time each one would take. In this way, the candidates had more control

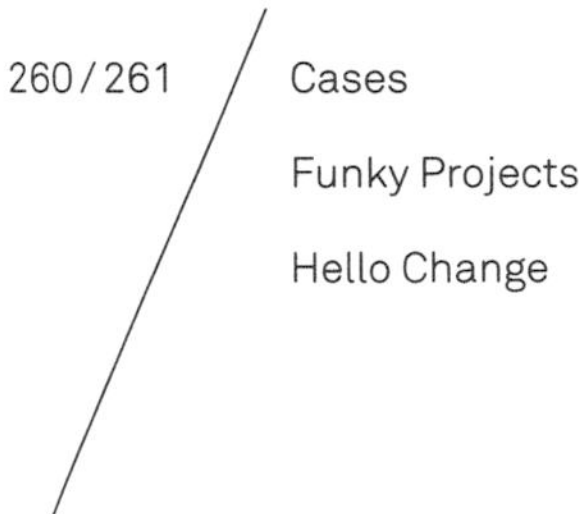

over the process and were able to evaluate their investment required in terms of time and effort. The web casting was rounded off with a workshop; a work day when face-to-face interviews with the final candidates were held, as well as individual exercises and a psychometric test. The day was also designed to meet the needs and characteristics of the employer company to stimulate the candidates and foment socialisation and especially to get to know and study them all.

During the whole process, the candidates knew whom they were competing against and had to bring out their best qualities in a constructive way through collaboration and building relationships with others.

Systematisation: service design as business design

The systematisation process of Hello Change turned into the design of a new kind of business, which became a start-up. In this process, systematisation required Funky Projects to incorporate economic and business management knowledge into the process, in order to design a business model which would give business viability to the Hello Change service.

Information provided by capital risk companies has been of great use for identifying the values and solutions that Hello Change would bring to the market, and for refining the sector analysis that had been undertaken at the beginning of the project. This new business direction that Hello Change took helped the team to reconsider the initial specification to turn the project into a system that would be applicable in and by any company. In order to do this, the team had to redefine the capacity for personalisation of the service, the interoperability of the service and the scale related with the number of users and the different processes that a company could be running at the same time.

Conscious that any service must be constantly refined, Hello Change has had to add systems for review and improvement that can be applied simultaneously within a project without interfering with it. In this way, while at first the service experience preceded the technological development, in the systematisation phase the order was reversed and both the technology and the communication design became the main focus of work.

Final statement

Hello Change is a recruiting system for talent based on mutual seduction. It helps the right people to meet the right company. And vice-versa. Hello Change lowers the risk in hiring and increases chances of a happy team story.

1

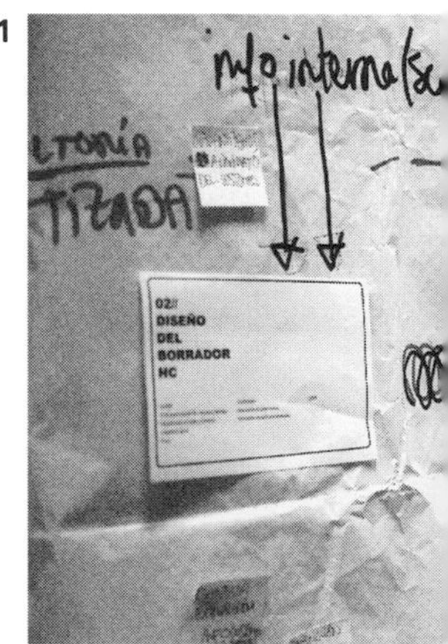

1 First drafts of the design process before setting technological requirements

2 Hello Change has become a business project that has to be redesigned for the market.

3 Gathering candidates' experiences through interviews.

2

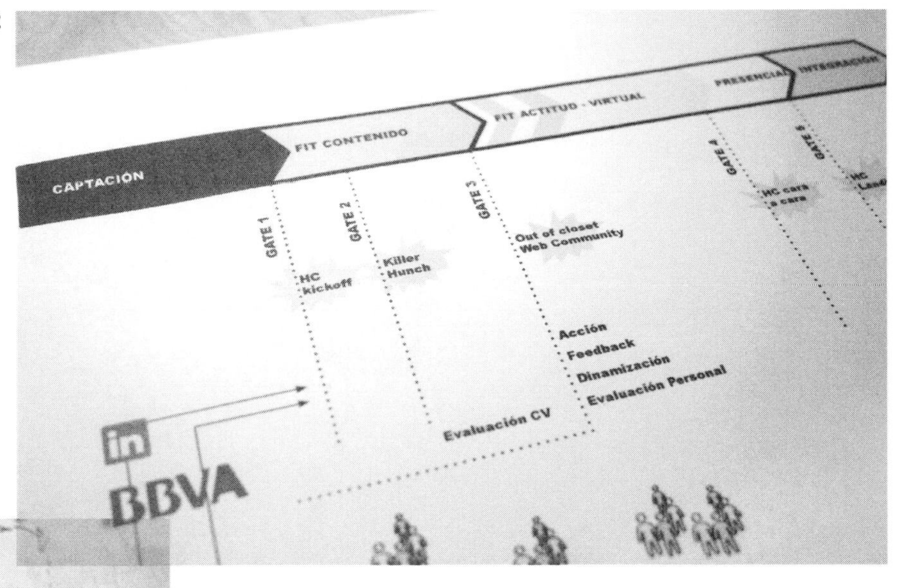

CAPTACIÓN
FIT CONTENIDO
FIT ACTITUD - VIRTUAL
PRESENCIAL
INTEGRACIÓN
GATE 1
GATE 2
GATE 3
GATE 4
GATE 5
HC kickoff
Killer Hunch
Out of closet Web Community
HC cara a cara
Acción
Feedback
Dinamización
Evaluación Personal
Evaluación CV
in
BBVA

3

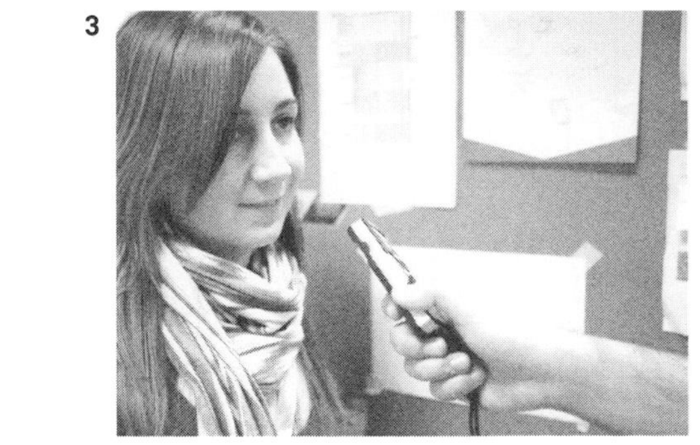

1

2

1 Part of Funky Projects' team with three Hello Change finalists after casting workshop

2 Web casting actions were communicated by the employer with videos embedded in the platform.

3 Web casting welcome page in HC platform. Candidates could see all the process activity and meet the other candidates.

4 Every candidate had a personal space to complete his/her profile beyond the CV.

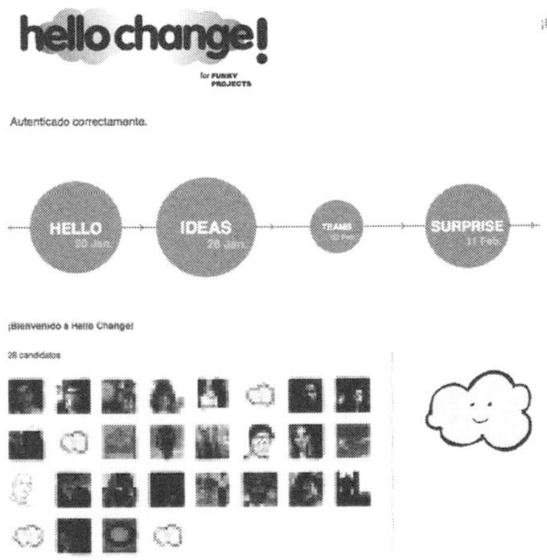
hello change!
for FUNKY PROJECTS
Autenticado correctamente.
HELLO
IDEAS
TEAMS
SURPRISE
¡Bienvenido a Hello Change!

3

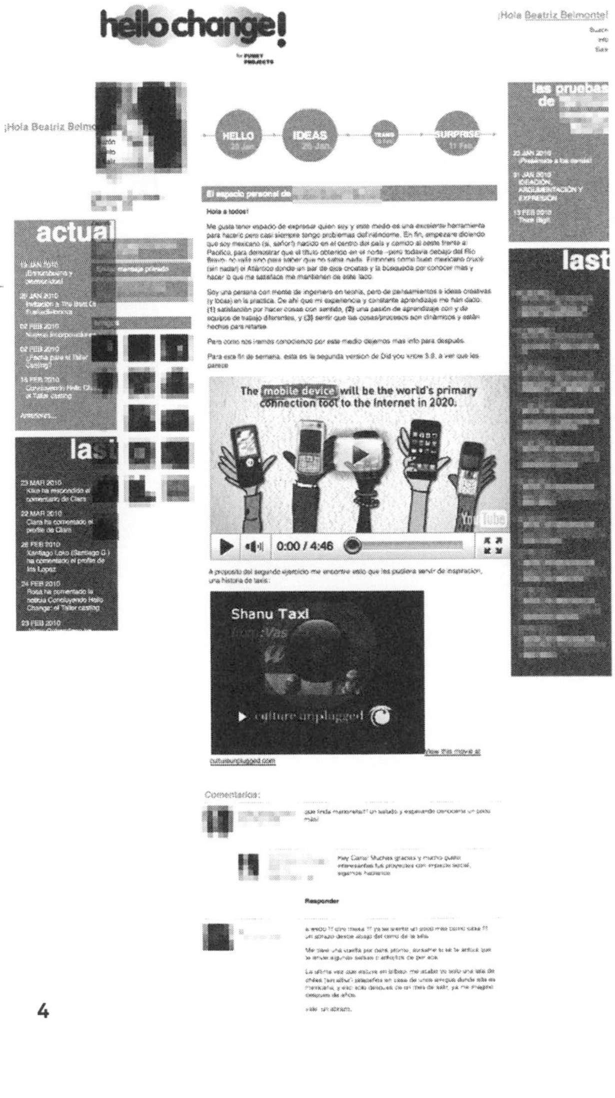
hello change!
for FUNKY PROJECTS
¡Hola Beatriz Belmonte!
actual
last
HELLO
IDEAS
TEAMS
SURPRISE
las pruebas de
last
The mobile device will be the world's primary connection tool to the internet in 2020.
0:00 / 4:46
Shanu Taxi
culture unplugged
Comentarios:
Responder

4

UPMC

CarnegieMellon
Design

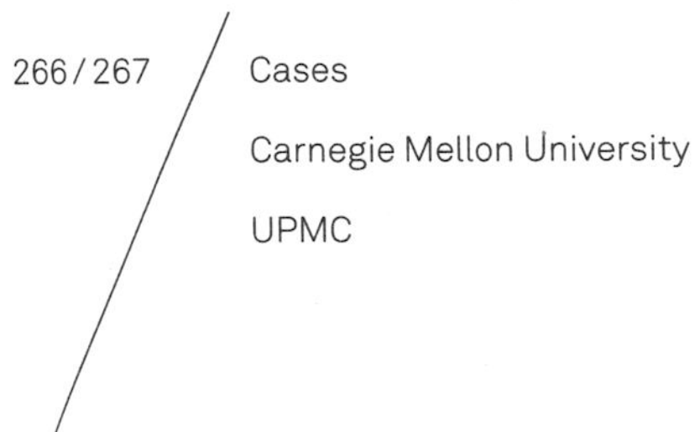

UPMC AND CARNEGIE MELLON UNIVERSITY

University of Pittsburgh Medical Center (UPMC)
The UPMC Center for Quality Improvement and Innovation provides quality improvement leadership, education, and support infrastructure to healthcare professionals across the system, in pursuit of excellence in care delivery. The Center's core mission is to help ensure that UPMC provides the best possible patient care by increasing the pace of improvements in quality and disseminating best practices throughout the health system.

Carnegie Mellon University
Carnegie Mellon University School of Design offers undergraduate degrees in communication and industrial design, and graduate degrees in interaction design and communication planning and information design. The design team for this case study was Melissa Cliver, Jamin Hegeman, Kipum Lee, Leanne Libert, and Kara Tennant, and was instructed by associate professor Shelley Evenson in 2007. The school has offered courses and collaborative projects in service design since 2004.

Clinic patients, family and staff

All clinic patients and family members, as well as the clinic doctor and staff were considered target stakeholders. Patients ranged from teenagers to the elderly.

Wait time, work flow and wayfinding

The neurosurgery clinic pioneered an innovative surgical technique used to remove brain tumours and lesions. The clinic operated once a week, during which the primary clinic doctor saw as many as eighty patients. The design team was tasked with improving wait time (some patients waited up to five hours), work flow for staff, and wayfinding.

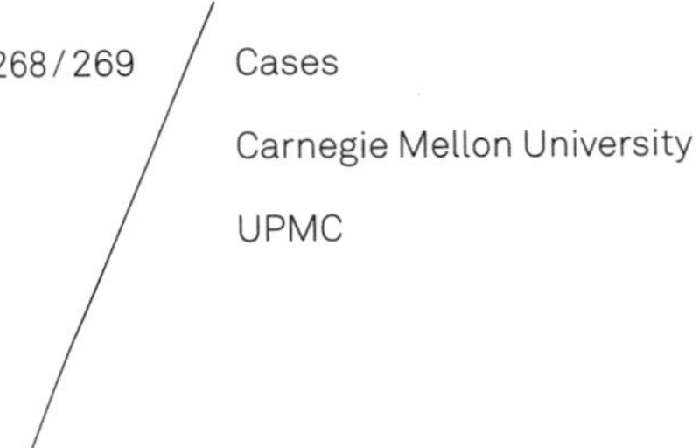

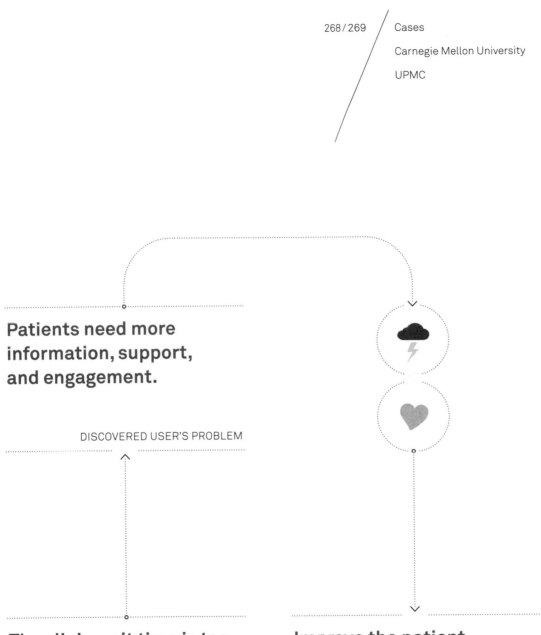

Patients need more information, support, and engagement.

DISCOVERED USER'S PROBLEM

The clinic wait time is too long, and staff workflow and wayfinding need to be improved.

COMPANY'S PROBLEM

Improve the patient experience through interaction, engagement, information, and support.

SERVICE VISION

JAMIN HEGEMAN EXPLAINS

CARNEGIE MELLON UNIVERSITY'S PROCESS

Exploration

Seeing the clinic with new eyes

After meeting with the Center for Quality Improvement and Innovation staff, the design team created a territory map to visualise the potential design opportunity space as well as our collective understanding of the problem area. A territory map consists of the stakeholders, environments, interactions, and assumptions about the design project. This is a first step at understanding the problem space.

However, to really understand the clinic experience and properly frame the design problem, the team visited the space and engaged with patients and staff. The team spent many days observing clinic interactions, usually spending the whole day to get an understanding of the experience. To get deeper insights, the team conducted one-on-one interviews with staff members and talked with patients in both the waiting room and the exam rooms.

Back in the studio, the team visualised findings through sticky notes and photos. These were arranged into categories to identify patterns and opportunities. The photos helped as a visual stimulus and aided the team in maintaining an empathic connection to the clinic experience.

Understanding the big picture

To understand the experience as a whole, the team mapped patient, staff, and physician interaction through a service blueprint. This served as a model of the typical patient visit. The visualisation revealed the front stage interactions patients had with various service touchpoints, as well as the systems and staff on the back stage that supported those

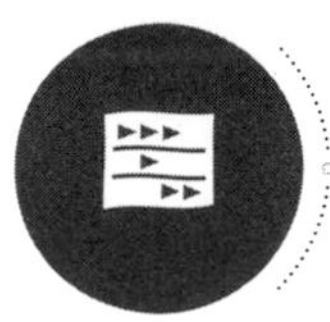

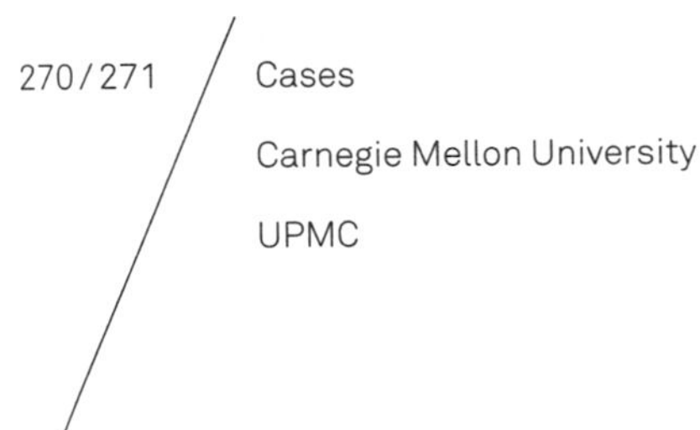

interactions. Mapping the service blueprint allowed the team to see the breakdowns in the clinic experience. In particular, we could see the different periods in the service experience where patients were waiting without any interaction with the service. These periods became opportunities for new interactions that could be designed to engage patients and support the clinic staff.

Engaging the staff

To deliver a great service, designers also need to engage the people who will ultimately be responsible for delivering the service. The team met with nurses and staff to share exploratory findings and engaged them in participatory design activities to better understand their perspective and experience.

Creation

Reframing the project

Organisations typically recognise when there is a problem with their service. But often the problem is unclear or assumed. As mentioned, the given problems were wait time, workflow, and wayfinding. While these were clearly issues, the team needed to prioritise and define the problem in a way that reflected the research findings and beliefs in what could be done to solve them.

During this problem reframing period, the team worked closely with the Center for Quality Improvement and Innovation staff to determine the best place to focus. Given the physician's desire to see many patients, we agreed that wait time could not be reduced. But instead of it being

an obstacle, the team argued to embrace wait time as an opportunity to engage patients in interactions that supported their needs. The team used the research insights to make its case for this direction, and the Center approved.

Providing co-creation tools

With the direction set, the team sought to build even greater empathy with patients by creating a set of experience cards to help them imagine alternative clinic experiences. For example, one card showed someone playing piano, another a row of computer terminals, and another showed someone taking a nap. The cards acted as prompts for patients to express desires or opinions about what-if scenarios that the designers used to inform concept generation.

Stepping into the operating room

To better understand every aspect of the patient experience, the team observed one of the endonasal procedures. Being in the operating room allowed the team further to empathise with the patient. It also allowed the team to see the other side of the physician's responsibility. And it gave them a greater appreciation and understanding of the family needs during the surgery.

Visualising the data

To better understand the qualitative information gathered, the team visualised the patient journey, then overlaid the emotions felt as well as the needs of the patient and family in terms of support, waiting, and information. Visualising this information helped the team to have a better understanding of the experience over time. Additionally, it was used

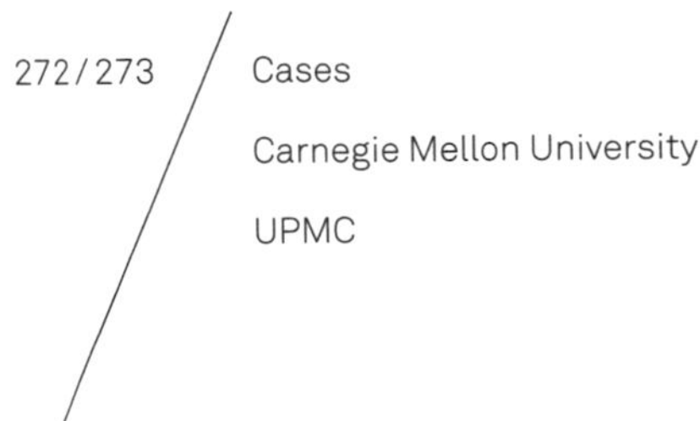

to identify opportunity areas. For example, it was clear to see in the visualisation that the patient needs during surgery are negligible, while the family needs are extremely high.

Reflection

Since the team had observed patients – especially those in wheelchairs – having trouble moving through the waiting room, they proposed removing chairs and reconfiguring the space. The clinic staff had never thought to do this. The result was very successful. People in wheelchairs could better enter the space, and were not relegated to the hallway or near the check-in desk, as the team observed previously. And there was enough room for them to sit with their families in any part of the waiting room.

Focusing the concepts

Using feedback received from discussions with patients about the experience cards, the team sketched new concepts on half sheets of paper. From a group of about seventy concepts, they selected ten that were turned into storyboards and used to validate the ideas with patients.

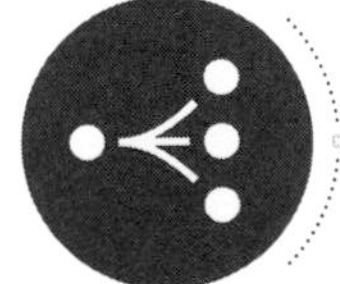

Getting patient feedback

The team again entered the exam rooms with patients and families while they waited for the physician. The privacy of the room gave the team an opportunity to talk in depth with patients and get their candid feedback about the concepts, as well as their experience with the doctor and the staff. With this final round of feedback, the team refined the concepts and prepared them for final delivery.

Delivering solutions

Rather than an individual concept, the team presented a collection of solutions that, while possible to implement individually, were intended to be parts of a whole aimed at improving the clinic experience for patients, families, staff, and physicians. As the clinic experience is co-produced by these four core stakeholders, the concepts were designed to engage all four in activities that affect the experience.

The concepts were presented with meaningful titles, like Wall of Hope, along with a description and storyboard that communicated the concept visually and included a narrative describing the experience. Two of the concepts were made more tangible. The team designed a welcome booklet to demonstrate a solution that could be implemented immediately. Conversely, the team delivered a more visionary concept called Clinic Chat that used technology to enable new ways for patients, staff, and physicians to communicate with each other. This concept was conveyed through a two-minute, narrative movie with illustrations and example interfaces and interactions.

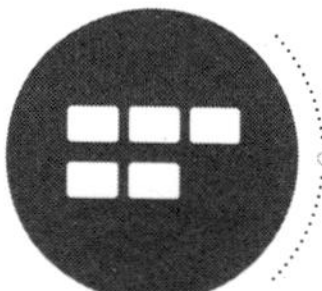

Implementation including results

The Center for Quality Improvement and Innovation and other UPMC staff that reviewed the final work really loved it. In addition, the clinic staff were impressed with the effort to understand both the patient needs and their needs. During the project, they even began to change their habits and to demonstrate to the design team how they were trying to address some of the problems we were highlighting by being there. In fact, one of the greatest successes the design team had was empowering the staff

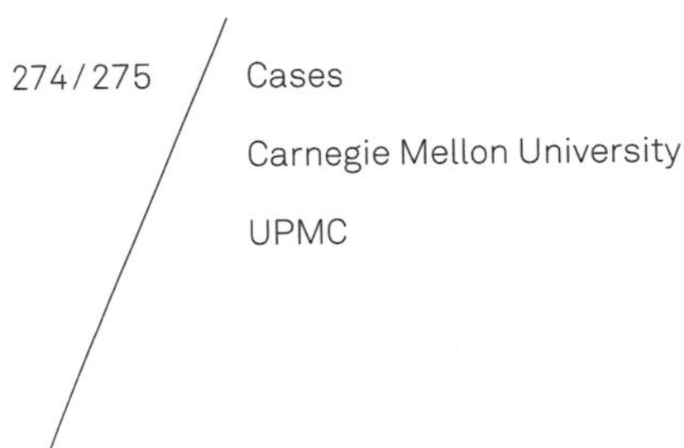

to believe that they could focus more on the patient experience and make small changes themselves.

In that sense, the project was a success. However, like many design consulting projects, it is unknown how or if the work will be implemented. In this case, the clinic underwent major leadership and organisation changes during the year after the design team's final work was delivered. The work was never implemented.

But in that failure comes a realisation that every designer of services must face. With such complexity, how can designers ensure that the work they do for an organisation actually makes it to implementation? When is the appropriate time to hand over the execution to the organisation? How can we best communicate and inspire others to ensure the great work that is co-produced by all stakeholders makes the impact that was envisioned?

Conclusion

While the work was never implemented, the experience of going through the service design process was invaluable. Only after the project did the team fully appreciate the difference between designing for products and designing for a service. The design constraints that the various stakeholders, touchpoints, and environments present cannot be appreciated or understood fully without going through the design process in a service design context.

Another key insight was the need to engage with staff as much as the team engaged with patients. Keeping the staff involved in the design process empowered the staff, made them advocates of the process, and helped the team achieve better access to the information they needed. The Center really appreciated the perspective of the design team and their ability to reframe the problem based on the exploratory findings. When examining a service as a whole, designers will uncover many problems and opportunities. One of the greatest challenges is deciding how to prioritise opportunities and direction.

Finally, service innovation does not need to be that innovative. Changing the layout of the clinic waiting room was simple and had no cost. A simple, humanised solution can have great impact.

Final statement

While the design of services has not traditionally taken a rigorous design approach, the time is coming. This project, along with other forays into the service design space, highlights the capability of designers to bring humanity to services in the same way they have been doing for products.

1 Research analysis
2 Single visit service blueprint

1

2

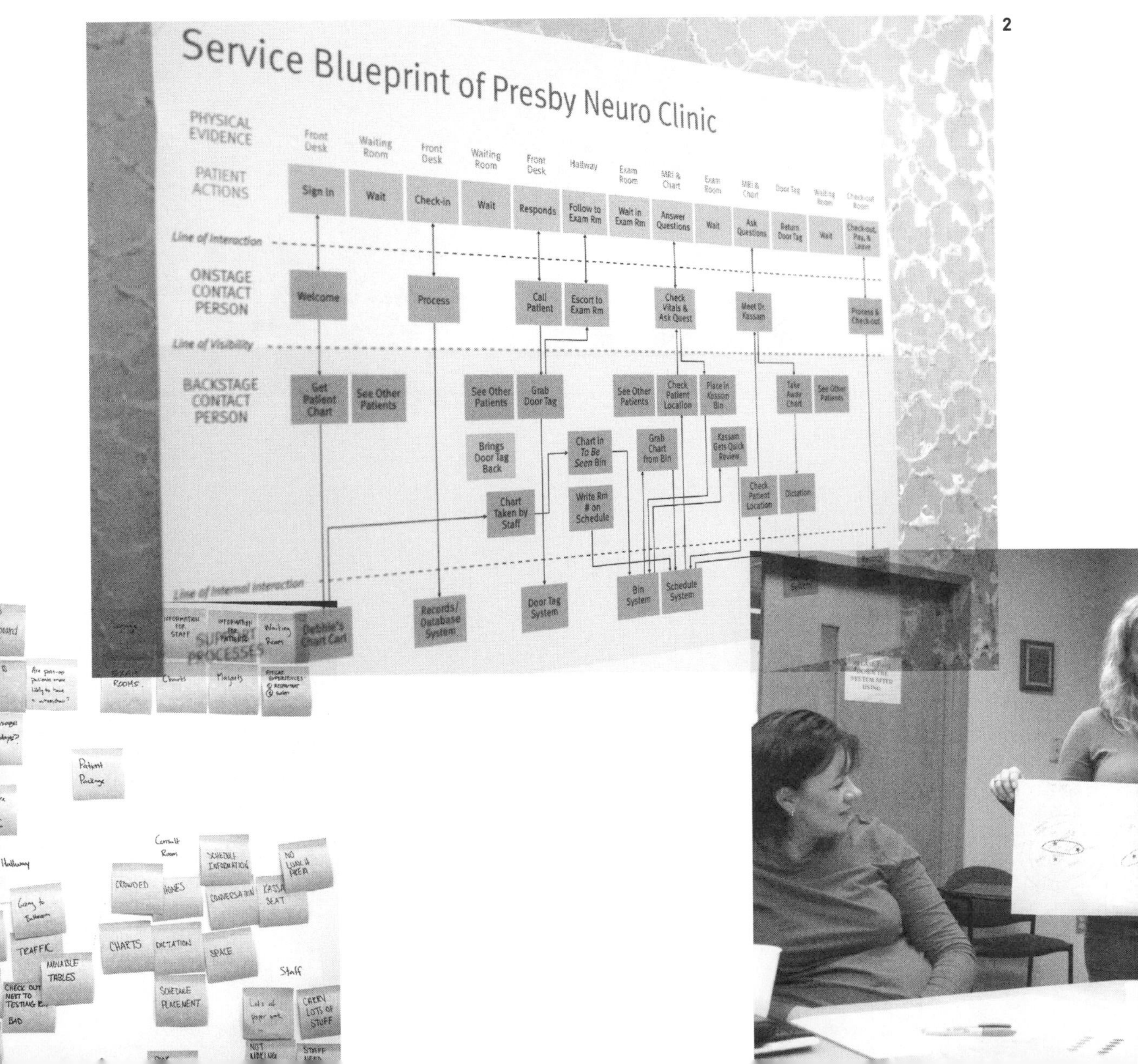
Service Blueprint of Presby Neuro Clinic
PHYSICAL EVIDENCE
PATIENT ACTIONS
Line of Interaction
ONSTAGE CONTACT PERSON
Line of Visibility
BACKSTAGE CONTACT PERSON
Line of Internal Interaction
SUPPORT PROCESSES
Front Desk
Waiting Room
Hallway
Exam Room
Sign In
Wait
Check-in
Responds
Follow to Exam Rm
Wait in Exam Rm
Answer Questions
Ask Questions
Return Door Tag
Welcome
Process
Call Patient
Escort to Exam Rm
Check Vitals & Ask Quest
Meet Dr. Kassam
Get Patient Chart
See Other Patients
Grab Door Tag
Check Patient Location
Place in Kassam Bin
Take Away Chart
Brings Door Tag Back
Chart in To Be Seen Bin
Grab Chart from Bin
Kassam Gets Quick Review
Chart Taken by Staff
Write Rm # on Schedule
Check Patient Location
Dictation
Records/ Database System
Door Tag System
Bin System
Schedule System
Debbie's Chart Cart
Patient Package
CROWDED
CHARTS
DICTATION
SPACE
TRAFFIC
STAFF
Staff

2

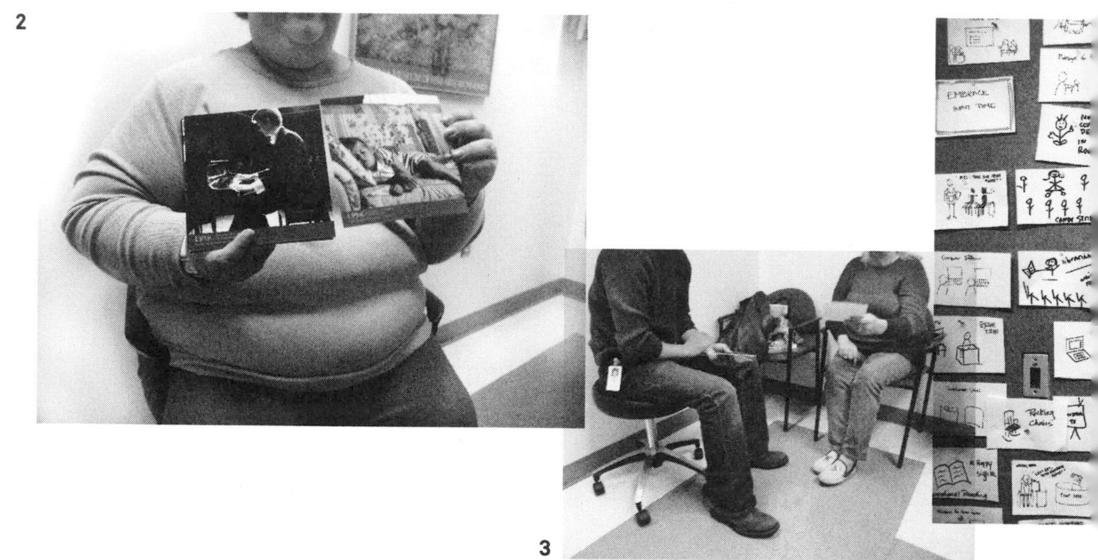

3

1

1 Generative research with nurses and staff
2 Co-creation with patients
3 Exam room interview
4 Concept generation
5 Observing brain tumor operation
6 Research analysis

4

6

5

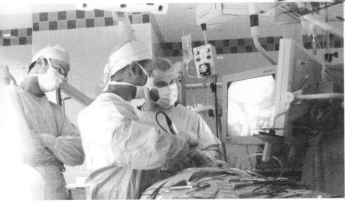

TRANSFORMATOR

SEB AND TRANSFORMATOR

SEB

The SEB bank was founded in 1856 and is now one of northern Europe's leading financial groups. SEB's target groups are companies and individuals with high demands for quality and they provide specialist expertise within all financial areas. SEB has over 20,000 employees in 21 countries and more than 600 branch offices of which one quarter are located in Sweden, another quarter in Germany and the rest in Estonia, Latvia, Lithuania, Russia and Ukraine. Even if the main focus is on northern Europe, SEB has offices in all the world's important financial centres such as Paris, New York and Shanghai. A strong entrepreneurship and an international presence are SEB's most important success factors as well as a long-term customer relationship and an innovative approach.

Transformator Design Group

Based in Sweden Transformator consists of consultants in the area of service design. Regardless of the type of touchpoint, Transformator sharpens the interface between the service company and their customers in order to create an extraordinary service experience. Aided by industrial design tools for both collecting user insights and creating innovations, Transformator helps organisations and companies to enhance the experience and increase the value in their interaction with their customers. Founded in 1998, Transformator has gained great service design experience from a wide range of industries such as security, banking, insurance, healthcare, logistics and recreation.

SEB customers

SEB's customers include around 2500 large companies and institutions, 400,000 small and medium-sized companies as well as five million private individuals. This project targeted about 350,000 private SEB customers. These customers would lower their banking costs by integrating all of their individual bank services into one package.

Package customers' separate services

The majority of SEB's private bank customers have a current account, a savings account, internet banking, telephone banking and a bank card. In addition to this, some customers have credit cards such as MasterCard. These services had previously all been introduced and sold separately, thus making the administration for SEB cumbersome and expensive. To streamline their system SEB wanted to package the customers' separate deals into one manageable package. This would give SEB a more efficient administration and a lower price for the customers.

SEB assumed that they needed each customer's consent to bundle the separate deals into one. Because of this they had to know exactly when, where and how to present this information so that it would be relevant, attractive and clear to the customer. SEB had an idea how this offer should be presented but no idea how it would be received.

Customers have a hard time understanding the language and logic often used when banks are presenting their services. The users often discard offers as "not relevant".

IDENTIFIED USER'S NEED

SEB was uncertain how to design, introduce and explain an offer that would benefit both them and their customers.

COMPANY'S NEED

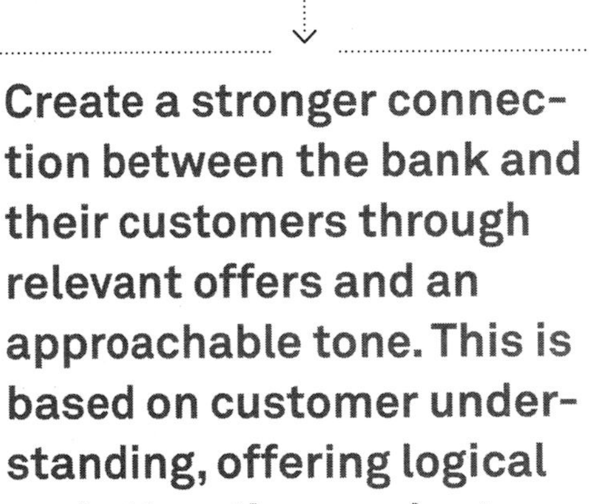

Create a stronger connection between the bank and their customers through relevant offers and an approachable tone. This is based on customer understanding, offering logical and attractive products.

SERVICE VISION

ERIK WIDMARK EXPLAINS

TRANSFORMATORS' PROCESS

The Swedish bank SEB had more than 350,000 customers with individual contracts that were both time consuming and expensive to handle. These customers had throughout the years added applications like telephone banking, internet banking and MasterCard to their bank services. All these different services had individual agreements and contracts. For SEB this meant that a lot of resources were spent on administration rather than on making the services better for the customers.

In an effort to rationalise this, SEB wanted to bundle all the most common services into one manageable package. So instead of handling all the individual agreements SEB would only have to manage one contract per customer. For the customers this wouldn't mean any change except that they would get a slightly lower yearly fee. It was truly a win-win situation. In charge of launching this deal was the Department for Retail Business Development (DRBD).

After discussions with the legal department, it was decided that in order to launch the offer SEB needed the consent of each and every one of the concerned customers. The solution that saved most cost and time seemed to be to promote the package on the internet banking page when the customer logged in.

DRBD had developed this promotion, and together with the IT department they designed an internet-based offer. The name of the offer was "Enkla Vardagen" (Everyday Simplicity). The offer had three purposes; to inform about the changes, to get the customer's consent to bundle their individual agreements and to offer them a credit card free of charge. SEB's ambitious goal was to connect 80% of their 350,000 strong target group to the "Enkla Vardagen" offer. SEB also wanted to acquire as many new MasterCard users as possible.

DRBD felt that they had developed an offer that from a banking perspective was very attractive, but had little knowledge if this offer would be desirable and relevant from a customer point of view. Transformator was appointed to try out and modify the offer based on customer insights.

The method

In this case Transformator decided to employ a method called "action research". This is an iterative approach divided into four stages:

- **PLAN:** Develop a theory of how to solve certain problems. This can, for instance, be based on previous research or observations of customer behaviour.
- **DESIGN:** Give shape to the service offer based on your theories and knowledge from the previous planning stage.
- **EXPLORE:** Try your service on real customers in the right environment. Here you collect insights both by observing the customers interacting with the service and by interviewing them about their experience using the service.
- **REFLECT:** To process all the research data and transform them into manageable insights. You map the customers' journey through the service and highlight problems as well as things that work well. After reflecting, you continue on to the planning phase.

The whole purpose of action research is to be concrete. By exposing customers to possible designs (even if they are really rough mock ups) you are giving them something to relate to. By observing how they act as well as interviewing them while interacting with your design you can get valuable information on not only how people are reacting but also why. These insights will form the foundation of your next, improved design. Action research is a method where the users are highly involved in the process by giving their immediate feedback. So instead of putting all your effort into making one final design you gradually improve and develop your concept through a dialogue with the end user.

In the case of SEB, Transformator decided to do four action research loops in order to try out and perfect their offer.

Action research loop 1

DESIGN

Since SEB had already planned the content of their web-based offer, Transformator started by putting it together into a simple mock-up. By using a PDF Transformator assembled the material into a simple clickable document that would work as a web page. To present the offer in an environment as close to reality as possible, screen shots of the log-in page for the internet bank were taken and this, together with banners promoting the offer were mounted into the PDF using Photoshop. The offer was pretty much text based with four stages where the customer had to read and fill in information in order to sign up for "Enkla Vardagen".

EXPLORE

To test the offer on real customers, Transformator went out to various bank offices and set up the computer with the PDF mock up. By asking people entering and exiting the bank to take part in a short survey on

a new bank offer, Transformator managed to collect a great number of interviews and observations in a short space of time. When interacting with the users it was important not to give them too much information about the project when we wanted their uninfluenced opinions about the offer. Transformator only gave them a short background to what they saw, for instance "You've logged into your internet bank, and you get to this page (the page with the banner showing the offer). Tell me what you would do", or when showing the page with the offer asking "what is this page about?"

REFLECT

The initial insights were very valuable. Hardly anyone saw, let alone clicked on the banner. This, people told us, was because they had a purpose when logging into the internet bank, usually to pay bills and certainly not to check out the bank's offers on display. Furthermore, the banner was perceived as public information and not specifically aimed at them. When Transformator guided the customers into the "Enkla Vardagen" page there was great confusion on what was being offered. Because "Enkla Vardagen" was really two offers in one and presented in the bank's terms, the customers had a hard time figuring out what this offer actually meant. Most people thought it was an offer for getting a credit card and a sly way of tricking them into getting a credit card they didn't want. Others thought it was aimed at new customers suggesting SEB's basic bank services in a package. Even if the "Enkla Vardagen" offer wouldn't mean any changes for the customer (except a lower yearly fee) people thought that the name suggested it was something new. Some thought that the interface of the internet bank would change and that they would have to relearn how to pay bills, etc. Since the offer was

conceived as ambiguous, people felt that there was something suspicious about it and that SEB was trying to trick them into something that would only benefit the bank. Transformator's test showed that less than 5% of the bank customers would sign up for "Enkla Vardagen" as it was designed. The test also showed certain elements on the page that were used by the customers to make sense of the offer. For instance, instead of reading all the text, a lot of the customers relied on a chart summarising the services, in order to make sense of the offer.

Action research loop 2–4

PLAN

The action research insights showed that the information had to be very straightforward using the language of the bank customers in order to reach out to them. Most people didn't have the energy to read through all the text, especially when they didn't know what the offer was about in the first place. It was also apparent that the multiple offers had to be separated so that it was clear what was being presented. In loop 2, 3 and 4 we took the insights from the previous stage and converted them into hands-on design solutions.

DESIGN

Transformator redesigned, according to customer feedback, the offer step by step in loop 2, 3 and 4 and created similar clickable PDFs. Based on the language the test participants used to verbalise what they were doing and thinking when interacting with the mock-ups, Transformator gave the new offers a more direct and clear vocabulary. It was also

apparent that the customers needed some kind of simple guidance and overview of what was being offered and what was expected from them. The design was therefore visually divided into two columns: one if you just wanted to sign up for "Enkla Vardagen" and one if you also wanted to add the MasterCard for free. The customer was asked on the page to choose one of the two offers. Simple headlines were put in to sum up the page so that the user could understand the offer without reading all the text. The texts were shortened and, where possible, "hidden" behind "read more" links. The chart was emphasised to sum up and give a visual overview of the offer.

EXPLORE

When tested Transformator realised that once clicking past the banner (which still wasn't noticed by most of the users), the more straightforward design and language gradually made the customers understand what the offer was all about. The clearer the message of the mutual benefit of changing to "Enkla Vardagen" the more positive the customers became. And by stressing that the credit card was an option free of charge the opinion went from being suspicious to feeling privileged. When the customers understood the mutual benefit in changing to "Enkla Vardagen" they started to wonder why they had to be active in this process. It was seen as the bank's duty to automatically give their customers the best offer possible. No one felt that they had to give their consent on lowering their bank costs.

REFLECT

The further the research went on, the more obvious it became that converting all the individual agreements into one package and thus lowering the prices was seen as a non-issue for the customers. If the customer actively had to be involved in the process of change, it was seen as an inconvenience since the cost reduction compared to the effort was so low. If the bank, on the other hand, automatically gave the customers a reduced price on their bank services it was perceived as something very positive.

THE SOLUTION

The solution was to follow the logic of the customers and simply skip the whole cumbersome process of consenting to the changes on the internet and, instead, automatically change the contracts and lower the costs of the services. Transformator drafted a letter based on the insights from the customer interactions. The letter that was sent out to all the affected customers informing them of the background to the change, the reason for the price reduction and what this would mean to the customer. In the letter the option of getting a MasterCard for free was gently presented so that it wasn't perceived as something that was pushed too heavily.

The result: SEB had a goal of signing up 80% of their customers to the "Enkla Vardagen" package. By the help of service design methods, Transformator and SEB managed to turn an offer that initially was regarded as suspicious and ambiguous into something perceived as a mutually beneficial and celebrated deal. The sign-up turnout for "Everyday Simplicity" was 100% and MasterCard sales by far exceeded the campaign targets that were set.

Final statement

In order to create relevant and profitable services, you have to truly understand the user's situation, need, mindset and driving forces. By involving and interacting with the customer as part of your business development process you not only ensure that the end result has customer relevance, you will also learn a great deal about your own business by looking at it from a customer perspective.

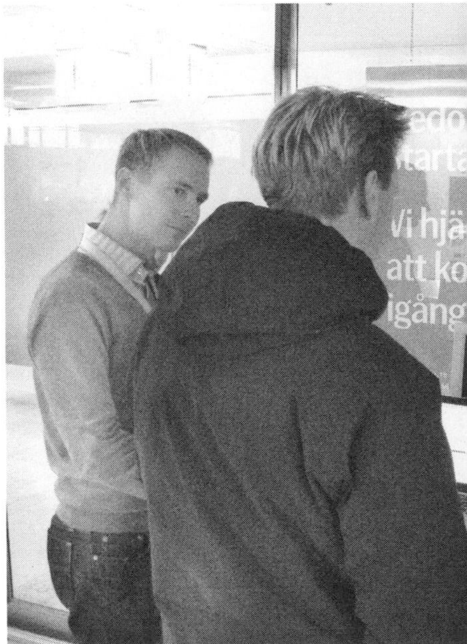

Interaction with customers

1

2

3

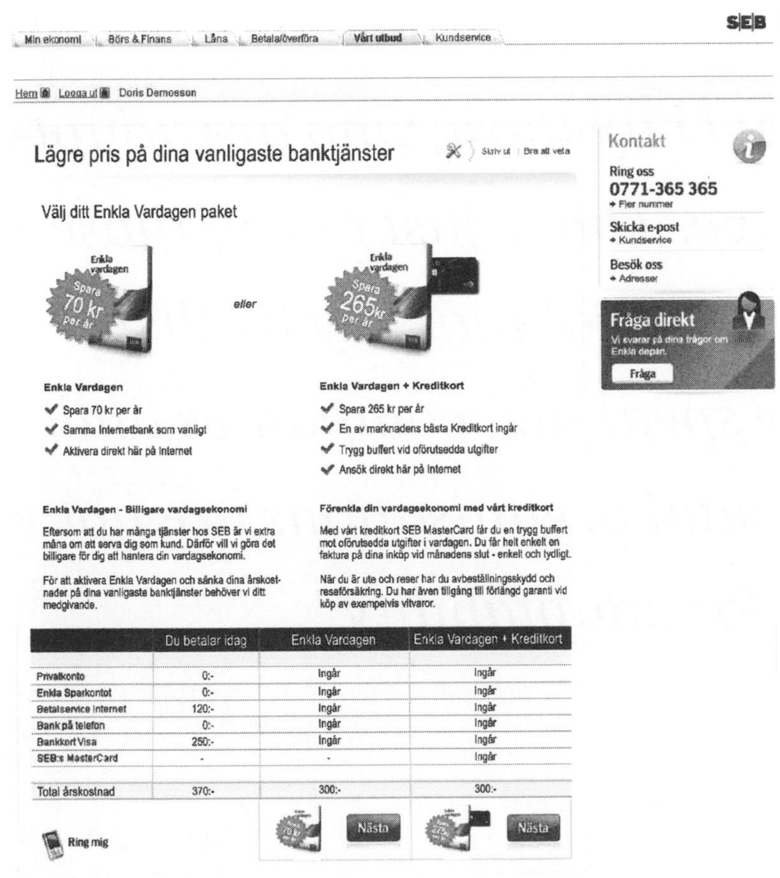

	Du betalar idag	Enkla Vardagen	Enkla Vardagen + Kreditkort
Privatkonto	0:-	Ingår	Ingår
Enkla Sparkontot	0:-	Ingår	Ingår
Betalservice Internet	120:-	Ingår	Ingår
Bank på telefon	0:-	Ingår	Ingår
Bankkort Visa	250:-	Ingår	Ingår
SEB:s MasterCard	-	-	Ingår
Total årskostnad	370:-	300:-	300:-

1 Interaction with customers

2 This is where the magic happens.

3 Simplified offer based on customer insights

Arne says: *Only those who are adaptable survive. That's just one of those inconvenient evolutionary truths! Generally speaking, companies and governmental organisations are not designed for adaptability.*

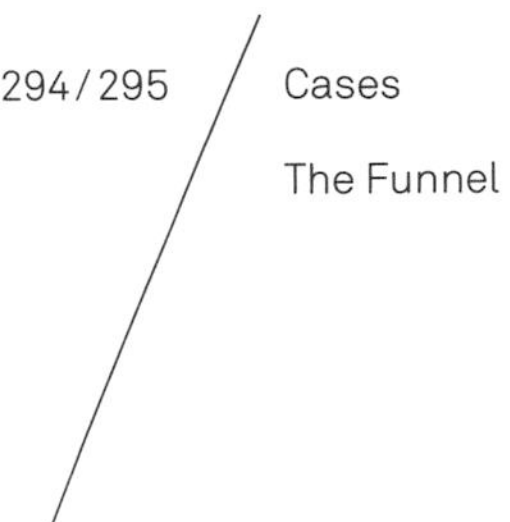

Jamin says: *Organisations often know when there is a problem with their service. But often the problem is unclear or taken for granted. One of the roles of service designers is to ensure that the stated problem is the best problem to design for.*

Erik says: *When trying to understand the end users, you really have to have an open mind and ask open-ended questions. You can't assume that you know what is essential to them. What seems important from a service company's point of view is not necessarily important to the end user.*

Beatriz says: *As this is a service designed for people by people, the identification of interests, desires and worries of the people involved marked the beginning of the experience design.*

Sarah says: *Considering how to reach out to all these people was tough but by using research (systems maps/personas/shadowing) it was possible to create a brand ethos that would work across all touchpoints.*

Deep Service Design Thinking

DEEP SERVICE DESIGN THINKING

The three following texts provide a particularly detailed description of selected service design aspects. The first text examines motivation as a precondition for successful service design thinking, while the second one summarizes recent research efforts in the field of service design. In conclusion, a rather philosophical perspective sets service design in a broader perspective.

FERGUS BISSET, UNITED KINGDOM
Integrating service design thinking and motivational psychology

JOHAN BLOMKVIST, STEFAN HOLMLID, FABIAN SEGELSTRÖM, SWEDEN
Service design research: yesterday, today and tomorrow

RENATO TRONCON, ITALY
Service design and biophilia

INTEGRATING SERVICE DESIGN THINKING AND MOTIVATIONAL PSYCHOLOGY

FERGUS BISSET

Following a comprehensive review of motivational psychology literature, this short chapter introduces the concept of motivation and considers its significance to service design thinkers as they approach complex human behavioural, social and ecological design problems. It concludes by suggesting how motivation might be helpfully incorporated with established service design journey mapping and customer journey visualisation tools to support service design thinkers as they begin to address some of society's most pertinent issues.

What is motivation?

Motivation has been described as the "energisation and direction of human behaviour" (Reeve, 2005) and is thus a fundamental concept for designers seeking to understand, regulate and support human behaviour. So much so, that motivation has been debated and discussed since time immemorial. From Confucian and Sanskrit philosophy in the East to the dialogues of the Greek political philosophers and writings of Christian biblical scholars in the West: theories of motivation attempt to understand the symbiotic relationship of the individual and their environment and more clearly articulate the governing principles of this relationship. The existential and philosophical questions that a study of motivation covers have throughout history been some of the most central questions to "energise and direct" humanity's beliefs, identity and creativity. These legacies define not only the social structures of the societies

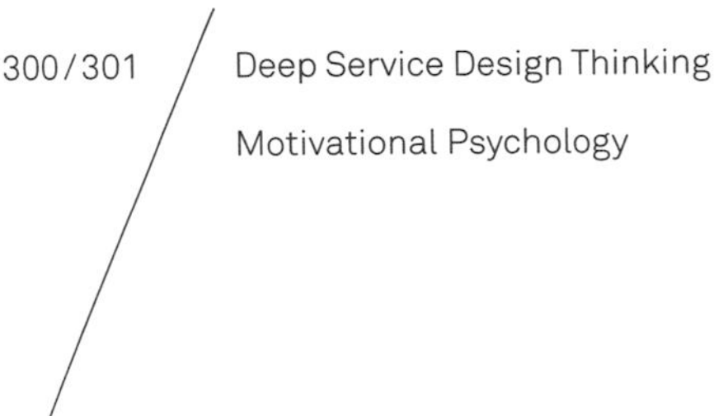

in which we live but also the political, educational and creative principles that continue to influence, govern and sustain the world around us today.

Despite these diverse social, political and cultural histories, in the developed world, we now live in a society where increasing individual autonomy and self-determination play more prominent roles in defining our individual philosophic, economic and social viewpoints. Case in point might be the manner in which new social-media technologies and the self-determination they facilitate, have supported much of the evolution of service design as an emerging field. The collaborative part-

Theories of motivation attempt to understand the symbiotic relationship of the individual and their environment and more clearly articulate the governing principles of this relationship.

nerships of service design thinkers, the like of which contributed to the development of this publication in your hands today, are now trascending institutional and national boundaries and in doing so offer the potential for new sources of inspiration and collaboration. That said, and despite the undoubted potential of such collaboration, there is little escaping the fact that our individual explanations and conceptualisations of motivation often dig deeper into our own psyche and that of the societies in which we live and work than very often we as designers are prepared, or even entitled, to acknowledge. If design thinking and service design hold the key to solving larger more complex social problems as Burns, Cottam, Vanstone, & Winhall (2006), Brown (2009), Løvlie (2009) and others have recently claimed, do we need to start to become more capable and comfortable at asking tough questions about the fundamental motives behind our own design interventions? If we endeavour to change or influence human behaviour, do we need to more clearly conceptualise, visualise and question our own motivations for doing so as well as the motives of the stakeholders with whom and for whom we are designing?

Visualising and codifying motivation in conjunction with existing and established service design tools, methods and processes gives us "service design thinkers" the opportunity to better understand, and more sustainably "energise and direct" human behaviour.

We are, as it happens, living in a golden age of motivation research (Reeve, 2005). This chapter seeks to give examples of how the modern day science of motivational psychology and its literature can support our "service design thinking". It will raise the view that visualising and codifying motivation in conjunction with existing and established service design tools, methods and processes gives us "service design thinkers" the opportunity to better understand, and more sustainably "energise and direct" human behaviour. It is proposed that this will help service design thinkers develop and evolve ever more innovative, democratic and empowering solutions to ever more "complex" behavioural, social and ecological problems.

Service design as a philosophy to support self-determination

White (1959) was one of the first to clearly define a distinction between motivation residing within humans and motivation that resides without. This notion of "intrinsic and extrinsic motivation" and the humanistic, organismic worldview that it underpins has since been further developed by, amongst others, Deci and Ryan (1985, 2004). This is perhaps best

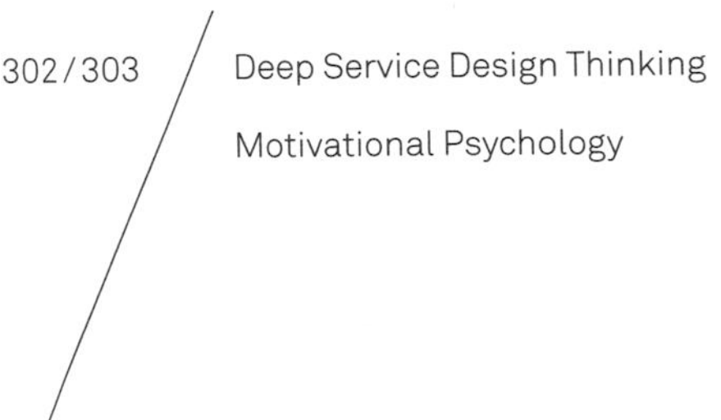

explained as White (1959) does with reference to the playful and curious behaviour of young children, which underpins their growth and development:

An organismic worldview posits that individuals are naturally predetermined (intrinsically motivated) to, over time, seek new sensory experiences, develop and refine skills and seek increased personal challenges as part of their acquisition of an ever broader comprehension of our world around us.

Alternatively, it can also be seen in observation of "expert performers" Ericsson (1998), Csikszentmihalyi (1998). Individuals and professionals continue to develop by seeking renewed challenge, refinement and understanding of their capabilities and interaction with the world around them. This can sometimes occur quite broadly or, alternatively, by the individual focussing on their performance within a narrow field, skill or specialism. Indeed, the notion of design for play (Kafai, 1995), designing for "flow" (Csikszentmihalyi, 1998) or using expert role models to guide decision making (Klein, 1999) are not new conceptualisations within the creative domains of industrial design, interaction design and ergonomics. However, these previous efforts have tended to conceptualise motivation deterministically rather than as a generative tool to guide further innovation. Deci and Ryan (1985) have argued over the past 25 years that an individual's human organismic growth, their motivation, is symptomatic of an individual seeking to expand their personal sense of autonomy, social relatedness and competence. Indeed, in assuming an organnismic perspective as a service design thinker, it becomes possible to see motivation as a dynamic and malleable entity. One way of conceptualising the role of a designer in this situation is by comparison with a sports coach or film director, working with the athlete or actor, supporting and

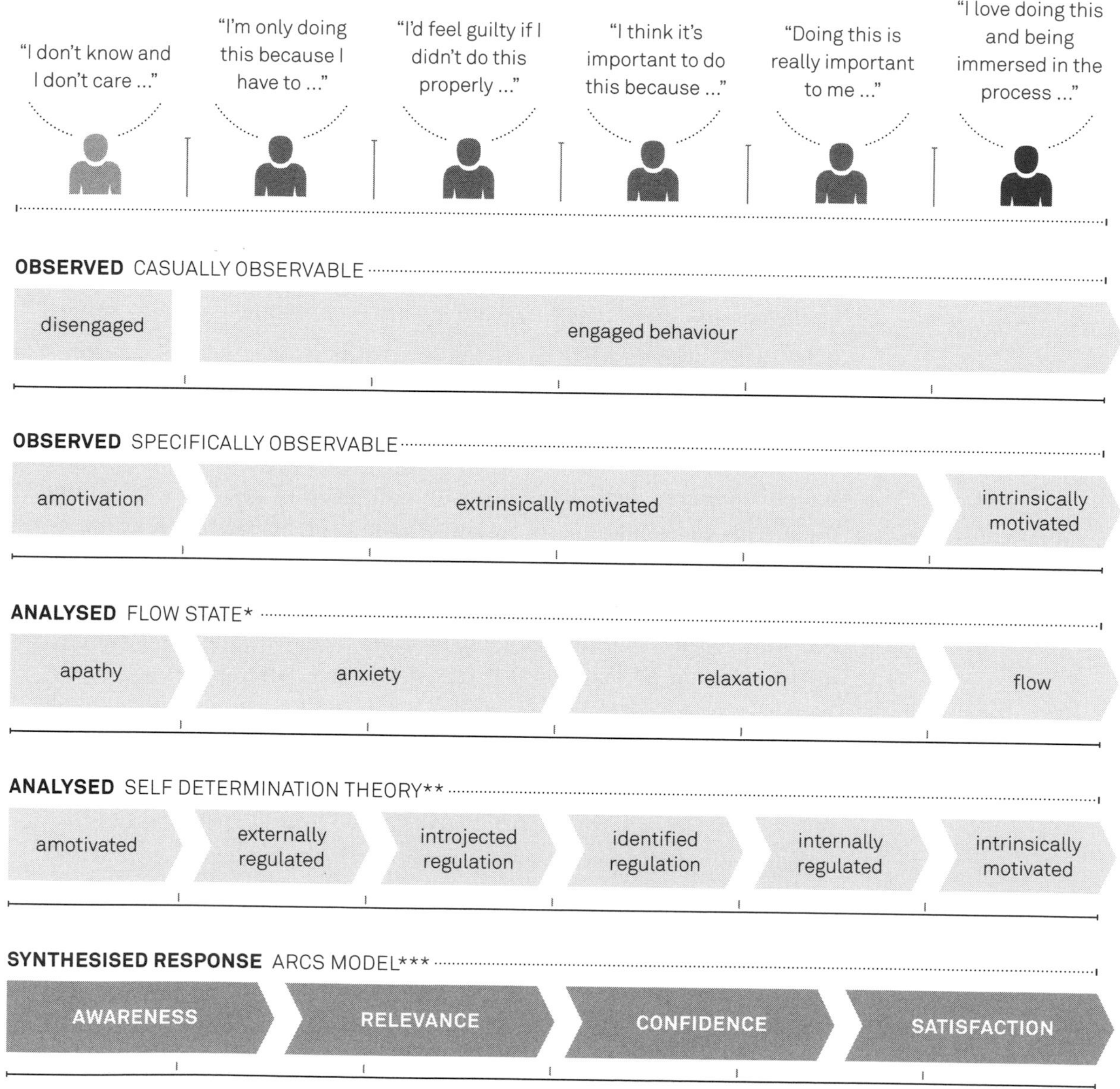
"I don't know and I don't care ..."
"I'm only doing this because I have to ..."
"I'd feel guilty if I didn't do this properly ..."
"I think it's important to do this because ..."
"Doing this is really important to me ..."
"I love doing this and being immersed in the process ..."
OBSERVED CASUALLY OBSERVABLE
disengaged
engaged behaviour
OBSERVED SPECIFICALLY OBSERVABLE
amotivation
extrinsically motivated
intrinsically motivated
ANALYSED FLOW STATE*
apathy
anxiety
relaxation
flow
ANALYSED SELF DETERMINATION THEORY**
amotivated
externally regulated
introjected regulation
identified regulation
internally regulated
intrinsically motivated
SYNTHESISED RESPONSE ARCS MODEL***
AWARENESS
RELEVANCE
CONFIDENCE
SATISFACTION

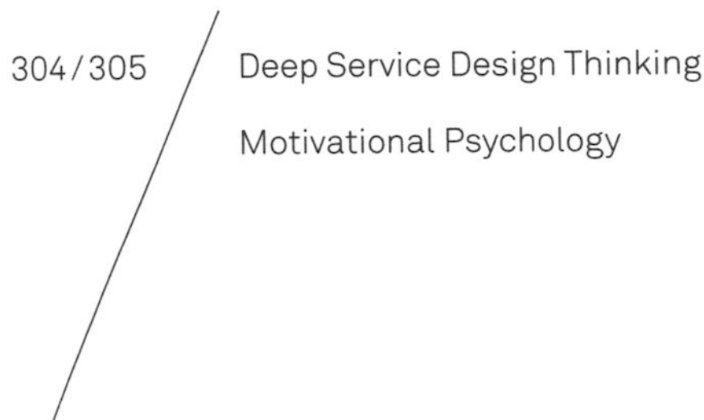

guiding him towards reaching your shared performance goals, or in less ambitious cases, simply ensuring that they do not produce a low-quality performance.

← FRAMEWORK OF MOTIVATED BEHAVIOUR (v0.1)

* Stavou, (2009) from Csikszentmihalyi, (1982)
** Deci and Ryan (2008)
*** Keller (1983)

Integrate motivation with journey mapping and service blueprinting

As is reflected throughout this volume, service design thinking offers a holistic, human-centred and temporal mindset – in both the physical and spiritual sense. For this reason it wouldn't be a drastic change for many service designers to reconsider their work and the value it generates from a motivational perspective. This is particularly true in the case of those already passionate about developing a deep understanding of users and empowering them in the creative process. Recent attempts to further develop tools for dynamic journey mapping and service evaluation such as MyServiceFellow (Stickdorn, 2009), in addition to recent work from Polaine (2009), represent efforts to highlight user mood or temporal engagement as signifiers of motivated or amotivated behaviour with and within product and service development. This is something that has also been considered in the motivational literature by Carver & Scheier (1998), amongst others. All this work highlighting the complexities involved in trying to visualise, codify and anticipate how or when motivating or demotivating events within a service encounter might occur and how they might impact on the overall user-service experience.

An organismic motivational perspective, with the literature and empirical studies that support it, gives this "engagement mapping" a structure – mapping an individual's dynamic motivational state from amotivated to intrinsically motivated along a six-stage continuum (Deci and Ryan's Self Determination Theory, 2004). This offers service designers a chance to incorporate a broad conceptualisation of motivation in parallel to existing customer journey visualisation techniques as a subtle but powerful addition to their established service design toolkits. Such a visualisation can be used deterministically, or more in keeping with the spirit exemplified in this publication it can be used as a tool to help designers see the services they are designing from a user's motivational perspective and indeed to help empower users in a generative approach to improving, refining and sustaining their service experiences.

It is the contention of this chapter that by becoming accomplished in conceptualising and visualising human motivation and seeing all human behaviour as "organismic" in its growth and potential, "service design thinkers" will be adopting an empowered view of the contexts within which they are working. In turn, it is hoped that this might effectively equip all of us, and those around us, with the motivational resilience to tackle large-scale "complex" problems and transform our world for the better.

Motivational Design Personas with Internally Regulated and Empowered States v0.1 →

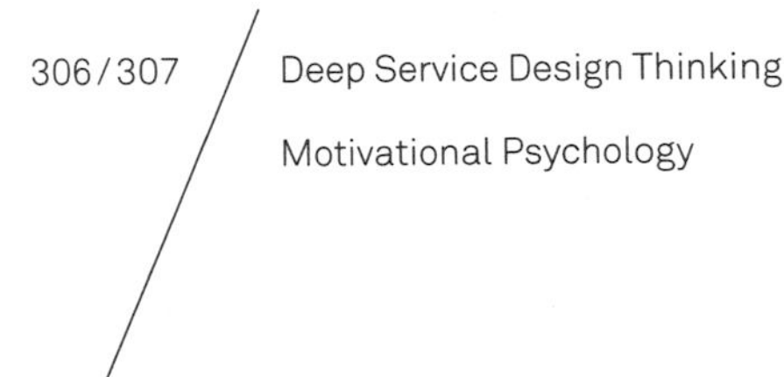

WHY?

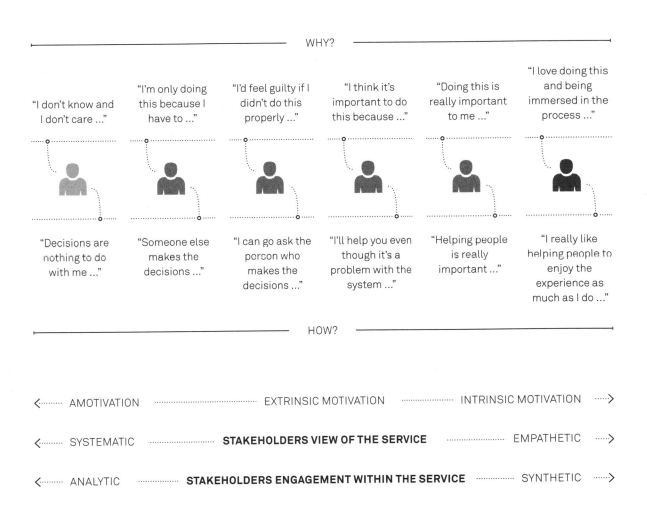

"I don't know and I don't care ..."

"I'm only doing this because I have to ..."

"I'd feel guilty if I didn't do this properly ..."

"I think it's important to do this because ..."

"Doing this is really important to me ..."

"I love doing this and being immersed in the process ..."

"Decisions are nothing to do with me ..."

"Someone else makes the decisions ..."

"I can go ask the person who makes the decisions ..."

"I'll help you even though it's a problem with the system ..."

"Helping people is really important ..."

"I really like helping people to enjoy the experience as much as I do ..."

HOW?

AMOTIVATION ... EXTRINSIC MOTIVATION ... INTRINSIC MOTIVATION

SYSTEMATIC ... **STAKEHOLDERS VIEW OF THE SERVICE** ... EMPATHETIC

ANALYTIC ... **STAKEHOLDERS ENGAGEMENT WITHIN THE SERVICE** ... SYNTHETIC

SERVICE DESIGN RESEARCH: YESTERDAY, TODAY AND TOMORROW

JOHAN BLOMKVIST
STEFAN HOLMLID
FABIAN SEGELSTRÖM

According to the service design myth, the field was born when live|work was founded in 2001. However, research on service design had been done since the early 1990s. A fairly small number of researchers conducted research in the field for about fifteen years until the subject gained widespread attention. The newfound traction has lead to a surge of publications on service design. This chapter reflects on the evolution of service design research by dividing the research overview into two parts: one for the early research focused on establishing service design and one for new research focused on expanding the knowledge of service design.

Early research

Much early research on service design focused on connecting the field to other design disciplines and arguing for service design in its own right. The first service design researchers were all trained in other disciplines and moved into service design gradually. Their various backgrounds have been reflected in the issues they performed researched on. One consequence has been that more research was done in the intersection of interaction design and service design than between product design and service design, as a large part of the early researchers had a background in interaction design.

Even though the early researchers were highlighting service design and differentiating service design from other fields (Manzini, 1993; Erlhoff, Mager, & Manzini, 1997; Mager, 2004; Maffei, Mager & Sangiorgi, 2005), it was supported by research in other fields. As in all research,

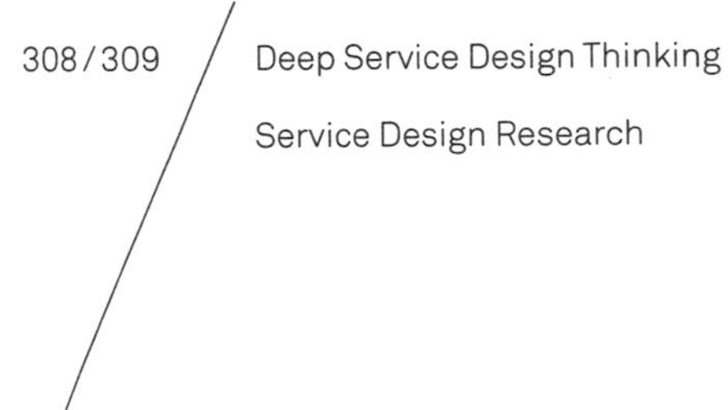

there is a need to be cumulative and e.g. blueprinting, servicescapes and personas were collected from other research fields (Shostack, 1984; Shostack, 1982; Bitner, 1992; Cooper, Reimann & Dubberly, 1999). Evenson (2005) took User Experience as the starting point for her work, and Holmlid (2007) grounded his framework in design theory. The two do/think tanks RED and Demos contributed to applied research of

Much early research on service design focused on connecting the field to other design disciplines and arguing for service design in its own right. The first service design researchers were all trained in other disciplines and moved into service design gradually.

methods and strategies for participation (Vanstone & Winhall, 2006; Burns & Winhall, 2006; Burns et al, 2006; Parker & Heapy, 2006). Additionally, a number of publications were produced by Italian researchers (as summarised by Pacenti & Sangiorgi, 2010). Among the more influential were Sangiorgi who grounded her work in Activity Theory (Sangiorgi, 2004; Sangiorgi & Clark, 2004), Pacenti with a basis in Interaction Design (Pacenti, 1998) and Morelli (2002; 2003) who published on Product-Service Systems.

Current research

In 2008–2009 the direction of academic publications changed. There was a surge of new researchers publishing on service design as well as a change of topics; from justifying service design to research on service design. This section highlights the research that was published in 2008 and 2009.

There seem to be two main approaches to this early research on service design. One is to widen the scope of service design and integrate practices and ideas from non-design fields, such as marketing, leadership and engineering. The other is to challenge and explore the basic assumptions in service design and the methods inherited from other disciplines. The sources are grouped according to trends we identify in current research. We limited the overview to material published in peer-reviewed research forums; this means that books and some conferences are not included here.

The first trend we see is in research in design theory, and it poses fundamental questions, such as explorations of co-creation (Tan & Szebeko, 2009), perspectives on service design (Singleton, 2009; Penin & Tonkinwise, 2009), and a language for service design (Jonas, Chow, & Schaeffer, 2009). It also includes writings on what service design can learn from other related disciplines, such as the various design disciplines focusing on the design of technology interfaces; examples include human-computer interaction (van Dijk, 2008) and participatory design (Holmlid, 2009). Sangiorgi (2009) discusses the rigour and direction of service design research; she critiques what she sees as a focus on methodologies rather than on the development of foundational theoretical frameworks. At IASDR in 2009 a special session titled "Adopting Rigour in Service Design Research" was held, in which the contributing authors reflected on various aspects of scientific research methods (Sangiorgi & Holmlid, 2009).

Among the efforts to ground research in service design with knowledge from related fields, management stands out.

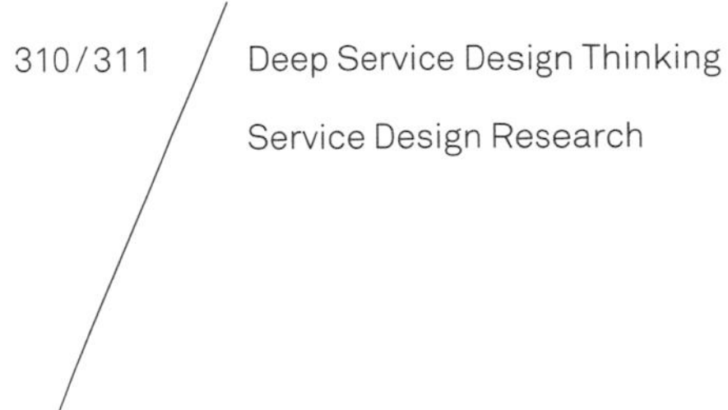

Among the efforts to ground research in service design with knowledge from related fields, management stands out. For the sake of simplicity various disciplines interested in services from economy perspectives such as Service Management, Service Marketing, Service Operations and Service Leadership are presented together under one heading here. Kimbell (2009) started her analysis of what service designers do in the writings of the management literature that has been built throughout the last thirty years. The First Nordic SDC (now known as ServDes)

Another perspective in research is the systemic perspective, also including an engineering aspect.

devoted a session to this topic; Gloppen (2009) explored how organisational leaders can be informed by design in managing services and Han (2009) turned her attention to how service designers manage their relationships to the stakeholders involved in the design process. Wetter Edman (2009) reflected on overlaps and differences between Service-Dominant Logic (SDL) and Design Thinking. The relationship between SDL and service design has also been explored by Cautela, Rizzo & Zurlo (2009) at IASDR 2009. Likewise at IASDR, Junginger & Sangiorgi (2009) reported a study on how organisational change can be aided by service design, and Candi & Saemundsson (2008) explores the use of design in service innovation. Studies on the relationship between management and design, in more general terms, can be found at European Academy of Design and Design Management Institute's conferences (de Borba & Remus, 2009; Gong, Suteu, & Shen, 2009).

Another perspective in research is the systemic perspective, also including an engineering aspect. One of the main concepts here is the idea of a Product-Service System, or PSS. In more specific cases this is referred to as functional sales, after-market services, etc. It has been suggested that designers contribute to the engineering of product-service systems through a shift in perspective as well as integrators (Morelli, 2009; Jung, Nam & Yu, 2009; Jung, Nam, 2008). Kim et al (2009) have presented techniques of representing value in ontological models of product-service

One of the main currents in present research can be characterised as research about design techniques, such as tools and processes.

systems. Akiyama, Shimomura & Arai (2009) developed a design engineering framework for resolution of design conflicts between product and service components of a PSS. Tollestrup (2009) showed how methods for concept development fit into a larger portfolio of design methods. Pinhanez (2009) views service systems as customer intensive and has produced an approach to service design based on this assumption. Popovic, Kraal & Kirk (2009) focused their attention on detailed activities of multiple actors in a service system.

One of the main currents in present research can be characterised as research about design techniques, such as tools and processes. Since service design is such a young field, many of the basic tools have been inherited from other disciplines, and research that explicitly concerns the design of services has been sparse and heterogeneous. Recent topics include; the development of new tools that meet the specific demands and challenges associated with designing for services (Clatworthy, 2009; Kaario et al, 2009), evaluations of and improvements to existing tools (e.g. blueprinting, see Wreiner et al, 2009; Lee & Forlizzi, 2009; Sparagen & Chan, 2008), and research relating to the bigger trend of co-creation

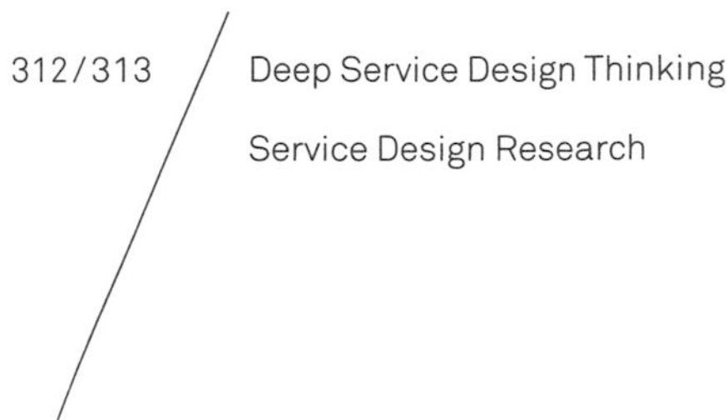

(Raijmakers et al, 2009; Kronqvist & Korhonen, 2009; Blomkvist & Holmlid, 2009). Research has also been done to further the understanding of visualisations in service design. Segelström has written about where and how in the process visualisations are made (Segelström & Holmlid, 2009) and the motivation for using visualisations (Segelström, 2009),

Although there are plenty of published case studies in service design, there is a lack of case studies in which the results have been scrutinised academically.

whereas Diana, Pacenti, & Tassi (2009) have created a way to categorise visualisations and understand the potential of certain techniques for service design. Another focus here has been the appropriations of ethnographic methods to service design (Raijmakers et al, 2009; Segelström, Raijmakers, & Holmlid, 2009; March & Raijmakers, 2008).

The final trend we see is to publish case studies. Although there are plenty of published case studies in service design, there is a lack of case studies in which the results have been scrutinised academically. The first larger attempt on a case study was the "Designing for Services" project (Kimbell, 2009; see also the project report by Kimbell & Siedel, 2008), although it was performed in a condensed way. During the second half of 2009 a few case studies were published with a longer perspective; Carr et al (2009) reported on a study in healthcare together with the NHS. Prendiville (2009) worked with a borough in London to improve stakeholder satisfaction with services of the local government. Akama (2009) studied the problems a design team consisting of visual and interaction designers had in adapting a service design approach to a project, and the negotiations which had to be made with the client.

There is also a small sub-community focusing on tourism and service design which has published a few cases (Stickdorn, 2009; Miettinen, 2009).

Challenges and looking ahead

One of the major challenges for service design as a research field is to establish its structure; to find and develop theories and methods which make research criticisable. Service design needs to find ways of structuring and presenting knowledge in a way that allows designers to utilise knowledge and researchers to cumulatively continue to develop knowledge. Furthermore, structures are needed to ensure that early-stage researchers are trained in fundamentals across the base disciplines. And as all fields of design research to develop strategies to perform research about design, research in design as well as research through design (Frayling, 1993).

The current focus of service design research seems to be changing from the focus in early research. Current research seems to focus less on distinguishing service design from other disciplines and more on the integration of perspectives. There seem to be two main approaches. One is to widen the scope of service design and integrate practices and ideas from non-design fields, such as marketing, leadership and engineering. The other is to challenge and explore the basic assumptions in service design and the methods inherited from other (design) disciplines and thus deepen the knowledge in and about service design.

We believe that we will see more of the widening type of studies than deepening in the upcoming years, but that this will change when the first generation of students who have been trained in service design throughout their education enter academia as PhD students. Examples of disciplines we think can contribute to the widening of service design

research are Cognitive Science, Service Science, Anthropology and Sociology. The depth of the knowledge in and about service design can be extended by methodologically more elaborate (case) studies and continued reflections on the values we inherit from other disciplines. Whether this evolution of service design research develops into competing schools of thought or into an interdisciplinary or transdisciplinary field, is still an open question. One thing is certain: the way provisions are set

Whether this evolution of service design research develops into competing schools of thought or into an interdisciplinary or transdisciplinary field, is still an open question.

up for doing service design research for early-stage researchers will implicitly define this trajectory. Requiring an interdisciplinary foundation and methodological rigour are key practices for universities in setting this trajectory. And a factor not to be underestimated; allowing researchers to study, experiment with and participate in service design projects and openly presenting the knowledge developed, is crucial to develop relevant knowledge. We can all contribute to making this happen, and open the space for emerging service design researchers to formulate questions, and construct knowledge we could not today imagine possible to formulate.

SERVICE DESIGN AND BIOPHILIA

RENATO TRONCON

Design: only things?

Books and treatises on design – even the most brilliant – often base their discussions on the idea that design means the production of objects. Chairs, lamps, walls, furniture, clothing or – at best – images: this is the concept of design accepted by professionals, researchers, the public and the publishing industry. Ask them in turn (indeed, ask yourself) and you will see that, even though the thought is a gross oversimplification, instinctively we revert to the idea that design means essentially the production of "things". But the same indistinct "buzz" of a thousand and one different objects that design introduces into daily life today requires even the most inattentive observer to consider that there are other issues in design besides the mere things in themselves – such as psychologies, the circumstances of life and income, geography, lifestyles, and so on. What then is the reason for this illusion? The fixation on the physicality of the object itself has very deep roots in our modern way of thinking about things. That goes back to the 1700s and 1800s, to the engineering sciences and even biology, which regarded living organisms as "shapes with a purpose". In these sciences no distinction was made between artefacts and machines, which were truly self-propelled contraptions consisting of separate parts that communicated with each other without ever losing their individuality. With such a mechanical science we could make excavators that tore down mountains and diverted rivers, carrying out their wonderful and impressive tasks in a completely autonomous manner.

The self-sufficiency of machines

In order to understand this point which, in my opinion, the digital era alone cannot change, no sophisticated studies are necessary: it is simply enough to look at and observe the various kinds of machinery around us. And if we want to know more, we can simply read the correspondence that the great pioneer of the machine age, the Scotsman

> Professionals, researchers, the public and the publishing industry: Ask them (indeed, ask yourself) and you will see that, even though the thought is a gross oversimplification, instinctively we revert to the idea that design means essentially the production of "things".

James Watt, maintained for many years. In his correspondence he documented the mechanical logic behind his most ingenious efforts to construct his various devices – in particular his most famous creation, the steam engine, documented by Patrick Muirhead via long extracts from his letters. We can see a similar delight in mechanisation in that now forgotten but very fine epistemological tract on the unlimited nature of the industrial era written in 1830 by Humphry Davy, praising a "chemical philosophy" that can alleviate man's labours, covering man's body "with the products of different chemical and mechanical arts", arranging them "in forms of beauty and variety". Thus we can see the identification of the productions of the human mind with the performance of a machine: an identity that still fuels our enthusiasm for the idea that science discovers with the aim of knowing and therefore applying, and not vice versa (a point that was made elegantly in 1986 by Edward Wilson, the biologist and pioneer of the field of biophilia).

Artefacts are strategies

In this world, the most prominent casualty is the idea that, while an artefact is a mechanism, it is also a "strategy" for the concrete and actual governing of the many forces that confront each other in a particular determined field. I open and close a window, I do this or that, I construct it in a certain way (this is the mechanism) but I also de facto use it to regulate the temperature, create a climatic and acoustic microcosm, exchange a multiplicity of other factors between an outside and an inside, and thus in fact create two spaces of the world that – incidentally – properly

The idea that an artefact (or a series of artefacts) should perform a service action in effect shatters, conceptually and methodologically, the conventional notion that centres it on its physical characteristics and its engineering aspects.

exist only after the creation of the window itself, not before (and this is the "governing" of forces). To understand this frame however we require new concepts: essentially a model of the circumstance that the world is not made of atoms but rather of molecules – with wholly new traits – not just of simple but of complex parts, not of singularities but of wholes, and with ourselves "inside" all this, not "outside". If designers were to read theoretical biology, social history and the philosophy of technology – see, for example, Stiegler – they would be greatly helped in their own work, and the universities too would offer a better education. Designers could above all benefit from a more mature aesthetic, an aesthetic that however would – in order to understand it – have to go beyond Kant and his dubious linkage of artistic artefacts with the imagination, or his conviction that the condition of the beautiful is the uselessness of its objects and the utilitarian's disinterest in them. This is an idea the legacy of which has confined aesthetic character to the insides of symphony halls, to galleries of paintings, to books of poetry, and has left designers and planners largely at the mercy of the utilitarianisms of functionalism.

A new aesthetic for design

An aesthetic that differs from this might be constructed on other foundations, and a particularly intriguing one is that of "service design". The idea that an artefact (or a series of artefacts) should perform a service action in effect shatters, conceptually and methodologically, the conventional notion that centres it on its physical characteristics and its engineering aspects. Whatever might be the thing intended for service, and even for "service design" (which is a broader term than it might first appear; it indicates an attitude to design and not simply a field of application), it is certain that simply to suggest the idea that at the forefront of design is a "dedication" or "concern" will shift the attention to its more immaterial and relational components. In "service design", then, the view is not monocular, fixed solely on the object itself, but binocular, seeing the "thing" but also all that this thing "provokes" or "claims" for itself. Closely linked to this "perspective" or "aspect" view, the idea also emerges from "service design" that designing requires investigation, "empathising" – see, for example, Dan Pink – and generally "knowing" the processes in which a certain artefact is to be inserted – and even to know them in their "qualities", and through qualitative means. Although it may seem curious, here too the study curricula and the bibliographies are not forthcoming and do not go beyond general recommendations. If a design course teaches the full range of marketing, from studying trends to project management, or if the arts are taught, why not also, in the spirit of "taking care", give primacy to the "cultural ecologies" such as those mentioned by Gay and Hembrooke or even (better still) those more deeply studied by philosophical anthropology? And why not recognise that so-called "artistic research", when applied, can offer invaluable gifts of knowledge? It is crucial not to teach students only how to make gloves without ever telling them to practice by shaking hands with their neighbours, or carelessly removing their gloves with the indolence of a great theatre actress; or to study interior furnishing without ever visiting the cell of the historically seminal monk and reformer Savonarola (1452–1498) in the Convent of Saint Marco, Florence. Why not study classics by Okakura or Huysmans?

The logic of the vital centres

The design catalogues printed by the publishing houses or universities often document the consequences of similar omissions – so much so that we often end up asking whether, before designing a certain lamp, it might not have been better to try to understand what reading means in general, and what it means to read by artificial light in particular. Or if, before building a famous name hotel in a certain place, it would not have been better to have a real idea of the nature of the activity that goes on there. The planning of aids for the elderly could also thus avoid the development of awkward bionic limbs or Formula One-style helmets for older people with motor or sensory deficits, or the development of the depressing "clinical" or "hygienic" design that holds an entire industry in its grip. The notion of "service design" in this sense requires a consistent application of the idea of the "vital centre" that the great architect and architectural theorist Christopher Alexander has advanced in his seminal writings. Beyond architecture, activities such as reading, shaking hands, removing gloves from our hands upon entering a room, and so on, are examples of these "centres". Service design is also a habit of study of the thousand practices, always different and always the same, that human beings have always engaged in. The field of service design also teaches that a certain "vital sequence" exists along the whole chain of an event, and that it cannot be dissociated from the variety of "media" – artefacts or others – on which it hinges. Such activities are not in fact "pure anthropology" of the sort that would exclude the concrete nature of things, or the actions and plans with which they are "interlaced"

The field of service design teaches that a certain "vital sequence" exists along the chain of an event, and that it cannot be dissociated from the variety of media – artefacts or others – on which it hinges.

but – even if this displeases the majority of academics and old-style aesthetics – their relationship is more like the way in which the aerodynamic performance of a pair of skis is intimately related to their profile and materials. Or it is like the quality of a film that forms a unity with the quality of its photographed subject, or the indefinable "touches" in the acting of a cast (Stanislavski gives a wonderful account of this). The legibility of the directions in an underground rail system or an airport cannot be said to be "excludable" from the relationship with their concrete (and thus quite varied) media.

One might use the analogy that if "being old" was a carpet, it would be woven from the interlacing of emotions, spatial perception, motor diagrams, culture, social positioning, building structures, laws, bureaucratic regulations, skills and ethos: all organically connected in order to aid or, sad to say, prevent an old person remaining for a longer or shorter period of time in their own home.

Loving and supporting life

This last aspect, on closer examination, has surprisingly revolutionary consequences for what should be the content of design in general, and the mission of service design in particular. If what we have said is true, it is difficult for design not to enter the fragile and sometimes unfathomable territory of the "action-patterns" of human existence. However, for the reasons set out above, design is not omnipotent and "service design" even less so. It must instead be "responsible" – that is, responsive – towards everyone and everything, young and old, rich and poor, beautiful and ugly, those blessed or spurned by life: it must do this without embracing invention for invention's sake in pursuit of self-sufficiency and innovation, but must rather marry the knowledge of "responding" to what is beautiful and ugly here and in the world. This type of design is in fact an "active philosophy" dedicated to making space for life. Why should not design – service design – be a love for life? And why should not life, in all its incredible variety, be the key giving us access to design?

This principle of biophilia – the love of life – thus offers us the basis for a new aesthetic of service design.

This type of design is in fact an “active philosophy” dedicated to making space for life.

Why should not design – service design – be a love for life?

Appendix

AUTHORS*

* in alphabetical order

8
22
7
4
11
6
12
1
15
9
2
16
21
23
19
14
18
13
20
17
3
10
5

AUTHORS*

1 Kate Andrews

Kate Andrews is a writer, designer and social communications consultant. She has a BA First Class Honors in Graphic Design, a Merit Award from the International Society of Typographic Designers, and is a Fellow of The Royal Society of Arts. On themes related to design's social impact, Kate has contributed to many design platforms, including Change Observer, Inhabitat.com, Eye Magazine and Design21sdn.com, and has lectured to design students in the UK and in Oslo. Her freelance clients include: Mencap, Visual Editions, The Affluenza Exhibition, Thinkpublic, ColaLife, The New Economics Foundation and Project H Design. She continually supports thomas.matthews and Kingston University as Digital Communications Strategist for their sustainability hub Greengaged, and is a jury member for the project Good 50x70.

Source of motivation

my father, Sir Ken Robinson, Edwin Abbott's Flatland

2 Beatriz Belmonte

Beatriz Belmonte is an information management and communication specialist. Her background includes History of Art, Museology, Information Management and Business Intelligence in different universities of Madrid and Barcelona. She has been involved in the design of e-learning and corporate communication projects, and since 2007 she has run her own site about communication and new technologies. Since 2008 she works at Funky Projects as a web and knowledge researcher looking for new ways to turn information into knowledge to trigger transformation.

Source of motivation

great people, travelling, challenges

3 Ralf Beuker

Ralf Beuker holds a diploma in Business Administration from the University of Paderborn, Germany. Beside his business projects he is a Professor for Design Management and Dean of the Design School at the University of Applied Sciences in Münster, Germany. Ralf's professional background is based on the areas of strategy consultancy, design management research and understanding technological innovation. Ralf has taught Strategy, Brand and Innovation Management at all leading design management programmes in Europe. These days Ralf is a guest/associate lecturer at EURIB Institute, Rotterdam; HGK Lucerne, Switzerland; and the Open University, United Kingdom. Since 1998 he has run design-management.de. Other than that he can be found as @iterations on Twitter.

Source of motivation

my wife & our two sons,
social media, endurance sports

4 Fergus Bisset

At the time of writing Fergus is a research assistant in the Human Centred Design Intitute in the School of Engineering and Design at Brunel University in West London, UK. He is developing a public engagement exhibition with The Design Museum, London titled "Ergonomics – Real Design". A social media enthusiast, Fergus is also an associate with Research in Practice for Adults and Destinable. When not wearing his design hat, Fergus can be found wearing his ski hat or running shoes.

Source of motivation

Google Reader, The British Library,
coffee, Twitter, cross-country skiing

AUTHORS*

5 Kate Blackmon

Kate Blackmon is currently an AIM ESRC Mid-Career Fellow in Services at the University of Oxford, where she is a Lecturer in Operations Management at the Said Business School and a Tutorial Fellow in Management Studies at Merton College. Trained as a Chemical Engineer, she has worked in a variety of public and private services during her career. Her current research focuses on service innovation, in sectors including health, culture, education, and the digital economy.

6 Johan Blomkvist

After about ten years working with care for the elderly and people with dementia, Johan got interested in human behaviour and took a bachelors in cognitive science. From there he went on to a masters in design, eager to apply his newly acquired knowledge about humans as social, communicative, and embodied beings situated in cultural and evolutionary contexts. During this time, Johan also started working with user innovation and managing projects where design students collaborated with organisations and companies. His current research, as a PhD student at Linköping University, aims to expand our knowledge about prototyping services.

Source of motivation

people, food, laughter

7 Simon Clatworthy

Simon is professor of Interaction Design at the Oslo School of Architecture and Design. He has been teaching service design for over four years, and is about to complete a major service design research project called AT-ONE. In an earlier life he managed a large brand and design department at a Scandinavian consultancy, has been research manager at Telenor and has had his own consultancy. He is passionately enthusiastic about the strategic role of design in organisations, and how designers add value to cross-functional development teams. When not designing, he admires the design of old sports cars, which he can't stop collecting (and repairing).

Source of motivation
designing great experiences, pottering in a garden, sunny days in a cabriolet

8 Lauren Currie

With an enthusiasm for service design, public services and working with people, Lauren Currie is focused on changing the lives of British people through service design and practical action. As the Director of MyPolice, Lauren is working closely with police and the public to ensure the police service is the very best it can be. Prior to being Director of Snook Lauren worked as a freelance Service Designer for Designthinkers in Holland, Deutsche Telekom Laboratories (T-Labs) in Berlin and London-based Future Gov. She mentors and teaches undergraduate students at universities all over Europe, running a variety of workshops and lectures on Service Design, Prototyping and Critical Thinking.

Source of motivation
daily life, all things red and the determination to make an impact

AUTHORS*

9 Geke van Dijk

Geke van Dijk is co-founder and Strategy Director of STBY (Standby) in London and Amsterdam. STBY is specialised in design research for service innovation, and works for clients in industry and the public sector. Geke has a background in ethnographic research, user-centred design and services marketing. She holds a PhD in Computer Sciences from the Open University in the UK. Geke is the initiator and co-founder of Service Design Network Netherlands, and publishes regularly about Service Design and Design Research.

Source of motivation

exploring life, keep on learning, make things happen

10 Sarah Drummond

Sarah Drummond focuses on making social change happen by rethinking public services from a human perspective. Sarah has been sponsored by Skills Development Scotland to work alongside their Service Design & Innovation Directorate to implement the design process. She is leading a process of change, putting design thinking at the heart of their organisaition; building capabilities of staff to innovate from the ground up. Her work challenges the role of design within the public sector, as the winner of the first Scottish Social Innovation camp Sarah ambitiously challenges the way governments operate and make policies through initiatives such as Mypolice and teaches at Universities all over Europe.

Source of motivation

organising complexity, people, common-sense

11 Jamin Hegeman

Jamin Hegeman is an interaction and service designer at Adaptive Path. His path meandered from poetry to journalism to editing to web design to a masters degree in design, where his passion for design flourished. He is interested in raising the awareness of design as an approach to addressing highly complex problems. Previously, he was a senior designer at Nokia, where he led efforts to define new services, experiences, and business opportunities for business development, strategic growth areas, and corporate social responsibility. He has produced solutions in various areas, including health care, education, communication, media, commerce, and social interaction.

Source of motivation
people, happiness, good, creativity, fun

12 Stefan Holmlid

Stefan Holmlid is assistant professor in interaction and service design at Linköping University, with fifteen years of experience in design research in academic as well as industrial settings. He pioneered studio teaching of interaction design and service design in Sweden, and continues to teach user-driven innovation, interaction and service design.

Currently his research interests are the expressive powers of and the involvement of stakeholders through design methods and techniques in service development and innovation. The idea that objects and materials can be both dynamic, and active and that the design is co-created "in use", drives his research of relevant theoretical grounding for design. His research is founded on a critical stance towards institutionalisation of user-centred design.

Source of motivation
good coffee and a book, sharing experiences, thinking and writing

13 Luke Kelly

Luke Kelly graduated from the University of Liverpool in 2007, obtaining a masters degree in Politics and the Mass Media. After working as a researcher for a UK politician, he spent a year living in Shanghai whilst lecturing at Xian-Jiaotong Liverpool University, before travelling to Amsterdam to work with STBY. Now based in STBY's London office, Luke's main interests concern the effect technology exerts on culture. He's currently using the ethnographic experience gained from working within service design to write a PhD proposal examining the impact of techno-cultural media on the Japanese public sphere. He's also woefully inept at playing football.

Source of motivation

tea, Isaac Asimov, proving my high-school English teacher wrong

14 Lucy Kimbell

Lucy Kimbell has taught an MBA elective on design management at Saïd Business School, University of Oxford, since 2005. She was principal investigator on a multidisciplinary research project on the design of services in science and technology-based enterprises involving academics from management and design; IDEO, live|work and Radarstation; and science entrepreneurs. Her main interest is establishing what is distinctive about a "designerly" approach to service design. Lucy originally studied engineering design, later did an MA in digital arts, and is completing doctoral work in design theory.

Source of motivation

watching and listening to people, climate change, playing

15 Satu Miettinen

Dr. Satu Miettinen works as a co-ordinator for the Competence Center of Industrial Design at the Savonia University of Applied Sciences. For several years she has been working with service design, and currently she is a research leader and director in the service design project called Service Design for Elderly funded by the Finnish Funding Agency for Innovation and Technology. She also worked as a principal investigator in the "Experiencing Well-being – Developing New User Interfaces and Service Platforms for Leisure" project, which was also funded by the Finnish Funding Agency for Innovation and Technology, TEKES. In the past she has worked as a project manager and specialist in the areas of crafts development, cultural and creative tourism in several international and European Union funded projects during the period 1997–2006.

Source of motivation
family, travel and design

16 Arne van Oosterom

Owner and Strategic Design Director at DesignThinkers, a strategic design agency based in Amsterdam, the Netherlands, that specializes in New Marketing and Branding, Social Innovation, Service Design and Customer Centered Design. Chairman of the Service Design Network Netherlands. Founder of the WENOVSKI Design Thinkers Network. Founder of the Healthcare Initiative CareToDesign. Arne is guest lecturer at Management Centre Innsbruck Austria, and has given lectures at Savonia University of Applied Science in Finland, Parsons New School New York, TU Delft, Rotterdam University of Applied Science and various other international institutions.

Source of motivation
learning, storytelling,
embracing the complexity of life

AUTHORS*

17 Asier Pérez

Asier Perez (born 1970) graduated in 1996 with an MFA from the École Régionale des Beaux-Arts de Nantes, France. Unhappy with the inefficiency of arts for social transformation, he decided to move into business after ten years of a successful career in arts. Asier Perez founded Funky Projects in 2002, after some other ventures, to stir-up innovation in organisations that aim to change themselves and their environment. Asier is a regular speaker, visiting teacher and media contributor in several European countries. He was teacher at the Fine Arts College of the University of the Basque Country from 1997 to 2001. Asier published Volatile Environments in Revolver Verlag in 2003 with his most representative art projects from 1996 until 2001.

Source of motivation
great people, travelling, challenges

18 Bas Raijmakers

Bas Raijmakers holds a PhD in Design Interactions from the Royal College of Art and runs his own design research company STBY (Standby) in London and Amsterdam with Dr. Geke van Dijk. Bas has a background in cultural studies, the internet industry, and interaction design. His main passion is to bring people into design and innovation processes, using visual storytelling in general and documentary film techniques in particular. He is the founder of the international Global Design Research Network "Reach" and also teaches and researches at Design Academy Eindhoven.

Source of motivation
family and friends, cooking, urban cycling, documentary film

19 Jakob Schneider

Jakob currently works at a design agency in Cologne. He graduated with a diploma in Communication Dcsign, with Distinction, from the University of Applied Sciences in Münster, Germany. Being a freelance design consultant and graphic designer since 2006, he has worked with a wide range of clients, from small cultural institutions to nationally operating trading companies.

Understanding processes and mechanisms behind things has always been fascinating to him. In his professional work he therefore strives not to separate branding from information design. A designer at heart, he suffers silently if circumstances destroy an initial concept, ending up with compromises. Besides the projects he undertakes on his own, Jakob gained work experience at MetaDesign, Berlin.

Source of motivation
friends, colleagues, outside

20 Fabian Segelström

Fabian holds an MSc in Design and a BSc in Cognitive Science, both from Linköping University. He is currently doing his PhD, in which he focuses on user involvement in the early stages of service design projects. He has published on visualisations in service design as well as appropriations of ethnography to service design and interaction design. When not in the office, he enjoys doing various sports and travelling to remote corners of the world, often to go diving there. You can follow him on Twitter: @segelstrom

Source of motivation
curiosity, new experiences, great music

AUTHORS*

21 Marc Stickdorn

Marc Stickdorn graduated in Strategic Management and Marketing from the University of Trier in Germany and worked in various tourism projects throughout Europe. Since 2008 Marc is a full-time staff member at the MCI – Management Center Innsbruck in Austria, where he lectures service design at the MA study program Entrepreneurship and Tourism. His main areas of interest are service design and strategic marketing management, particularly in a tourism context. This involves research such as the development of a mobile ethnography application for mobile phones and various publications and presentations. Marc is co-founder and consultant of Destinable – Service design for tourism and guest lecturer at different European and US universities. When not working, Marc is hard to find since he loves travelling and outdoor sports.

Source of motivation

friends, outdoor sports, backpacking

22 Renato Troncon

Renato Troncon is Professor of Aesthetics and Coordinator of the Centre for Aesthetics in Practice at the University of Trento. He is author and/or editor of about 15 books and 50 scientific articles, presenter of more than 50 lectures at scientific congresses, scientific coordinator and organizer of more than 30 scientific national and international meetings as well as member of various scientific academies and networks for anthropological philosophy, design, cultural policies. His researching / teaching is devoted both to philosophy (aesthetics, aesthetics in practice, cultural ecologies, phenomenology, philosophical anthropology, theories of colour, German philosophy from the 1700s to the 1900s, German Romanticism) and to design research and practice.

Source of motivation

beauty, goodness, justice

23 Erik Widmark

Erik Widmark graduated 2006 as a MFA from the Konstfack, University College of Arts, Crafts and Design in Stockholm, Sweden. Puzzled that everything in design school revolved around design being a handicraft (modelling, sketching etc.), Erik and three class-mates explored the area of design thinking as their master project. With no one wanting to employ radical design thinkers, Erik and his colleagues had no option but to start their own business. Since 2007 Erik has been working as a design strategist and service designer at Transformator Design Group, which has pioneered in the area of service design in Sweden. In his spare time Erik collects vinyl records, reads books about pirates and explorers and has just taken up beekeeping.

Source of motivation

auctions, Salsoul, weather (all kinds)

REFERENCES

The design beyond the design

20

— Design thinkers network by Wenovski: www.designthinkersnetwork.com

— ServDes 2009: First Nordic Conference on Service Design and Service Innovation, 24–26 November 2009, Oslo/Norway: www.aho.no/servicedesign09

— Service Design Network: http://www.service-design-network.org

— TiSDT PanorEmo, online from 1 November 2009 to 1 August 2010: http://www.susagroup.com/marcstickdorn

— TiSDT Uservoice, online from 1 May 2009 to 1 August 2010: http://tisdt.uservoice.com

— TiSDT Wordpress, online from 1 November 2009 to 1 March 2010: http://service.engagement.ac

— Wenovski MiniUnConference 2010: 22 January, Münster, Germany.

Definitions

28

— 31 volts service design (2008). One line of Service Design by Marc Fonteijn. Retrieved 10 August 2010, from http://www.31v.nl/2008/03/one-line-of-service-design/

— Buchanan, R. (2001). Design research and the new learning. Design Issues, 17 (4), 3–23.

— Continuum (2010). Service Design: What. Retrieved 10 August 2010, from http://www.dcontinuum.com/content/expertise_page.php?pageid=62

— Engine service design (2010). Service design. Retrieved 10 August 2010, from http://www.enginegroup.co.uk/service_design/

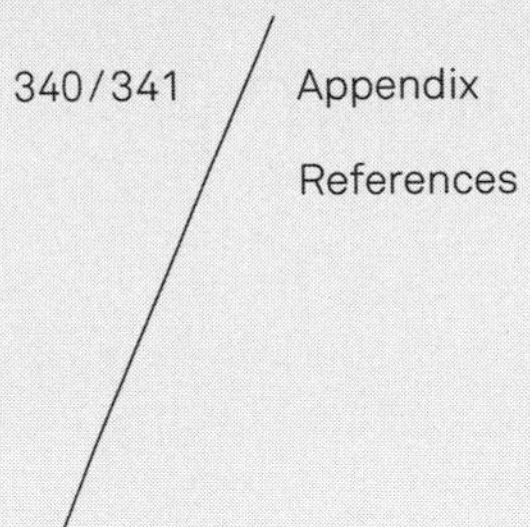

— frontier service design (2010). About Service Design. Retrieved 10 August 2010, from http://www.frontierservicedesign.com/about-us/about-service-design/

— live|work (2010). Service Design. Retrieved 10 August 2010, from http://www.livework.co.uk/articles/creating-customer-centred-organisations

— Mager, B. (2009). "Service Design as an Emerging Field". In: Miettinen & Koivisto (Eds.): Designing Services with Innovative Methods, Helsinki: Taik Publications, p. 28–42.

— Stefan, M. (2005). Service Design: Practical access to an evolving field (M.A. Thesis: Köln International School of Design). Retrieved 10 August 2010, from http://stefan-moritz.com/welcome/Service_Design_files/Practical%20Access%20to%20Service%20Design.pdf

— The Copenhagen Institute of Interaction Design (2008). What is Service Design? Retrieved 10 August, 2010, from http://ciid.dk/symposium/sds/

— UK Design Council (2010). What is service design? Retrieved 10 August 2010, from http://www.designcouncil.org.uk/about-design/Types-of-design/Service-design/What-is-service-design/

Marketing – Connecting with people, creating value

46

— Booms, B. & Bitner, M.J. (1981). "Marketing Strategies and Organisational Structures for Service Firms", in Donnelly, J. & George, W. (eds.), Marketing of Services. Chicago: American Marketing Association, pp. 47–52.

— Grönroos, C. (2000). Service Management and Marketing: A Customer Relationship Approach. 2nd ed., Chichester, UK: Wiley.

REFERENCES

- Lovelock, C. & Gummesson, E. (2004). "Whither Services Marketing? In Search of a New Paradigm and Fresh Perspectives". Journal of Service Research. 7(1), pp. 20–41.
- Norman, R. & Ramírez, R. (1993). "Designing Interactive Strategy: From Value Chain to Value Constellation" Harvard Business Review, 71 (4), pp. 65–77.
- Vargo, S. & Lusch, R. (2004a). "Evolving to a New Dominant Logic in Marketing", Journal of Marketing, 68 (1), pp. 1–17.
- Vargo, S. & Lusch, R. (2004b). "The Four Service Marketing Myths: Remnants of a Goods-based Manufacturing Model". Journal of Service Research. 6 (4), pp. 324–335.
- Zeithaml, V. & Bitner, M. (2003). Services Marketing: Integrating Customer Focus across the Firm, 3rd ed., New York: McGraw-Hill.
- Zeithaml, V., Parasuraman, A. & Berry, L. (1985). "Problems and Strategies in Services Marketing". Journal of Marketing, 49 (Spring), pp. 33–46.

Product design

- Apple (2010). Corporate Website. Retrieved 16 August 2010, from http://www.apple.com/
- Brown, T. (2008). "Design Thinking". Harvard Business Review. June 2008. Retrieved 10 March 2010, from http://hbr.org/2008/06/design-thinking/ar/1
- Buchanan, R. (2001). "Design Research and the New Learning". Design Issues. Autumn 2001, Vol. 17, No. 4, Pages 3–23.
- Gould, J.D. & Lewis, C. (1985). Designing for Usability: Key Principles and What Designers Think. Communications of the ACM March 198.5 Vol. 28 No. 3.

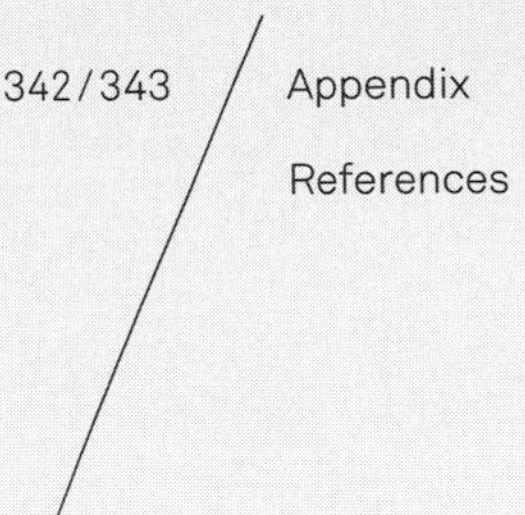

— Industrial Designers Society of America (2010). Retrieved 10 March 2010, from http://www.idsa.org/absolutenm/templates/?a=89

— Jones, M. (2010). Lead for Service Design and Innovation, IDEO. Interview by Satu Miettinen.

— Keinonen, T. (2006). "Introduction to Concept Design". In Product Concept Design. A Review of the Conceptual Design of Products in Industry. Keinonen, T. & Takala, R. (Eds.) Springer.

— Keinonen, T. (2009). "Design Contribution Square". Advanced Engineering Informatics. 23 (2009), pp 142–148.

— Koivisto, M. (2007). Mitä on palvelumuotoilu? Muotoilun hyödyntäminen palvelujen suunnittelussa. Taiteen maisterin lopputyö. Taideteollinen korkeakoulu.

— Kone (2010a). Corporate Website. Retrieved 16 August 2010, from http://www.kone.com/

— Kone (2010b). Corporate Website. Retrieved 16 August 2010, from http://www.kone.com/corporate/en/lab/design/innovationsdesign/konedeco/Pages/default.aspx

— Lehtinen, L. (2010), Assistant Vice President, Service Innovations, KONE Corporation. Interview by Satu Miettinen.

— Myyrmanni (2010). Corporate Website. Retrieved 16 August 2010, from http://www.myyrmanni.fi/

— Sanders, E. B.-N. (2005). Information. Inspiration and Co-creation. The 6th International Conference of the European Academy of Design. March 29–31, 2005. University of Arts, Bremen, Germany. August 27, 2010, from http://www.maketools.com/articles-papers/InformationInspirationandCocreation_Sanders_05.pdf

— Sato, K. (2009). Perspectives on Design Research. In Poggenpohl, S. & Sato, K. (Eds): Design Integrations: Research and Collaboration. Chicago: The University of Chicago Press.

REFERENCES

— Valtonen, A. (2007). Redefining Industrial Design: Changes in the Design Practise in Finland. University of Art and Design Helsinki A74. Gummerus Printing.

Graphic design

68

— Gilmore, J. H. & Pine B. J. (2007). Authenticity: What customers really want. Boston, MA: Harvard Business School Press.

Interaction design (further reading)

— Designing for Interaction: Creating Innovative Applications and Devices (Voices That Matter) by Dan Saffer. → This is a slim book with a good design approach that nicely covers the basics. Covers some service design too.

— Interaction Design: Beyond Human-Computer Interaction by Dr Helen Sharp, Professor Yvonne Rogers, and Dr Jenny Preece. → This used to be the bible for interaction design about five years ago. Now in its second edition its still good, but it has its focus upon usability rather than desirability.

— The Design of Everyday Things by Don Norman. → This is not a practitioner's book, but explains some basic principles of interaction design, and why things are the way they are. An easy read, that gives you the big picture.

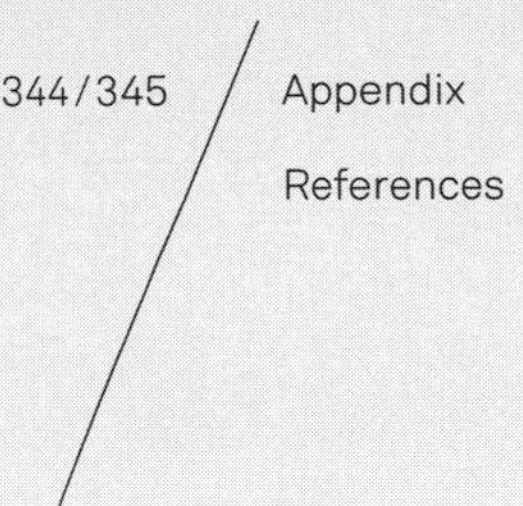

Social design

88

- Brown, T. (2009). Change By Design. Collins Business.
- Martin, Roger L. (2009). Design of Business: Why Design Thinking is the Next Competitive Advantage. Harvard Business School Press.
- O'Toole, R. (2009). Design-Thinking-Learning Essay. Retrieved 16 August 2010, from http://blogs.warwick.ac.uk/inspireslearning/entry/design-thinking-learning_essay/
- Kemerling, J. (2010). The Volunteer Design. Chronicles (Lincoln, NE). Retrieved 16 August 2010, from http://www.designobserver.com/changeobserver/entry.html?entry=12768
- Rawsthorn, Al. (2009). Design: Trying to Be Responsible and Cutting-Edge, Too. The New York Times: Arts. Retrieved 16 August 2010, from http://www.nytimes.com/2009/12/28/arts/28iht-design28.html?_r=1
- ColaLife: http://colalife.org/blog

Strategic management

94

- Kim, W. C., & Mauborgne, R. (2004). Blue Ocean Strategy. Harvard Business Review. October, pp. 76–85.
- Kim, W. C., & Mauborgne, R. (2005). Blue Ocean Strategy: How to Create Uncontested Market Space and Make the Competition Irrelevant. Boston (MA): Harvard Business School Press.
- Martin, R. (2007). The Opposable Mind: How Successful Leaders Win Through Integrative Thinking. Boston: Harvard Business School Press, 2007.
- Miettinen, S. & Koivisto, M. (2009). Designing Services with Innovative Methods. Helsinki: Taik Publications.
- Porter, M. (1979). "How competitive forces shape strategy". Harvard Business Review, March/April 1979.

REFERENCES

- Porter, M. (1980). Competitive Strategy. New York: Free Press.
- Porter, M. (1985). Competitive Advantage. New York: Free Press.
- Zeithaml, Valarie. Selected publications: http://bit.ly/zeithaml

Operations management

- Chase, R.B. (1981). "The Customer Contact Approach to Services: Theoretical Bases and Practical Extensions". Operations Research, Vol. 29, No. 4, pp. 698–705.
- Levitt, T. (1972). "Production Line Approach to Service". Harvard Business Review, Vol. 50, pp. 41–52.
- Sasser Jr., W.E., Olsen, R.P. & Wyckoff, D.D. (1978). Management of Service Operations: Text, Cases and Readings. Boston, MA: Allyn and Bacon, Inc.

Design ethnography

- Kelley, T. & Littman, J. (2005). The Ten Faces of Innovation. Doubleday: Random.
- Monaghan, J. & Just, P. (2000). Social & Cultural Anthropology: A Very Short Introduction. Oxford: University Press.
- Raijmakers, B., Gaver, W. & Bishay, J. (2007). Design Documentaries. Inspiring Design Research Through Documentary Film. Proceedings of DIS2006 conference, State College, Pennsylvania.
- Rouch, J. & Morin, E. (1960). "Chronicle of a Summer" (film). Original title in French is "Chronique d'un été".

The iterative process of service design thinking

124

— Best, K. (2006). Design Management: Managing Design Strategy, Process and Implementation. Lausanne: AVA Publishing SA.

— Cameron, E. & Green, M. (2009). Making Sense of Change Management. London: Kogan Page.

— Designthinkers (2009). DT 5 Steps Service Innovation Method. Retrieved 2 August 2010, from: http://www.designthinkers.nl

— Engine (2009). Engine service design – Our process. Retrieved 2 August 2010, from http://www.enginegroup.co.uk/service_design/v_page/our_process

— Hegeman, J. (2008). The Thinking Behind Design. Retrieved 2 August 2010, from http://jamin.org/portfolio/thesis-paper/thinking-behind-design.pdf

— live|work (2009). What we do. Retrieved 2 August 2010, from http://www.livework.co.uk/what-we-do

— Mager, B. (2009). Service Design. Paderborn: Fink.

— Miettinen S, & Koivisto, M. (2009). Designing Services with Innovative Methods. Taik Publications, Helsinki.

AT ONE

136

— Isaksen, S. G., Dorval, K.B. & Treffinger, D.J. (2000). Creative approaches to problem solving (2nd ed.). Dubuque, IA: Kendall/Hunt.

— Pine, B.J. & Gilmore, J.H. (1999). The experience economy. Boston: Harvard Business School Press.

REFERENCES

Tools

BLOGS (IN ALPHABETICAL ORDER)

- Business Model Alchemist: http://www.businessmodelalchemist.com/
- Design for Service: http://designforservice.wordpress.com/
- Insights Observed: http://noreally.wordpress.com/
- Service Design Tools: http://www.servicedesigntools.org/
- Design Crux: http://designcrux.netfirms.com/index.html
- Think Vitamin: http://thinkvitamin.com/
- Smart Storming: http://smartstorming-blog.com/
- The Agile Manifesto: http://agilemanifesto.org/
- Thoughtbits: http://www.well.com/~mb/thoughtbits/blogger.html
- Usability Post: http://www.usabilitypost.com/
- Work, Play, Experience: http://workplayexperience.blogspot.com/

PEOPLE AND ORGANISATIONS (IN ALPHABETICAL ORDER)

- 7daysinmylife: http://www.7daysinmylife.com
- Adaptive Path: http://www.adaptivepath.com/
- Anne Fairbrother: http://annefairbrother.co.uk/
- Business Model Generation: http://www.businessmodelgeneration.com/
- DesignThinkers: http://www.designthinkers.nl/
- Engine: http://www.enginegroup.co.uk
- Live Work: http://www.livework.co.uk/

- myServiceFellow: http://www.myservicefellow.com/
- Snook: http://www.wearesnook.com/
- STBY: http://www.STBY.eu
- The Design Council: http://www.designcouncil.org.uk/
- Work, Play, Experience: http://www.workplayexperience.com/
- WQ Usability: http://www.wqusability.com/index.html

MEDIA (IN ALPHABETICAL ORDER)

- Baldridge: http://www.baldrige.com/
- Dartmouth Engineer: http://www.dartmouthengineer.com/2010/03/engineering-by-design/
- The Guardian: http://www.guardian.co.uk/service-design/

BOOKS AND PAPERS (IN ALPHABETICAL ORDER)

- Agar, M. H. (1996). The Professional Stranger: An Informal Introduction to Ethnography, 2nd edition. USA: Academic Press.
- Gaver B., Dunne T., Pacenti E., (1999). “Design: Cultural Probes.” Interaction 6(1): 21–29.
- Miettinen S, & Koivisto, M. (2009). Designing Services with Innovative Methods, Helsinki: Taik Publications.
- Osterwalder, A. & Pigneur, Y. (2009). Business Model Generation: A Handbook for Visionaries, Game Changers, and Challengers. Amsterdam: Self Published.
- Segelström, F., Raijmakers, B., & Holmlid, S. (2009). Thinking and Doing Ethnography in Service Design. Proceedings of the International Association of Societies of Design Research, IASDR 2009. Seoul.
- Shostack, L. (1982). How to Design a Service. European Journal of Marketing (161), 49–63.

REFERENCES

Case: NL Agency

234

— DesignThinkers: http://www.designthinkers.nl/

— NL Agency – Dutch Ministry of Economic Affairs: http://www.agentschapnl.nl

Case: Mypolice

234

— Snook: http://www.wearesnook.com/

— Mypolice: http://www.mypolice.org/

— BBC News (2010). Government reviews hundreds of "unnecessary" websites. BBC News – Technology, 25 June 2010, Retrieved 18 August 2010, from http://www.bbc.co.uk/news/10412216

— Evenson, S. & Dubberly, H. (2010). Designing for Service: Creating an Experience Advantage. Retrieved 18 August 2010, from http://www.dubberly.com/wp-content/uploads/2010/03/ddo_article_designing_service.pdf

— Kershaw, C., Nicholas, S. & Walker, A. (Eds.) (2008). Crime in England and Wales 2007/08. Home Office Statistical Bulletin 07/08. London: Home Office. Retrieved 18 August 2010, from http://www.homeoffice.gov.uk/rds/pdfs08/hosb0708.pdf

— Macaskill, M. (2009). Warning over "shop a cop" website: Online forum may be hijacked by disgruntled members of the public making unfounded claims, say police leaders. The Times, 28 June 2009, Retrieved 18 August 2010, from http://www.timesonline.co.uk/tol/news/uk/scotland/article6591191.ece

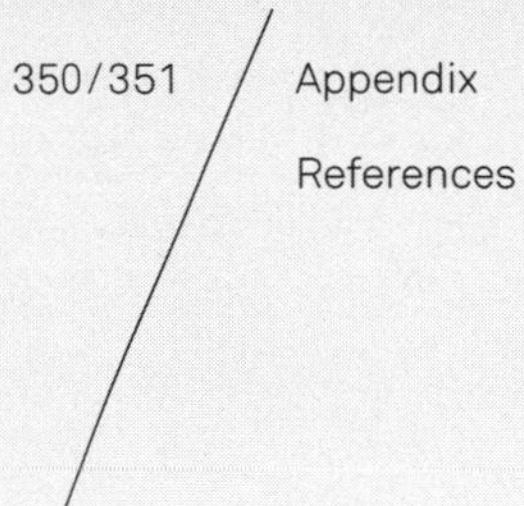

— Nielsen (2010). Led by Facebook, Twitter, Global Time Spent on Social Media Sites up 82% Year over Year. Retrieved 18 August 2010, from http://blog.nielsen.com/nielsenwire/global/led-by-facebook-twitter-global-time-spent-on-social-media-sites-up-82-year-over-year/

— Sanders, E. & Simons, G. (2009). A Social Vision for Value Co-creation in Design. Retrieved 3 January 2010, from http://www.osbr.ca/ojs/index.php/osbr/article/view/1012/973

Case: Hello Change

250

— Funky Projects: http://www.funkyprojects.com

— Hello Change: http://www.hellochange.net

— Jobsite (2008). Insider: SMEs' £ 69 million recruitment waste. Retrieved 15 August 2010, from http://www.jobsite.co.uk/insider/smes-69million-recruitment-waste-116/

— NESTA (2009). Everyday innovation: How to enhance innovative working in employees and organisations. Retrieved 13 August 2010, from http://www.nesta.org.uk/library/documents/Every-day-innovation-report.pdf

— Schön, D. (1983). The Reflective Practitioner: How Professionals Think in Action. London: Temple Smith.

Case: UPMC

250

— Carnegie Mellon University – School of Design: http://www.design.cmu.edu/

— University of Pittsburgh Medical Center – Center for Quality Improvement and Innovation: http://www.upmc.com

REFERENCES

Case: SEB

250

- Transformator: http://www.transformator.net
- SEB: http://www.seb.se

Integrating service design thinking and motivational psychology

298

- Brown, T. (2009). Change by Design: How Design Thinking Transforms Organizations and Inspires Innovation. HarperBusiness.
- Burns C., Cottam, H., Vanstone C. and Winhall, C. (2006). Red Paper 02: Transformation Design. Design Council, London.
- Carver, C. S., & Scheier, M. F. (1998). On the Self-Regulation of Behaviour. New York: Cambridge University Press.
- Csikszentmihalyi, M. (1998). Finding Flow: The Psychology of Engagement With Everyday Life. Basic Books.
- Deci, E., & Ryan, R. (2004). "Intrinsic Need Satisfaction: A Motivational Basis of Performance and Well-Being in Two Work Settings". Journal of Applied Social Psychology, 34, 2045–2068.
- Deci, E., & Ryan, R. (1985a). Intrinsic Motivation and Self-Determination in Human Behaviour. New York: Plenum.
- Ericsson, K. A. (1998). "The Scientific Study of Expert Levels of Performance: General Implications for Optimal Learning and Creativity". High Ability Studies, 9(1), 75–100.
- Kafai Y. B. (1995). Minds in Play: Computer Game Design as a Context for Children's Learning. Hillsdale, NJ: Lawrence Erlbaum Associates.
- Klein, G. (1999). Sources of Power: How People Make Decisions. Cambridge, MA: MIT Press.
- Loevlie, L. (2009). How service thinking through design creates new service opportunities. Nordic Service Design Conference, Oslo, Norway.

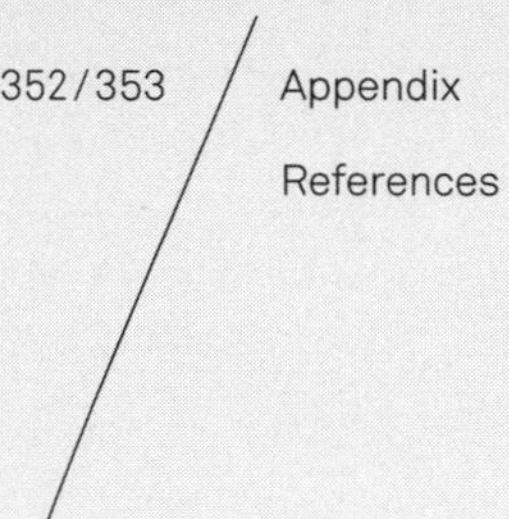

— Polaine, A. (2009). Blueprint+: Developing a tool for Service Design. Service Design Network Conference, Madeira, Portugal.

— Reeve, J. (2005). Understanding motivation and emotion (4th ed.). Hoboken, NJ: John Wiley & Sons, Inc.

— Stickdorn, M. & Schneider, J. (2009). MyServiceFellow. Experience Service Design Conference, Kuopio, Finland.

— White, R. W. (1959). Motivation reconsidered: The concept of competence. Psychological Review, 66, pp. 297–333.

Service design research

308

— Akama, Y. (2009). Warts-and-all: the real practice of service design. First Nordic Conference on Service Design and Service Innovation. Oslo, Norway.

— Akiyama, Y., Shimomura, Y., & Arai, T. (2009). A Method of Supporting Conflict Resolution for Designing Services. 1st CIRP Industrial Product-Service Systems (IPS2) Conference, (pp. 54–61). Cranfield, UK.

— Bitner, M. J. (1992). Servicescapes: The Impact of Physical Surroundings on Customers and Employees. Journal of Marketing 56(2), pp. 56–71.

— Blomkvist, J., & Holmlid, S. (2009). Examplars in Service Design. First Nordic Conference on Service Design and Service Innovation. Oslo, Norway.

— Burns, C., & Winhall, J. (2006).

The Diabetes Agenda. London, UK: Design Council.

— Burns, C., Cottam, H., Vanstone, C., & Winhall, J. (2006). Transformation Design. London, UK: Design Council.

REFERENCES

— Candi, M., & Saemundsson, R. J. (2008). "How different? Comparing the use of design in service innovation in Nordic and American new technology-based firms". Design Studies 29: pp. 478–499

— Carr, V., Sangiorgi, D., Büscher, M., Cooper, R. & Junginger, S. (2009). Clinicians as service designers? Reflections on current transformation in the UK health services. First Nordic Conference on Service Design and Service Innovation. Oslo, Norway.

— Cautela, C., Rizzo, F., & Zurlo, F. (2009). Service Design Logic: An approach based on the different service categories. Proceedings of the International Association of Societies of Design Research, IASDR 2009. Seoul, Korea.

— Clatworthy, S. (2009). Bridging the gap between brand strategy and customer experience. The target experience tool. First Nordic Conference on Service Design and Service Innovation. Oslo, Norway.

— Combined Systems. Design Research Society Conference, DRS 2008. Sheffield, UK.

— Cooper, A., Reimann, R., & Dubberly, H. (2003). About Face 2.0: The Essentials of Interaction Design. Hoboken, NJ: John Wiley & Sons, Inc.

— de Borba, G. S., & Remus, B. D. (2009). Service Design: A Study of the Innovation Process in Brazilian Soccer Clubs. 8th European Academy of Design Conference, (pp. 61–66). Aberdeen, UK.

— Diana, C., Pacenti, E., & Tassi, R. (2009). Visualtiles – Communication tools for (service) design. First Nordic Conference on Service Design and Service Innovation. Oslo, Norway.

— Erlhoff, M., Mager, B., & Manzini, E. (1997). Dienstleistung braucht Design – Professioneller Produkt- und Markenauftritt für Serviceanbieter. Berlin, Germany: Hermann Luchterhand Verlag GmbH.

— Evenson, S. (2005). Designing for Service. Proceedings of DPPI. Eindhoven, Netherlands.

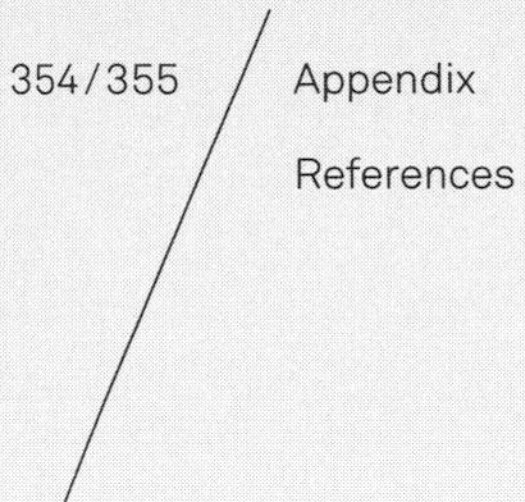

- Frayling, C. (1993). Research in Art and Design. Royal College of Art Research Papers, 1(1): pp. 1–5.
- Gloppen, J. (2009). Service Design Leadership. First Nordic Conference on Service Design and Service Innovation. Oslo, Norway.
- Gong, M., Suteu, I. M., & Shen, J. (2009). Chita 08: Colloborative Service and Mobile Communication: A Service Design Workshop on Chinese Sustainable Lifestyles and Inter-Culture Experiences. 8th European Academy of Design Conference, (pp. 174–179). Aberdeen, UK.
- Han, Q. (2009). Managing Stakeholder Involvement in Service Design: Insights from British service designers. First Nordic Conference on Service Design and Service Innovation. Oslo, Norway.
- Holmlid, S. (2007). Interaction design and service design: Expanding a comparison of design disciplines. Nordic Design Research Conference, NorDes 2007. Stockholm, Sweden.
- Holmlid, S. (2009). Participative, co-operative, emancipatory: From participatory design to service design. First Nordic Conference on Service Design and Service Innovation. Oslo, Norway.
- Jonas, W., Chow, R., & Schaeffer, N. (2009). Service Design Descriptors: A Step Toward Rigorous Discourse. 8th European Academy Of Design Conference. Aberdeen, UK.
- Jung, M. J., Nam, K. Y., & Yu, H. (2009). Design as the Integrator in Service-Product Systems: With cases on Public Bike Rental Systems. Proceedings of the International Association of Societies of Design Research, IASDR 2009. Seoul, Korea.
- Jung, M., J., Nam, K., Y. (2008). Design Opportunities in Service-Product.
- Junginger, S., & Sangiorgi, D. (2009). Service Design and Organizational Change: Bridging the Gap Between Rigour and Relevance. Proceedings of the International Association of Societies of Design Research, IASDR 2009. Seoul, Korea.

REFERENCES

— Kaario, P., Vaajakallio, K., Lehtinen, V., Kantola, V., & Kuikkaniemi, K. (2009). Someone Else's Shoes – Using Role-Playing Games in User-Centered Service Design. First Nordic Conference on Service Design and Service Innovation. Oslo, Norway.

— Kim, Y. S., Wang, E., Lee, Y. C., & Cho, Y. C. (2009). A Product-Service System Representation and Its Application in a Concept Design Scenario. 1st CIRP Industrial Product-Service Systems (IPS2) Conference, 1–2 April 2009 (pp. 32–39). Cranfield, UK.

— Kimbell, L. (2009). Insights from Service Design Practice. 8th European Academy of Design Conference, (pp. 249–253). Aberdeen, UK.

— Kimbell, L., & Siedel, P. (2008). Designing for Services – Multidisciplinary Perspectives: Proceedings from the Exploratory Project on Designing for Services in Science and Technology-based Enterprises. Oxford, UK: Saïd Business School.

— Kronqvist, J., & Korhonen, S.-M. (2008). Co-Designing Sustainable Solutions – Combining Service Design and Change Laboratory. First Nordic Conference on Service Design and Service Innovation. Oslo, Norway.

— Lee, M. K., & Forlizzi, J. (2009). Designing Adaptive Robotic Services. Proceedings of the International Association of Societies of Design Research, IASDR 2009. Seoul, Korea.

— Maffei, S., Mager, B., & Sangiorgi, D. (2005). Innovation through Service Design. From Research and Theory to a Network of Practice. A Users' Driven Perspective. Joining Forces. Helsinki, Finland.

— Mager, B. (2004). Service design: A review. Cologne, Germany: KISD.

— Manzini, E. (1993). Il Design dei Servizi. La progettazione del prodotto-servizio. Design Management (7).

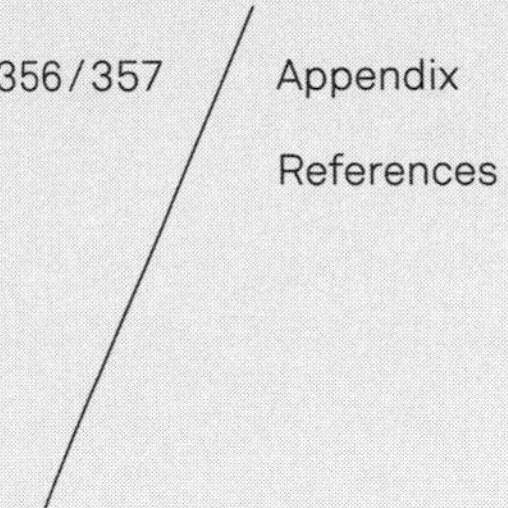

— March, W., & Raijmakers, B. (2008). Designing in the Street: Innovation In-Situ. Proceedings of DRS2008, Design Research Society Biennial Conference. Sheffield, UK.

— Miettinen, S. (2009). Prototyping Social Design in Finland and In Namibia: Service Design as a Method for Designing Services for Wellbeing. Proceedings of the International Association of Societies of Design Research, IASDR 2009. Seoul, Korea.

— Morelli, N. (2002). Designing Product/Service Systems: A Methodological Exploration. Design Issues, 18(3): pp. 3–17.

— Morelli, N. (2003). Product-service systems, a perspective shift for designers: A case study: the design of a telecentre. Design Studies 24: pp. 73–99.

— Morelli, N. (2009). Service as Value co-production: reframing the service design process. Journal of Manufacturing Technology and Management, 20 (5), 568–590.

— Pacenti, E. (1998). Il progetto dell'interazione nei servizi. Un contributo al tema della progettazione dei servizi. (Vol. PhD thesis in Industrial Design). Milan, Italy: Politecnico di Milano.

— Pacenti, E., & Sangiorgi, D. (2010). Service Design research pioneers: An overview of Service Design research devoloped in Italy since the '90s. Design Research Journal 2010 (1), pp. 26–33.

— Parker, S., & Heapy, J. (2006). The Journey to the Interface. London, UK: Demos.

— Penin, L., & Tonkinwise, C. (2009). The Politics and Theatre of Service Design. Proceedings of the International Association of Societies of Design Research, IASDR 2009. Seoul, Korea.

— Pinhanez, C. (2009). Services as Customer-Intensive Systems. Design Issues, 25 (2), pp. 3–13.

REFERENCES

— Popovic, V., Kraal, B. J., & Kirk, P. J. (2009). Passenger experience in an airport: an activity-centred approach. Proceedings of the International Association of Societies of Design Research, IASDR 2009. Seoul, Korea.

— Prendiville, A. (2009). "Love Lewisham", improving stakeholder satisfaction in local government service: A case study of strategic public sector service innovation. First Nordic Conference on Service Design and Service Innovation. Oslo, Norway.

— Raijmakers, B., van Dijk, G., Lee, Y., & Williams, S. A. (2009). Designing Empathic Conversations for Inclusive Design Facilitation. Include 2009. London, UK.

— Sangiorgi, D. (2004). Il Design dei servizi come Design dei Sistemi di Attività. La Teoria dell' Attività applicata alla progettazione dei servizi. (Vol. PhD in Industrial Design in Industrial Design). Milan, Italy: Politecnico di Milano.

— Sangiorgi, D. (2009). Building Up a Framework for Service Design Research. 8th European Academy Of Design Conference, (pp. 415–420). Aberdeen, UK.

— Sangiorgi, D., & Clark, B. (2004). Toward a participatory design approach to service design. Participatory Design Conference, PDC 2004. Toronto, Canada.

— Sangiorgi, D., & Holmlid, S. (2009). Rigor in Service Design Research. Special Session in Proceedings of the International Association of Societies of Design Research, IASDR 2009. Seoul, Korea.

— Segelström, F. (2009). Communicating through Visualizations: Service Designers on Visualizing User Research. First Nordic Conference on Service Design and Service Innovation. Oslo, Norway.

— Segelström, F., & Holmlid, S. (2009). Visualization as tools for research: Service designers on visualisations. Nordic Design Research Conference, NorDes 2009. Oslo, Norway.

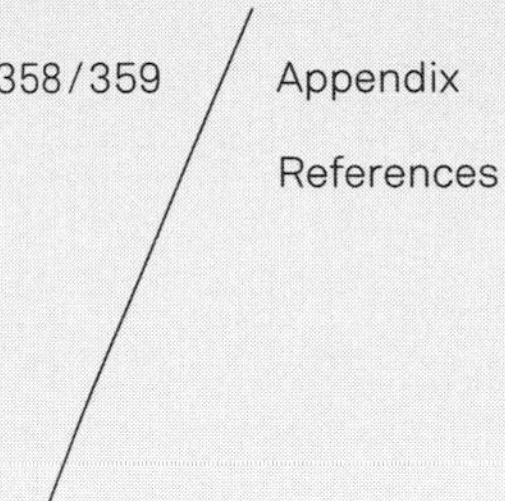

— Segelström, F., Raijmakers, B., & Holmlid, S. (2009). Thinking and Doing Ethnography in Service Design. Proceedings of the International Association of Societies of Design Research, IASDR 2009. Seoul, Korea.

— Shostack, L. (1982). How to Design a Service. European Journal of Marketing (161), pp.49–63.

— Shostack, L. (1984). Designing Services that Deliver. Harvard Business Review, 62 (1), pp. 133–139.

— Singleton, B. (2009). Services Design in New Territories. Proceedings of the International Association of Societies of Design Research, IASDR 2009. Seoul, Korea.

— Sparagen, S. L., & Chan, C. (2008). Service Blueprinting: When Customer Satisfaction Numbers are not enough. International DMI Education Conference. Cergy-Pointose, France.

— Stickdorn, M. & Zehrer, A. (2009). Innovation in Tourism. First Nordic Conference on Service Design and Service Innovation. Oslo, Norway.

— Tan, L., & Szebeko, D. (2009). Co-designing for dementia: The Alzheimer 100 project. Australasian Medical Journal, 1 (12), pp. 185–198.

— Tollestrup, C. (2009). Conceptualising services – developing service concepts through AT-ONE. First Nordic Conference on Service Design and Service Innovation. Oslo, Norway.

— van Dijk, G. (2008). HCI informing Service Design, and visa versa. HCI08 Workshop: HCI and the Analysis and Design of Services. Liverpool, UK.

— Vanstone, C., & Winhall, J. (2006). Activmobs. London, UK: Design Council.

— Wetter Edman, K. (2009). Exploring Overlaps and Differences in Service Dominant Logic and Design Thinking. First Nordic Conference on Service Design and Service Innovation. Oslo, Norway.

— Wreiner, T., Mårtensson, I., Arnell, O., Gonzalez, N., Holmlid, S., & Segelström, F. (2009). Exploring Service Blueprints for Multiple Actors: A Case Study of Car Parking Services. First Nordic Conference on Service Design and Service Innovation. Oslo, Norway.

Service design and biophilia

— Alexander, C. (2002). The Nature of Order, vol.1: The phenomenon of Life. The Center for Environmental Structure, p. 79 ff. and 116 ff.

— Buchanan, R. (1995). "Wicked Problems in Design Thinking", In Margolin V. & Buchanan, R. The Idea of Design. Cambridge (Mass.): MIT Press, pp. 3–20.

— Davy, H. (1838). Consolations in travel or, the last days of a philosopher, London: John Murray, p. 229.

— Gabbay, D.M., Meijers, A., Thagard, P., Woods, J. (2009). Philosophy of Technology and Engineering Sciences. Elsevier, p. 1021 and 1167.

— Gay, G. & Hembrooke, H. (2004). Activity-centered design: an ecological approach to designing smart tools and usable systems. Cambridge (Mass.): MIT Press, pp. 7–14.

— Huysmans, J.-K. (2003). Against nature (À rebours, 1884). Penguin Classics, Chap. 2.

— Kant, I. (1790). Critique of Judgement, §2, §9

— Mager, B. & Gais, M. (2009). Service Design. Paderborn: Wilhelm Fink Verlag, pp. 19–37.

— Mehaffy, M. (2007). "Notes on the Genesis of Wholes: Christopher Alexander and his Continuing Influence", in Urban Design International 12, March 2007, pp. 41–49.

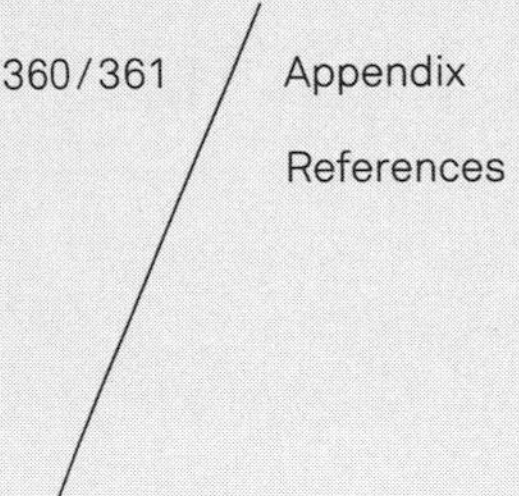

— Muirhead, J. P. (1846). Correspondence of the late James Watt on his discovery of the theory of the composition of water: With a letter from his son. London: John Murray, pp. xv and xvi.

— Muirhead, J. P. (1859). The life of James Watt: With selections from his correspondence. London: John Murray.

— Okakura, K. (1906). The Book of Tea. New York, Chap. iv.

— Phillips, A. (2007). The erotic life of electric hair clippers. In Calhoun, C.J. & Sennett, R.: Practicing culture. London: Routledge, pp. 193–214.

— Pink, D. (2006). A Whole New Mind: Why Right-Brainers Will Rule the Future. Riverhead Trade.

— Stanislavski, K. (1988). An Actor Prepares (1936). London: Methuen.

— Stiegler, B. (2009). Technics and time. 3 vols., 1998–2009, Stanford: Stanford University Press.

— Troncon, R. (2004). Aesthetics in Practice and Cultural Planning: The Perspective of "Festiveness", in Journeys of Expression III: Tourism & Festivals as a Transnational Practice, "Review of Tourism Research", Texas A&M University, Vol. 2, Issue 3, June 2004.

— Williams, N. (2008). Tuscany & Umbria. Lonely Planet, p. 120.

— Wilson E. O. (1986). Biophilia. Cambridge: Harvard University Press, p. 58.

REFERENCES

Image credits

NUMBERED FROM LEFT TO RIGHT / DIAGRAMS AND VISUALISATIONS NOT STATED BELOW REFER TO THE EDITORS

— 19: Photos by Jakob Schneider.

— 65/66: Photos by KONE.

— 71: Illustration by Henry C. Beck, courtesy of London Transport Museum

— 74/75: Photos by schneiter meier külling AG, courtesy of schneiter meier külling AG
http://smek.ch

— 79: Photos by Christian Richters, courtesy of büro uebele and Christian Richters.
http://www.uebele.com
- Client: Projektgesellschaft Neue Messe
- Architect: Wulf & Partner
- Design: Katrin Dittmann (project management), Beate Kapprell, Katrin Häfner, Benedikt Haid, Andreas Uebele
- Product design: Büro für Gestaltung, Diane Ziegler

— 87: Diagram by Simon Clatworthy, adapted by Jakob Schneider.

— 91/92: Photos by Tim Dench of TOAD Charity, courtesy of ColaLife
http://www.toadcharity.com

— 97: Diagram by Jakob Schneider based on:
Porter, M.E. (1979)
"How competitive forces shape strategy",
Harvard Business Review, March/April 1979.

— 101: Diagram by Jakob Schneider based on:
Kim, W. C., & Mauborgne, R. (2005).
Blue Ocean Strategy: How to Create Uncontested Market Space and Make the Competition Irrelevant.
Boston (MA): Harvard Business School Press.

— 105: Table by Kate Blackmon, adapted by Jakob Schneider.

— 111: Diagram by Geke van Dijk, adapted by Jakob Schneider.

— 125: Diagram by Damien Newman.

— 127: Diagram by the British Design Council, adapted by Jakob Schneider.

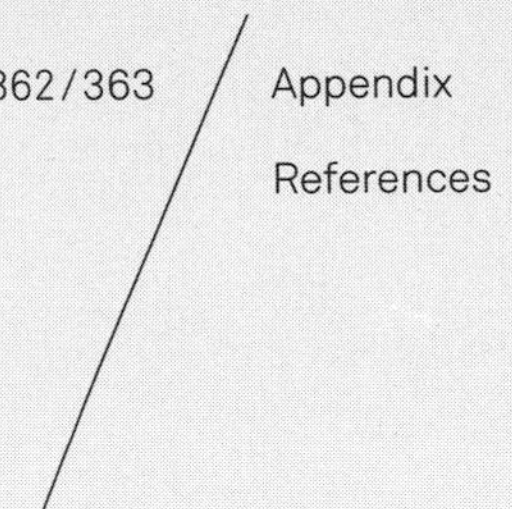

- 142/143: Diagram by Jakob Schneider based on www.service-innovation.org (courtesy of Simon Clatworthy).
- 152/153: Diagram by Jakob Schneider, Marc Stickdorn and STBY.
- 155: Photos by STBY (courtesy of Deutsche Telekom Creation Center Berlin).
- 157: Photos by STBY (courtesy of Nokia).
- 160: Diagram by Jakob Schneider, Marc Stickdorn and STBY
- 161: Photos by [1] Marc Stickdorn and [2] Lauren Currie.
- 164/165: Photos and interview materials by [1, 2, 3, 5] STBY (courtesy of Southern Water and ZuidZorg) and [4] Lauren Currie.
- 167: Diagram by STBY and Jakob Schneider.
- 170/171: Photos by [1, 4, 5] STBY and Spur (courtesy Deutsche Telekom Creation Center Berlin and Heartlands Cornwall) and [2, 3] Anders Mellbratt.
- 173: Photos by [1, 2, 3] Marc Stickdorn and [4] Erik Roscam Abbing.
- 175: Photos by STBY (courtesy of Sony).
- 177: Photos by Marc Stickdorn.
- 179: Photos by [1, 3] Arne van Oosterom and [2] STBY (courtesy of Southern Water).
- 181: Photos by [1] STBY (courtesy of IB-Groep) and [2] Marc Stickdorn.
- 183: Photo by Spur (courtesy of Deutsche Telekom Creation Center, Berlin).
- 185: Photos by [1] STBY (courtesy of Sony) and [2] Work, Play, Experience (courtesy of Stimmt AG).
- 188: Photos by Jakob Schneider (courtesy of Reetta Kerola).
- 189: Photos by Lauren Currie.
- 191: Photos by STBY (courtesy of Heartlands Cornwall).

REFERENCES

- 193: Photos by STBY (courtesy of Deutsche Telekom Creation Center, Berlin).
- 195: Photos by [1, 2] STBY (courtesy of Heartlands Cornwall) and [3] Work, Play, Experience (courtesy of Stimmt AG).
- 197: Diagram by Jakob Schneider and Marc Stickdorn.
- 200/201: Photos by [1, 4, 5] STBY (Deutsche Telekom Creation Center, Berlin) and [2, 3] Lauren Currie.
- 203: Diagram by STBY and Jakob Schneider.
- 206/207: Diagram by Jakob Schneider and Marc Stickdorn, based on: Service blueprint for Service Design panel, online: http://www.flickr.com/photos/brandonschauer/3363169836/ (courtesy of Brandon Schauer).
- 209: Photos by Work, Play, Experience (courtesy of Stimmt AG).
- 211: Diagram by Jakob Schneider and Marc Stickdorn.
- 213: Pictures by Rannie Turingan, Marc Stickdorn & Patrick Van Der Pijl (all courtesy of Alexander Osterwalder).
- 220: Logos courtesy of NL Agency and DesignThinkers.
- 227: Photo by Arne van Oosterom.
- 232/233: Photos by Arne van Oosterom.
- 234: Logos courtesy of mypolice and Snook.
- 240: Photo by Sarah Drummond.
- 246/247: Photos by Sarah Drummond.
- 248/249: Photos by Sarah Drummond.
- 250: Logos courtesy of Hello Change! and Funky Projects.
- 256: Photo courtesy of Funky Projects.
- 262/263: Photos courtesy of Funky Projects.
- 264/265: Photos courtesy of Funky Projects.

- 266: Logos courtesy of University of Pittsburgh Medical Center and Carnegie Mellon University – School of Design.

- 276/277: Photos by Jamin Hegeman (courtesy of Carnegie Mellon University – School of Design).

- 278/279: Photos by Jamin Hegeman (courtesy of Carnegie Mellon University – School of Design).

- 280: Logos courtesy of SEB and Transformator.

- 292/293: Photos courtesy of Transformator.

- 304/307: Diagram by Fergus Bisset adapted by Jakob Schneider.

INDEX

INDEX

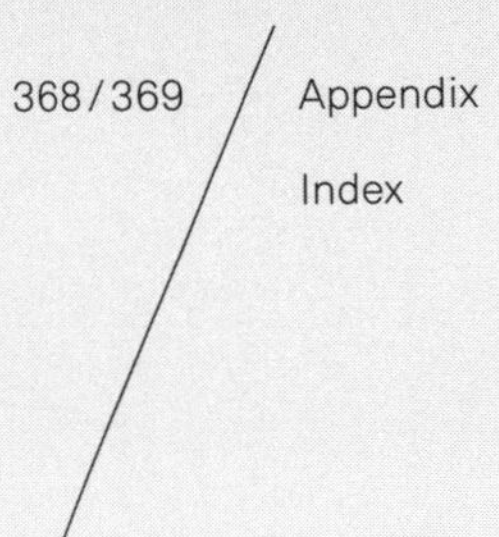

INDEX

INDEX

Appendix

Index

ICONS USED IN THIS BOOK

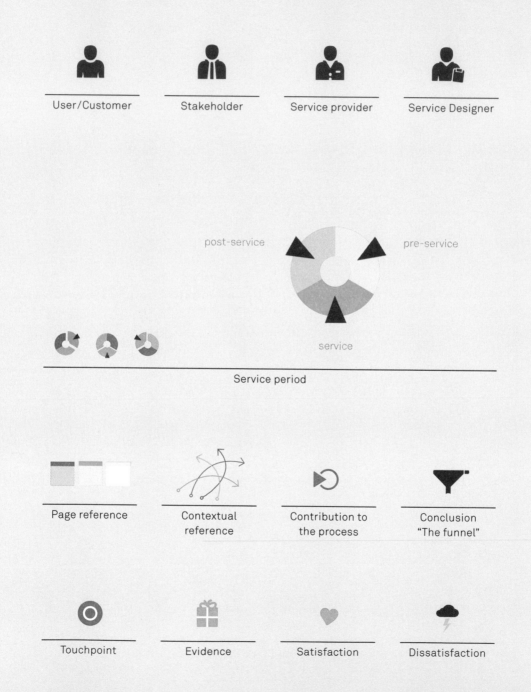

User/Customer

Stakeholder

Service provider

Service Designer

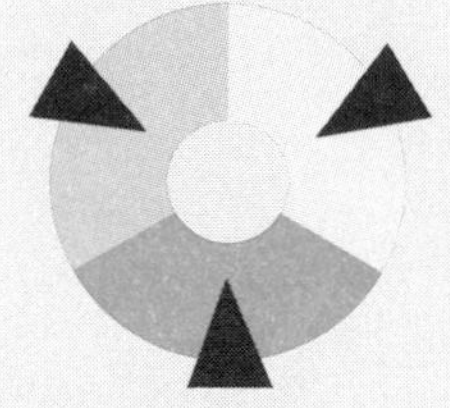

Service period

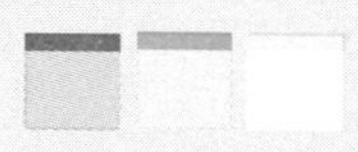

Page reference

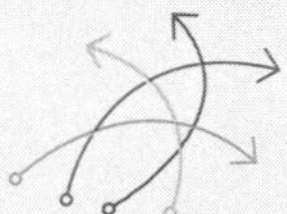

Contextual reference

Contribution to the process

Conclusion "The funnel"

Touchpoint

Evidence

Satisfaction

Dissatisfaction

Stakeholder Maps

Service Safaris

Shadowing

Customer Journey Maps

Contextual Interviews

The Five Whys

Cultural Probes

Mobile Ethnography

Day in the Life

Expectation Maps

Personas

Idea Generation

What if ...

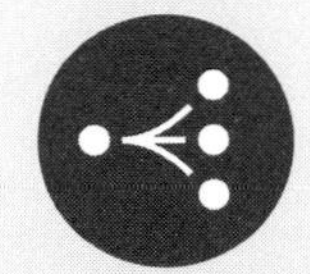
Design Scenarios

Storyboards

Desktop Walkthrough

Service Prototypes

Service Staging

Agile Development

Co-Creation

Storytelling

Service Blueprints

Drama Coaching

Customer Lifecycle Maps

Business Model Canvas